PUBLIC RELATIONS   Made Simple

The Made Simple series
has been created
especially for self-education
but can equally well
be used as
an aid to group study.
However complex the subject,
the reader is taken
step by step,
clearly and methodically,
through the course. Each volume
has been prepared by experts,
taking account of
modern educational requirements,
to ensure the most
effective way of
acquiring knowledge.

In the same series

Accounting
Acting and Stagecraft
Additional Mathematics
Administration in Business
Advertising
Anthropology
Applied Economics
Applied Mathematics
Applied Mechanics
Art Appreciation
Art of Speaking
Art of Writing
Biology
Book-keeping
British Constitution
Business and Administrative
  Organisation
Business Economics
Business Statistics and Accounting
Calculus
Chemistry
Childcare
Commerce
Company Law
Computer Programming
Computers and Microprocessors
Cookery
Cost and Management Accounting
Data Processing
Dressmaking
Economic History
Economic and Social Geography
Economics
Effective Communication
Electricity
Electronic Computers
Electronics
English
English Literature
Export
Financial Management
French

Geology
German
Housing, Tenancy and Planning
  Law
Human Anatomy
Human Biology
Italian
Journalism
Latin
Law
Management
Marketing
Mathematics
Modern Biology
Modern Electronics
Modern European History
New Mathematics
Office Practice
Organic Chemistry
Personnel Management
Philosophy
Photography
Physical Geography
Physics
Practical Typewriting
Psychiatry
Psychology
Public Relations
Rapid Reading
Retailing
Russian
Salesmanship
Secretarial Practice
Social Services
Sociology
Spanish
Statistics
Teeline Shorthand
Transport and Distribution
Twentieth-Century British History
Typing
Woodwork

PUBLIC RELATIONS   Made Simple

Frank Jefkins
BSc(Econ), BA(Hons), FIPR, MCAM, MInstM

Made Simple Books
HEINEMANN : London

Printed and bound in Great Britain
by Richard Clay (The Chaucer Press) Ltd, Bungay, Suffolk
for the publishers, William Heinemann Ltd.,
10 Upper Grosvenor Street, London W1X 9PA

SBN 434 98518 X casebound
SBN 434 98506 6 paperbound

Preface

Although this book covers the syllabus for the CAM Certificate in Communications Studies Public Relations paper—but presents the material in a more logical order than the confusing CAM syllabus—its interest and value are not confined to CAM Certificate students.

It should help to explain the complexities of public relations to those preparing for appropriate examinations held by the Associated Examinations Board, Business Education Council, London Chamber of Commerce and Industry and Institute of Marketing.

The book will also be helpful to overseas students since it is international in approach, and draws on the author's observations while lecturing in and visiting many countries. Moreover, comparisons are made between UK practice and that in other countries. Most textbooks are either UK or American-orientated: this one is not.

In addition, the book should be enlightening to many people who realise that PR is not restricted to professionals. PR concerns all people in all organisations who have to communicate.

In the final chapter, the future of PR is discussed in relation to new fields for PR activity, technological media changes and the need for a totally new concept of training for entry into PR.

FRANK JEFKINS
Croydon, January 1982

Other Books by Frank Jefkins

Acknowledgements

To deal with such a broad subject as public relations, and to attempt to make it relevant on an international scale, I have invited many people in the UK and overseas to assist me with information. I have also quoted from a variety of sources. For this very generous help I am extremely grateful, and wherever possible acknowledgements are given in the text.

Many of the thoughts, ideas and examples contained in this book have resulted from the courses which I have run in the UK and some 16 countries, bringing me into contact with PR practitioners from more than 70 countries. To all the participants on my courses I would also like to express my gratitude for their stimulating participation which has helped me to broaden my vision of public relations.

As an examiner in public relations for many years I have also learned much about aspects of the subject which needed explanation in a comprehensive textbook. I would therefore like to thank these candidates for their indirect assistance in producing a book which I hope will be of benefit to examination candidates.

This book is dedicated to my wife Frances, my son John, and my daughter Valerie

Contents

PART 1

PUBLIC RELATIONS AS A MANAGEMENT FUNCTION

1

INTRODUCTION TO PUBLIC RELATIONS

What do we mean by Public Relations?

Few subjects are more misunderstood or maligned than public relations. Journalists and others who work for the media of the press, radio and television tend to suspect that PR is something which it isn't, while some businessmen who should know better expect it to do things which it cannot.

Perhaps the fault lies with the name itself, and with dislike of the term 'PRO' for public relations officer. Some journalists refer to PROs as PRs, which is a meaningless expression. The situation is not improved by the multiplicity of alternative titles, ranging from communication manager to public affairs officer. There is really nothing wrong with the self-explanatory term 'public relations', which simply means relations with the public.

Very plainly, PR is about communicating in order to achieve understanding through knowledge. The techniques of PR are to do with the sending and receiving of messages so that both sides understand each other: in other words, two-way education.

This may sound remarkably like good human relations. It is, except that certain communication skills are called for when a Government addresses the people, a company communicates with its customers, a charity informs its donors, or an employer has a dialogue with employees.

Consequently, all organisations—and many individuals—are concerned with public relations. It exists whether they like it or not. Bad public relations result from ignorance and misunderstanding rebounding in ill-will and a poor reputation. Good public relations—that is, the conscious effort to inform and be informed—produces knowledge, understanding and, if it is truly deserved, goodwill and a good reputation.

Historical Background

Public relations is not as new as is often supposed. Organised PR dates back to 1948 when both the Public Relations Society of America and the Institute of Public Relations in Britain were formed. But long before that—even if it had no name—PR was being carried out. Where does the history of PR begin? Probably as soon as people found it necessary to communicate. It would not be improper to suggest that there are many instances in the Bible, right back to the Old Testament.

More modern examples belong to the need for businesses and governments to communicate. The house journal has been used for nearly a century and a half, with the *Lowell Offering* of 1842, *I. M. Singer & Co.'s Gazette* of 1855, and *Protector* of 1865 being among the first American ones, while in Britain a staff magazine was published by Lever Brothers towards the end of the nineteenth century. Ivy Ledbetter Lee was handling PR for US coal and railway interests in 1906. In Britain during the 1920s the Lloyd George Government used PR to announce its programme of health, pension and housing schemes. The various UK marketing boards of the 1930s used PR, product publicity stories in the press were called quaintly 'aditorials', and Shell made their classic film about refuelling an Imperial Airways *Heracles* airliner at Croydon Airport. The author was writing and publishing news releases in 1938, when he was a teenage publicity assistant in a London store. After the Second World War a number of London PR consultancies were founded by ex-wartime Government information officers. The first President of the Institute of Public Relations was Sir Stephen Tallents, a pioneer of marketing board PR in the 1930s. The evolution of PR is not quite as all-American as is sometimes supposed. It is significant that right from early days, and contrary to the belief that press relations is the beginning and the end of PR, the house journal and the documentary film have predominated as primary PR media.

Publics

In PR we refer to 'publics' rather than to 'the general public' (as in some dictionary definitions, e.g. *The Oxford Paperback Dictionary*, 1979, which is misleading). We do so because PR messages, unlike mass advertising, are addressed to specific groups of people or special sections of the general public. These **publics** may be members of the local community, employees, investors, members, electors, ratepayers, donors, distributors or various kinds of consumers and users, according to the type of organisation. These groups can be subdivided into even more specialised groups—for example, a company has many grades of staff. When we consider that PR is undertaken by every kind of organisation, commercial or non-commercial and in both the public and private sector, the identification of publics, and the use of different techniques to reach them, becomes a very important aspect of campaign planning. We shall consider publics more closely in a later chapter.

The Total Organisation

PR embraces the total communications of the entire organisation, and enters into the activities (and ideally into the job specification) of most members of an organisation from the chairman or chief executive to the telephonist or gate-keeper. It is not only to do with the work of the staff public relations officer or the outside public relations consultant. Thus PR may be described as 'a management philosophy', even if PR is often lacking from much of the training undertaken by management.

A major element in the 'British disease' of industrial strife is poor communication between management and staff. The late John Methven, when director of the Confederation of British Industry, was right when he said that productivity was not so much about people working harder but of management being more efficient. Successful management depends on good communication and understanding of the attitudes of an organisation's relevant publics, including employees. An organisation is also judged by the behaviour of salesmen, clerks, telephonists, drivers, service staff and other employees who can give it a good or a bad reputation. The great trading success of Marks & Spencer owes much to the inherent PR in that company from top management right through to shop assistants, and that includes buying policy, staff relations and customer relations. Marks & Spencer do have some critical suppliers who complain that M & S buyers are perfectionists!

In marketing, PR is not merely press relations or 'product publicity' used to support advertising. It enters into every phase of the 'marketing mix', which includes naming, packaging, dealer relations, market education and after-sales service. So, PR can be regarded as part of 'marketing management philosophy', helping marketers to maintain good relations throughout their activities. Marketing and PR have a lot in common, and it is a pity that there is so much mutual antipathy between marketing and PR people. Often, they are talking about the same thing in different words. So-called 'social marketing' is something PR people have been undertaking for decades.

The financial side of an organisation also relies on PR, whether it be with banks or investors. The money market forms a vital public, and there are specialist consultancies which deal only in corporate and financial PR. For instance, share prices could fall through lack of confidence simply because buyers and sellers of shares—such as big pension fund and other institutional investors—were ill-informed about a company's successes, plans and prospects.

Public relations is therefore a very broad and complex activity, although its basic objectives and principles of creating and maintaining knowledge and understanding are very simple. Confidence depends on understanding. Much-criticised organisations may be less criticised if there is better understanding of their problems. Many public institutions may never be popular, but at least they can be understood and respected. Typical examples are tax and census collectors, the Army and the Police, and public services such as the Post Office, public transport, gas and electricity suppliers.

Every Kind of Organisation

Because PR affects every kind of company, department, board or body, it is conducted by both non-commercial and commercial organisations of all kinds. In fact, PR is often more evident in the public than in the private sector if we include central and local government departments, public corporations, state-sponsored boards and commissions (quangos), plus all the hundreds of voluntary bodies from charities to trade unions.

In the Third World this situation is all the more apparent, and PR plays a major part in explaining new ideas and public services to the population. Development may depend upon personal hygiene, family planning, pest control, road safety, growing more food or sending children to school. Ignorance and traditional prejudices may have to be overcome in spite of problems of language, illiteracy, religion or tribal attitudes. Thus, PR techniques and media can be very important to the authorities in developing countries.

Feedback

A factor which has already emerged in this chapter is that PR is not only to do with the transmitting of messages but is also responsible for receiving reactions and information about publics and their attitudes. This special nature of PR is described as 'a two-way process', PR acting as an intelligence system. Feedback of information—complaints, suggestions, press cuttings and monitored radio and television broadcasts, attitude, opinion poll and image research—can all contribute to this service.

The Image

An important part of all this is the **image**. What exactly do we mean by image? There are many confusing and sometimes false ideas about the image, usually by those who misunderstand PR as mentioned in the first paragraph of this chapter. An image cannot be manufactured, although we often hear of so-called image-makers. An image is the impression gained according to knowledge and understanding of the facts. Wrong or incomplete information can result in an imperfect image. For instance, many Europeans who lack sufficient information imagine that Africa is a single country, not a continent made up of some fifty countries. It was not until some time after the IRA troubles erupted in Northern Ireland that many people in Britain appreciated that Ulster was part of the UK and not of the Irish Republic. Thus, the image of anything or anybody should be a correct impression, and that is what the PRO will aim to achieve by distributing information and creating or improving knowledge.

The PRO cannot 'polish an image' (as is sometimes supposed—the expression is frequently used loosely and wrongly by media and advertising people), but he can act as a windscreen-wiper and provide clearer vision of the image. To issue false information in a deliberate attempt to create a fictitious image may be propaganda (which will be discussed presently) but it is not PR. The difference should be remembered. To be successful—that is, to spread knowledge and win confidence—PR messages must always be *credible*. Their strength springs from trust and belief.

This means that we have to be careful about doubtful expressions such as 'favourable image'. The true image can only be what it is. It will be favourable or good only if the facts are to its credit and the good image is deserved. An unfavourable image can be the result of unfortunate or discreditable facts. If an airline suffers a number of crashes nothing short of better aircraft, better crews and better training and servicing resulting in a creditable safety record will recapture public faith. The image of the airline will be either bad or good according to the evidence.

But sometimes a poor image is not deserved, and results from *ignorance, hostility, prejudice* or *apathy*. Much PR activity aims to convert these antagonistic or indifferent attitudes into *sympathy, acceptance, interest* and *knowledge*, which may be called the 'PR transfer process'. This is possible only if the positive attitudes are deserved. Smokescreens quickly blow away and reveal the truth.

The informative and educational role of PR is thus emphasised here together with its ability to inform those responsible internally about the reasons for a bad image. Once again we see the value of feedback.

From these remarks it will be seen that it is misleading to call PR practitioners image-*makers* or to expect them to be such. Sometimes we hear of attempts to create images for politicians—but it will be noticed that the experts called in are *advertising agents* (who are expert in projecting product images and emphasising their selling points) and *not* PR consultants. The so-called 'making of a president' is an advertising, not a PR, exercise, and as we shall see the two techniques are very different.

PR Professionals and Others

It must be admitted that there are regrettably two kinds of PR practitioners.

There is the professional who probably holds a professional qualification, belongs to his professional institute, and acts in accordance with a professional code of conduct: there are others who are unqualified by examination, would never qualify by experience for membership of an institute, and may combine poor performance with unethical behaviour.

Sometimes, neither clients nor the general public, and certainly not novelists and television playwrights, know the difference between professional and unprofessional PR practitioners.

PR Defined

Let us analyse the well-known definition of the (British) Institute of Public Relations which reads:

Public relations practice is the deliberate, planned and sustained effort to establish and maintain mutual understanding between an organisation and its public.

This is an excellent definition because it can apply to any sort of organisation, commercial or non-commercial, anywhere in the world. Therefore it is worth remembering in its whole and in its parts.

The three words *deliberate*, *planned* and *sustained* are important. They support what has been said so far in this chapter. They mean that PR should not be haphazard but should have a well defined purpose. The PR programme should be planned, not 'played by ear'. And the PR effort should be continuous, not spasmodic—or even seasonal, which might be justified with an advertising campaign. It should be a *sustained effort*. It should not be what is sometimes called 'a fire-fighting exercise'—that is, a rescue operation in times of trouble. A lot of trouble, such as public criticism, takeover bids or industrial strikes, results from lack of information and understanding, which implies an absence of sustained PR effort. There have been cases of famous companies nearly being taken over because their shareholders did not realise how good these companies were, while strikes have occurred because workers have listened to rumours instead of being told the facts.

The results of PR activities are seldom quickly forthcoming, and time is needed for continuous activity to build up knowledge, appreciation and response. A corporate identity, for instance, does not come about overnight, however brilliant the design of the symbol or however striking the colour scheme—nor does understanding of, say, a new building component, a Government policy, or the work of a charitable institution. Painstaking effort, consuming much time, is necessary, perhaps for months, a year or years. Gimmicks do not work in PR—they are like fireworks that rocket into the sky and perish. Reputation accrues with familiarity and faith.

To achieve this, *mutual understanding* is required, and this (as we have said earlier) is a two-way system of communication. The PRO has to be the eyes and ears as well as the tongue of the organisation. A submarine needs radar as well as a periscope before torpedoes or missiles can be fired.

The definition finally refers to *public* although it is the jargon of PR to speak of *publics* since it is necessary, when planning PR programmes, to define the different groups of people who are to be addressed, and so that particular media may be used for this purpose. Thus we may use a house journal to communicate with employees, a seminar to reach technicians, a trade journal to bring news to retailers, financial editors and journals for business affairs, and more popular media in order to address consumers. Publics and media go together in planning an effective campaign.

PR, Advertising and Propaganda

These three forms of communication are not the same. It therefore becomes essential to distinguish between public relations and both advertising and propaganda with which they may be confused.

The purposes of advertising and propaganda are quite different from those of PR. If PR is to work—that is, inform, educate and so create knowledge and understanding and present a clear image—it must be unbiased. For instance, a news story must state facts, not utter self-praise. These facts are like the components which may be assembled to build a motorcar or a piece of electronic equipment. If the story is written otherwise it will not be credible, trustworthy and newsworthy, and it will be rejected by editors before it ever reaches readers.

But advertising occupies purchased space or time, and provided he is not unethical or illegal, the advertiser can boast and be as biased in his own favour as he likes. An advertisement is like an actor wearing stage make-up while PR is like a man in the street. Selling requires the highlighting of selling points, and advertising does so dramatically in order to be noticed or to compete with other advertisers. This is not unlike the actor having to throw his voice.

Propaganda is similarly prejudiced in its own favour for it aims to persuade people to sacrifice their time, money or minds. It may be deceptive like a person in disguise. But unlike advertising there is no exchange of goods or services for money. The supporter may be rewarded only by mental or emotional satisfaction, a sacrifice really. Propaganda may be for good or bad causes. It dates from 1662 when a committee of Cardinals in Rome took up the propagation of the Gospels through overseas missions. Political dictatorships have tended to give propaganda a bad name, and it is of course used by both sides in wars and other conflicts. Propaganda is therefore information which is faulted by a one-sided point of view.

Advertising has suffered at the hands of unscrupulous *advertisers*—there is nothing wrong with advertising, which is merely a tool, but there are voluntary controls such as the British Code of Advertising Practice (administered by the independent Advertising Standards Authority), and legal controls such as the Trade Descriptions Acts. Similar controls exist to a greater or lesser extent throughout the world, while the EEC has made even more stringent recommendations concerning the control of advertising in Europe. In the USA the Federal Trade Commission seeks to abate abuses of advertising.

PR and Advertising

One association between PR and advertising is that advertising is more likely to be effective if there has been prior PR activity to educate the market—both distributors and consumers—so that the advertising does not have to fight a barrier of ignorance or hostility, let alone indifference. Unfortunately, some advertisers rely on unnecessarily heavy (and costly!) initial advertising to break into a new market when an earlier PR programme could have created a favourable market reaction.

Again, PR can establish the image of an advertiser so that when a new product or service is launched it enjoys the well-known reputation of the maker. This is sometimes called the **halo effect**. 'Made by the makers of . . .' can be a good recommendation. Another example of this is when a company puts new shares on the stock market: if share buyers are appreciative of the company's good record the prospectus will attract investors, and the share issue may even be oversubscribed.

Meanwhile, existing products are likely to sell better if customers are told about the ways in which these goods may be used—perhaps correctly or in new ways. This type of PR can apply to almost anything, to mention only cooking ingredients, sewing machines or decorating materials. The demonstration theatres of gas and electricity suppliers are good examples. Yet again we see the explanatory, informative and educational role of PR as distinct from the more promotional, bombastic and high-pressure role of advertising. Nor is it a case of one being better than the other for in a competitive world PR and advertising are necessary. But even in a less competitive world in which the supply of both goods and money is less plentiful, PR can play a big part in advising people about public services or about new products which are becoming available. Some products may require very careful instruction: in hot countries brewers have had problems because beers have not been kept in cool places, while mothers have eked out supplies of milk-powder and so caused malnutrition in their babies.

This introductory chapter has sought to define PR and to bring out its value to all concerned, not just its sponsors but also its audiences. Most kinds of organisation can benefit from being properly known and understood, and from properly knowing and understanding those with whom they do or could have relations. Most people can benefit from being better informed.

2

DEFINITION, CONCEPT AND PRINCIPLES OF PUBLIC RELATIONS

To define public relations in such a way that it explains the concept and principles of PR as it applies to every kind of organisation, and even certain individuals, is not easy. The Institute of Public Relations' definition already given in Chapter 1 sets a good standard, and it has persisted in spite of a search by the IPR for a better one. But let us consider the variety of definitions which have appeared over the years. Some of them show limited, different or broader approaches to the subject. There is also some confusion due to the attempt to find another name for public relations, or to seek new divisions.

The chief alternative expression is **communication**, but simpler though that sounds it is liable to be indefinite, or to have other meanings connected with transportation or electronics. Also, should it be singular or plural? Because of the same initials, *press relations* and *public relations* are confused, but the former is only part of the latter, and is dependent on literacy and the extent of the mass media so that it can be less relevant in developing countries. As PR activities become more extensive, and new private media such as video cassettes are introduced, press relations becomes no more than the tip of an expanding iceberg.

Public affairs (and other deviations such as **external affairs**) are sometimes attempts either to make PR more respectable, or to hive off special areas of PR. These areas include corporate PR, and activities to do with social conscience such as relations with pressure groups concerning the environment, pollution, consumerism and company behaviour with which the public, politicians and activists are concerned. But it is still PR and there is no need for the Americanism 'public affairs'.

Essentials of a PR definition

What should a definition of PR embrace? To be all-embracing it should make clear that:

1. PR is planned and conducted in a businesslike way.
2. It is a two-way or mutual activity.
3. It is not a form of advertising.
4. It deals with many different groups of people.
5. It seeks to spread knowledge and educate people in order to achieve understanding according to the prescribed objectives.
6. It has universal application to all organisations, commercial or non-commercial, in both the public and private sectors.

There are also certain things which the definition should not do. It should:

1. Not suggest that PR is free or unpaid advertising, or an alternative to advertising.

2. Not pretend that PR is a 'soft sell'.

3. Not claim that PR can influence or persuade, since this may be going too far, can be a matter of semantics, suggest bias, and may properly belong to the realms of propaganda or advertising.

4. Not regard PR as merely a means of creating a favourable image, climate of opinion or impression. It *may* do this, but there are many occasions when the PR task is to create a fair or honest understanding of an unfavourable situation, or of a subject which people do not necessarily have to endorse. It may be a case of winning understanding or tolerance rather than support or acceptance. This could apply to many controversial subjects such as strikes, political parties, religious creeds, the policies of other countries, homosexuals, race relations, or the activities of activist groups.

5. Not suggest that PR consultancies are the major part of the profession, when in fact PR operates differently from advertising, and most PR is an in-house activity even where a consultancy is also employed.

6. Not imply that PR is confined to the commercial world (by including words like *company*), when in reality the bulk of PR work is conducted elsewhere.

7. Not give the impression that PR is only an external activity when internal relations are an important part of PR.

These 13 considerations impose great demands on our definition if it is to be truly comprehensive and meaningful. We are moving a long way from the typical dictionary definition, especially the kind that refers to 'the general public'.

There are several inadequate definitions such as *relations with the public, gaining credit for achievement, the skilled propagation of prestige,* or *the creation and maintenance of confidence.* It is all these things and more, but we have to be careful of words like *propagation* which could have sinister implications if taken to mean more than sowing the seeds of knowledge.

In arriving at a perfect definition we have to dispel many familiar misconceptions, abuses and inhibitions, and show that it is *not* what some politicians, journalists, businessmen, marketing, advertising and sales people believe PR to be, or may even wish it was! With a proper understanding of PR, its scope and limitations become clear and its benefits and possibilities can be better appreciated. Having said this, and when various definitions have been analysed, it may be decided that no definition is wholly adequate.

We also have to appreciate that the emphasis may depend on the country or part of the world in which PR is being conducted, although the basic principle of communicating information in order to achieve understanding remains identical. In North America, where there are fewer inhibitions about selling, PR may veer closer to sales promotion, while in a developing country where it is necessary to encourage people to adopt new ideas and life styles PR may be termed *'enlightenment'* and tend to more propagandist. In the UK the media are vigilant about 'puffery' and hostile to propaganda so that PR messages will succeed best as factual information.

In *The Nature of Public Relations* (McGraw-Hill, 1963) appears John Marston's well-known definition: *'Public relations is planned persuasive communication designed to influence significant publics'*. This is an American definition and if *public relations* was replaced by *advertising* it would serve as an excellent definition of advertising even if it does not spell out the sales objective of advertising. It only goes to show how dangerous it is to read British and American books without recognising the fundamental differences in British and American concepts of PR. This can be very confusing for overseas students preparing for British examinations.

We have only to look at the role of the PRO as performed in American cinema and television films; note the role of so-called PR in certain American corruption exposures; observe that press agents (in the guise of PROs) have been appointed to attend members of the British royal family when visiting the USA; and note that advertising agents have been appointed to present the images of American presidential candidates to realise that American concepts of PR can be wildly different from those of British ones. It does not help when the transatlantic concept is imported into Britain, Europe (and other parts of the world) by American multinationals and American-owned PR consultancies, many of which have offices in London and other cities outside the USA. Two examples are the insistence on evaluating press cuttings on an advertisement rate card basis, and—in Africa—the dressing up of salesgirls as nurses in order to promote powdered baby milk.

Henry James, a past-president of the IPR, has very sensibly said that 'public relations was not the business of making or changing images—it was the business of disseminating truthful information about a product, organisation or policy. But absolute truth was as unattainable as absolute zero. PROs had to disseminate the truth as it was presented to them—that was possible in "our inexact profession".' Henry James said this while addressing the North West Spectrum Conference (organised by the NW Group IPR) at Lancaster University, on September 28, 1979.

It is important, therefore, to accept that truthfulness is a basic criterion for all effective PR activity. This contradicts the popular concept of PR as a confidence trick aimed at misleading people into accepting distortions of the truth. It also challenges those people—often in places of authority—who think they can employ PR techniques and practitioners to distort the truth for them. We shall return to this when we consider professional codes of practice in Chapter 8.

Walter Raven, writing in the *Campaign* Public Relations Special Report (August 24, 1979) favoured the word 'communication'. He wrote: 'Public relations is nothing more than one aspect of communications, and its prime function is to inform.' Communications is a word familiar to management—indeed, it has been its central concern for more than half a century. If, then, we accept the communications function of public relations, we can arrive at a much more comprehensive definition of what constitutes public relations. Mr Raven's recommended definition reads:

> *Public relations is the effective communication, on a sustained and controlled basis, of all information concerning the company which may in some way influence those persons whose actions and decisions, now or at some future time, affect the fortunes and actions of that company.*

Mr Raven prefers his definition to that of the IPR, which he considers to be a statement of objectives, not an explanation of what PR is. Perhaps we need a definition which combines both? There are still three faults with Mr Raven's fulsome definition. It is limited to an *outflow* of information whereas the *inflow* is equally important; in both his preamble and definition he says nothing about the essential objective of creating *understanding*, let alone *mutual understanding*, which is the essence of PR; and he limits himself to the *company* when we must consider every kind of organisation, most PR being outside the business world. Mr Raven was writing about PR in relation to business management, but he did claim to offer 'a more comprehensive definition', which he did not do.

In his book *The Management of Public Relations* (Wiley, New York, 1977), Robert D. Ross offers probably the simplest of all definitions when he says that: 'The single purpose of the public relations function should be to help the organisation develop and maintain a social climate in which it can prosper best.' Another American view is that 'Good public relations results from good performance publicly acknowledged and appreciated' (Cutlip and Center, *Effective Public Relations*, Prentice-Hall, 1964).

But as pointed out with our list of 13 considerations, an adequate definition cannot be as glib as this. It is necessary to explain the process of public relations as well as its nature. We need something which will encompass both the scope and limitations of PR. The following is the author's own development of the IPR definition, given in the previous chapter, which lacks recognition of the tangibility of PR. Too many people wrongly assume that PR is intangible—that is, that its results cannot be assessed. In Part 3 we shall show that properly planned PR can be tangible for if objectives are set it is reasonable to expect that these objectives should be achieved. So here is a definition which introduces objectives as a vital facet of PR:

Public relations consists of all forms of planned communication, outwards and inwards, between an organisation and its publics for the purpose of achieving specific objectives concerning mutual understanding.

But even this does not satisfy every requirement laid down at the beginning of this chapter, and probably the most comprehensive and satisfying definition yet devised is the 'Mexican Statement'. This was agreed at the world assembly of public relations associations held in Mexico City from August 8 to 10, 1978, and reads:

Public relations practice is the art and science of analysing trends, predicting their consequences, counselling organisation leaders, and implementing planned programmes of action which will serve both the organisation's and the public interest.

The special merits of this definition are that it recognises the need for research before advice can be given and PR programmes planned, and that the public interest must be served as well as that of the organisation. It declares both the professionally efficient and the socially responsible role of public relations. It also blends very well with the six-point PR planning model which is the basis of operational PR as discussed in Part 3.

The Mexican Statement is about objective, tangible PR because it insists upon the initial analysing of trends (or appreciation of the situation) before any PR action is proposed or carried out. Organisation leaders will be counselled or advised on how to bring about a change in the situation, and here we are once again confronted by the PR transfer process (see Fig. 1), of changing from a negative to a positive situation by creating knowledge which produces understanding. The extent of that change and that knowledge must be observable or measurable.

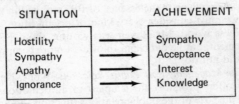

Fig. 1. The PR transfer process.

Even so, the Mexican Statement is not perfect. 'Plans of action' could be for any purpose, and it is a pity that it does not state that these plans of action are for the purpose of *achieving mutual understanding between an organisation and its publics*. With this addition we would have a very comprehensive definition and one which frees public relations from any confusion with advertising. Thus we arrive at the following:

Public relations practice is the process of analysing trends, predicting their consequences, counselling organisation leaders, and implementing planned communication programmes which by achieving mutual understanding, will serve both the organisation's and the public interest.

Public Relations and Advertising

Public relations and advertising are two utterly different worlds, although in some ways and on some occasions they may be related. In no way is public relations a form of advertising, although there are times when PR will use advertising such as to announce a catalogue of PR films, or for the purpose of institutional or corporate advertising. Although less money may be spent on it (and for that reason it may be thought to be less significant than advertising) PR is nevertheless a much bigger activity than advertising. Not every organisation needs advertising but every organisation is involved in PR whether it likes it or not. Similarly, it is a bigger activity than marketing since marketing is only one function of a business, and not every organisation is involved in trade.

To emphasise and distinguish the differences between PR and advertising let us consider four areas in which these differences occur. They are:

1. The people addressed—the target audiences or publics.
2. The media through which these people are addressed.
3. The costs and methods of payment.
4. The purpose of the communication.

1. The People Addressed

Advertising campaigns are usually concentrated on the largest number of potential buyers. PR programmes are dispersed to many different groups of people. Advertising addresses the target audience: PR addresses many publics. While advertising is aimed mostly at distributors, users and consumers in order to sell, and to possible recruits and suppliers in order to buy, PR publics—as we shall see—can include all kinds of people with whom the organisation does or should communicate. But not all organisations are in industry, trade or commerce. We have already mentioned that most PR exists outside the business world, and to substantiate this claim here are some of the non-business organisations in which PR is very important:

(*a*) The police, Armed Forces, prison service, fire brigades, ambulance services.

(*b*) Hospitals and other health services.

(*c*) Universities, polytechnics, schools and other educational establishments.

(*d*) Societies, institutes and associations representing special interests, including professional and trade bodies.

(*e*) Churches and various religious organisations such as missionary and denominational educational societies.

(*f*) Cultural organisations, e.g. libraries, museums, art galleries, symphony orchestras, and choirs and choral societies.

(*g*) Sports clubs representing every kind of amateur and professional sport.

(*h*) Political parties, political societies, trade unions.

(*i*) Central Government, ministries and departments and the hundreds of quasi-autonomous national government organisations (quangos) set up by government.

(*j*) Local government authorities.

(*k*) Charities and voluntary bodies ranging from Dr Barnardo's to the Royal National Lifeboat Institution.

From this brief list it will be realised that many thousands of organisations make up this vast world of non-commercial activity. Some of them, it is true, use advertising techniques to raise funds but even so they are usually non-profit-making and the funds derived from trade are required for administrative or charitable purposes. They are the very fabric of civilised society.

2. The Media

If the lists below are compared side by side it will be found that there are differences in the use of some similar or identical media, while there are many media used only by advertising, and yet more which are specially created for PR purposes. The latter may be called private or sponsored media and they are seldom mass media, whereas advertising exploits existing mass media which operate to make a profit. Advertising tends to be mean in its choice of the fewest possible economically effective media whereas PR is greedy and almost profligate in its use and creation of media.

Media comparisons

Advertising media	*PR media*
(i) Display and classified ads in newspapers, consumer magazines, trade, technical and professional journals.	(i) News stories, feature articles, pictures for the press. Internal and external journals.
(ii) Commercials (film or video-tape) and advertising films for showing on television and cinema screens.	(ii) Documentary, sponsored or industrial films, video-tapes, video-discs, slides, television programme material, television news.

(iii) Radio commercials.

(iii) Taped radio interviews, studio interviews, phone-ins, news.

(iv) Posters, signs and other outdoor and transportation advertising.

(iv) Educational visual aid posters.

(v) Public, trade, private, mobile exhibitions.

(v) PR aspects of all exhibitions and exhibitions for PR purposes.

(vi) Sales promotion and merchandising schemes.

(vi) Educational literature—printed information.

(vii) Point-of-sale displays.

(vii) Sponsored books.

(viii) Sales literature—leaflets, catalogues.

(viii) Seminars, and conferences—spoken word sometimes combined with film shows, slide presentations, and exhibits.

(ix) Direct mail.

(ix) Press facility visits, works visits.

(x) Door-to-door mail drops of sales literature.

(x) Annual reports and accounts.

(xi) Sponsorship with direct marketing and advertising purposes.

(xi) Participation in events, e.g. floats at carnivals, awards of prizes, sponsorship of events and causes.

(xii) Special forms of advertising: aerial, shopping bags, novelties, etc.

(xii) Corporate identity: house style, livery, symbols (logos), colours, typography.

These lists are by no means complete but they help to show that advertising and PR communicate differently by means of different communication media.

3. Costs and Payment

The financial sides of advertising and PR can be compared in a similar way. By costs we mean what has to be bought; by payment (or remuneration) how an advertising agent or a PR consultant receives monies to recover what has been spent on a client's behalf and to make a profit.

In advertising it is usual to refer to **above-the-line** and **below-the-line** costs, the first covering the main five media of the press, television, radio, outdoor and cinema. All the other media—which do not usually pay the advertising agent a commission—are termed below-the-line. It is wrong to include PR in this second category for it is not a part of advertising and needs its own budget.

To explain the advertising agency commission system more thoroughly, agencies may be 'recognised' (or 'accredited' as it is called in some countries) by bodies representing publishing houses and broadcasting stations or contractors. It is more convenient for the media to deal with a small number of space and airtime buyers (advertising agents) than with large numbers of advertisers, provided accounts are settled promptly, say, in 30 days. The media owners' bodies (e.g. Newspaper Publishers' Association and the Independent Television Contractors Association) grant these agents 'recognition'—on the basis that they have sufficient cash flow to pay their bills promptly—and invoice less 10–15 per cent so that the agent can charge his client the full amount and gain the difference. The commission is seldom adequate and agents commonly charge their clients a supplementary percentage. Agents also earn commission on work which they put out in order to produce advertisements, e.g. typesetting and photography, but in some cases, e.g. printing, the supplier does not deduct a commission but adds a percentage which represents the agent's handling cost. Thus, it could be cheaper for the client to buy print direct, whereas it would not be cheaper for him to buy space or airtime direct. The agent's sources of income are therefore various and complicated. There are some agents who reject the commission system and work more professionally for fees which represent man-hours and expertise, expenditures for clients being charged net.

Public relations consultancies are not in the commission business; mainly they are selling time which is representative of man-hours and expertise, plus materials and expenses. The hourly rate for PR services covers salaries, overheads and profits. We shall deal with this in the chapters on PR consultancy and budgeting, but here let us examine costs under sets of comparative lists.

Cost comparisons

Advertising costs	*Agency payment*
(i) Advertising space in the press.	(i) Commission on space, airtime and screen bookings, poster site rentings.
(ii) Airtime on television, radio.	
(iii) Rent of poster sites.	(ii) Charges for artwork and costs of production.
(iv) Screen time on cinemas.	
(v) Stand space at exhibitions.	(iii) On-costs on work farmed out to suppliers such as printers.
(vi) Production costs of: (a) Press advertisements. (b) Television commercials. (c) Radio commercials. (d) Cinema screen commercials. (e) Exhibition stands. (f) Print, display material.	(iv) Discounts from suppliers such as photographers, film and video-tape makers. (v) Fees for work which bears no commission.

PR costs	*Consultancy payment*
(i) Time—salaries.	(i) Fee based on hourly rate.
(ii) Materials—stationery, postage, photography.	(ii) Recovery of cost of materials, usually at cost.
(iii) Expenses—travelling, hotels, hospitality.	(iii) Recovery of expenses at cost.

Whereas the advertising agent's main cost is on space, airtime and the production of advertisements, the PR consultant's main cost is on man-hours to service the account. This leads to another difference: agency commission covers the cost of the account executive who services the account and acts as the liaison between the client and the agency. Commission also covers administrative costs such as media planning and buying. The PR consultant has to charge for every minute spent on servicing the account, including talking to the client. Quite simply, there are only two payers of the consultant's costs, 'them and us'. Anything not paid by the client has to come out of the consultant's pocket and is a loss.

3

AN ORGANISATION AND ITS PUBLICS

'Publics' is part of the jargon of public relations, an invented word not to be found in the orthodox dictionary, and one which is reduced to the more grammatical 'public' in the pedantic IPR definition of public relations. At the risk of offending the purists, **publics** is used in the author's *Dictionary of Marketing and Communication* (under **public relations**) to explain that *PR concerns communications between any sort of organisation, commercial or non-commercial, and various publics with whom it has contact*.

From this example it will be seen that 'publics' is a very meaningful expression and one peculiar to PR. This special word also helps us to strike yet another contrast with advertising, which has its own distinct jargon.

Advertising campaigns are usually directed at a target audience consisting of the largest number of potential buyers, or at a market segment of particular buyers. This selectivity is implied by the definition of advertising used by the Institute of Practitioners in Advertising, the professional body of advertising agencies:

Advertising presents the most persuasive possible selling message to the right prospects for the product or service at the lowest possible cost.

The right prospects can be defined precisely for an advertising campaign. For example, research may show that the prospects for an inexpensive battery-operated kitchen clock might be C^2 housewives aged 24 to 34, or sales of a small, economical family car may be aimed at that segment of the motorcar market which is concentrated on family urban driving.

Such an identification of the sales market will be taken into account when planning a PR programme, but it is much smaller and less diffused than the 'various publics with whom it (an organisation) has contact'.

The identification of PR publics is fundamental to the planning of a PR programme (as will be seen in Chapter 15), for unless the publics are defined it is impossible to select media which will convey our PR messages to them. Unlike the *Oxford Dictionary* misconception of PR, we are not addressing the general public.

Moreover, it may be necessary to list all possible publics in order to decide priorities because constraints of the budget, manpower and other resources have to be applied. But how can we choose priorities or media unless we first of all write down *all* the publics we would like to communicate with in an ideal world free of constraints? The problem will vary from one organisation to another. Some will have such a diversity of minority group publics that it would be costly to try to reach them; others will have majority group publics which can be reached simultaneously through the mass media, especially if there is considerable **role playing** by the same people.

To explain role playing, a man may be a city office worker, a husband, a parent, a motorist, a golfer, a gardener and an amateur photographer who enjoys motoring holidays abroad. These are his roles. Such a person may read a lower middle-class newspaper, listen to his car radio and watch television and is easily reached by the mass market media. Now, supposing an organisation such as a bank, building society, travel agent, rose grower, camera dealer or car ferry operator wanted to reach some of the publics represented by this man's different roles it could do so very easily because such players of several roles enjoy the same popular media. But this would not be so if people with more specialised interests had to be reached, e.g. those who drove performance cars, played in golf championships, grew orchids, or made home movies or video-cassettes.

Let us look at the example of a bank and its publics, the role playing of its potential customers and the ease of reaching them through the existing mass media. The bank's commercial objective may be to lend money to people who require finance for the purchase of houses, house improvements and extensions, motorcars, photographic equipment or holidays abroad. The PR objective may be to educate relevant publics about the bank's services. The role playing aspect is important because it will show that many of the bank's prospects or publics are in fact the same people playing out different roles at different times. They can be reached simultaneously through the same media with the same PR effort.

Nevertheless, this can be an oversimplification and concern only those publics containing large groups of people not unlike the advertising target audience. Most organisations will have numerous publics, as we shall see.

Understanding the nature of publics helps to determine the feasibility of reaching them economically within the budget. For example, because of their specialised minority interests it may be necessary to create private media in order to reach them—media such as slides, films, video-tapes, house journals, educational literature or seminars.

Basic Publics

The basic publics that apply to most commercial organisations may be generalised as follows:

1. The community.
2. Potential employees.
3. Employees.
4. Suppliers of services and materials.
5. The money market.
6. Distributors.
7. Consumers and users.
8. Opinion leaders.

Now we can see how much more varied are PR publics than the target audiences or market segments of advertising. We are also spreading through the entire organisation, taking in the production and financial functions of a business in addition to marketing. This immediately positions PR in relation to top management and the board of directors, and indicates that it is unrealistic to place PR within the marketing function. Further, it shows how limiting it is to combine advertising and PR within the one job specification. More and more we see that advertising and PR are worlds apart, although it does follow that in those companies that do little advertising—such as industrial companies—advertising may well come within the responsibilities of the PRO.

According to the nature of the business, the eight basic publics may be subdivided or extended, so let us now review each of these publics in greater detail.

1. The Community

The community consists of the organisation's neighbours who may live or work close to the factory, office, store, airport, seaport, power station, research laboratory or whatever may be the organisation's premises. Some complex organisations will have a number of premises of different kinds and will have relations with various communities. Sensible companies are careful to develop and sustain a 'good neighbour' policy. After all, the community may contain potential customers, employees, actual customers and employees (and their families), and many people who can be friends or enemies.

The activities of the company may affect the community. Noise, dirt, fumes, smells—even the very presence of the organisation—may provoke antagonism. Deliberate efforts may be made to overcome these problems and to make the organisation acceptable. Tall chimneys, garden frontages, tastefully obscured buildings, waste disposal or conversion plants and noise abatement all contribute to good relations. But so also will more obvious PR activities such as 'open days', participation in local events and the regular supply of company news to the local press.

Some manufacturers who make goods which are sold outside the community sometimes forget they are part of the community, and their works attain an almost 'Dracula's Castle' image. The author once visited the country house headquarters of a well-known company, and was surprised to find that local people had nicknamed it 'The Rattery' because it had a research laboratory. Firms like Cadburys and W. D. & H. O. Wills have, of course, been very much part of the community while others, like Bata, are sometimes accused of going too far with the creation of company towns.

Community relations can be matters of delicacy and diplomacy but, as with so much PR activity, they represent thoughtfulness. Unlike the aggressiveness of advertising, PR is about human understanding. The department store will try not to offend the job applicants it does not employ—they could be customers; provision of a car park will be a convenience appreciated by customers; good carriers (like those of Marks & Spencer) protect clothes on their journey home from the shop—and back to the shop if they have to be changed, but if form-filling formalities make the return or exchange of goods an embarrassment good relations will be sacrificed.

Some organisations take great pride in their community relations, supporting local theatres, musical festivals, flower shows, sports events and plainly being seen to be a responsible member and patron of the local society. In fact, some are great benefactors and down through history they have paid for churches, schools, hospitals, libraries, art galleries, parks and other important parts of the infrastructure. But one does not need to be part of the community fabric: brand new industries, perhaps located on a somewhat isolated trading estate which invites anonymity, still need to develop community relations.

2. Potential Employees

Some future employees may live in the vicinity of the workplace—relatives or friends of present staff, local schoolchildren and students, employees in other local firms—but this will depend on the kind of employment.

Those who criticise the increase in immigration to Britain in post-war years forget that Britain had labour shortages in the 1950s and employers in the transportation and catering trades recruited staff from the West Indies. Similarly, hotels import staff from all over the world, just as early British railway builders imported Irish navvies, the Americans imported Chinese, and British colonists in Africa imported Indians for their railway construction. Migrant and immigrant labour is usually attracted by money, opportunity and better living conditions, and employers have great PR responsibilities in today's race relations situation. The sons and daughters of immigrants and refugees are British-born citizens.

Recruitment may be from schools, colleges and universities where it is important that information about career opportunities is supplied to careers masters, advisers and appointments officers. Viewdata systems such as the Post Office's Prestel are an excellent means of providing updated information on career opportunities, and this is one of the many examples of the value of teletext as a PR medium. This may be augmented by films, displays for careers evenings, visits to plants, and student weekends at training centres such as those organised by banks. Here we see PR techniques being allied to the efforts of the personnel and training departments.

Other employers and industries may be sources of recruitment. Redundant workers may be attracted and trained in new jobs. The motorcar industry has recruited workers from coalmining and agriculture, and PR itself has drawn staff from many spheres—not only from journalism. Where skilled staff are scarce they will have to be won from competitors. Vacancy advertisements alone will not always succeed: applicants of the right type will emerge more readily if they are aware of the merits of the employer seeking recruits. Public relations is about reputation: is the job advertiser a reputable employer, is the industry one with worth-while prospects? Young people may be deterred by prejudices towards certain industries, as we have seen with engineering and chemicals, and PR is about correcting false ideas.

3. Employees

Management–employee relations are considered to be one of the growth areas of PR. In Britain—as compared with north European countries—lack of worker participation on the one hand and old-fashioned craft unions on the other tend to maintain a 'man and master' class division which does not encourage ideal industrial relations. Nevertheless, more open management, the training of shop stewards in new technologies, the encouragement of communications from the bottom up, the use of 'speak up' schemes, explanations of annual reports and accounts by means of house journals, films and video-tapes, and so on are improving internal communications and relations.

This public may have many subdivisions, and it is seldom satisfactory to rely on a single staff newspaper to cover the whole work force. Some typical subdivisions may be:

(*a*) Management and executives, branch managers.
(*b*) Section leaders and foremen.
(*c*) Office workers.
(*d*) Factory workers.
(*e*) Field sales force.
(*f*) Transport workers.
(*g*) Overseas staff.
(*h*) Casual labour.

An airline is a good example of an employer with a great mixture of staff on the ground, in the air, at the home base and at overseas locations. On the other hand, a departmental store will have its staff concentrated within one building. It also depends on whether a large organisation is structured vertically or horizontally. This kind of integrated structure results from amalgamations and mergers, a vertical company being an empire of complementary interests covering resources, supplies, manufacturing and distribution while a horizontal one is a combination of similar interests. Unilever is typical of the first; Air UK of the latter. Then there are conglomerates—holding companies like Tillings which own companies of unrelated interests operating independently, and there are also consortiums of companies which may cooperate in a major venture as has been seen with construction projects in the Arab oil states.

These complicated structures may have considerable industrial communications problems. An obvious place to begin is at the recruitment and training stage to which PR can contribute valuable induction material such as literature, slide presentations, films and video-cassettes, the effort being sustained by house journals and other regular forms of communication.

If there is a complete mixture of technologies and jobs, as with vertical amalgamations and conglomerates, each unit may have to be treated separately yet given a certain unity. For example, ICI has special house journals for the staffs at different plants, and a central information unit which supplies headquarters news (such as the annual report and accounts) to each editor. But an amalgamation of similar interests, such as Allied Bakeries, could have its own national radio station covering factories in London, Manchester and Glasgow until, after several years of successful operation, it was able to replace this with the broadcasts from local radio stations. The purpose of the radio was to overcome the noise in the bakeries, scores of loudspeakers being positioned strategically so that workers could listen to music and request programmes while they worked. Thus, different types of employee publics provide special communication problems.

This is an area in which the International Association of Business Communicators is developing internal communications beyond the traditional staff newspaper. Although based in San Francisco, the IABC has a British chapter.

4. Suppliers and Services

These two external groups may include:

Suppliers: (*a*) Sources of raw materials.
(*b*) Sources of components.
(*c*) Suppliers of print and packaging.
(*d*) Suppliers of fuel.

(e) Suppliers of transportation.
(f) Suppliers of finished goods if it is a marketing organisation, retailer, caterer, etc.

Services: (a) Professional—advertising, PR, legal, accountancy, etc.
(b) Public services—health, water, refuse, police, fire brigade.
(c) Educational—day-release training, industrial training board.
(d) Advisory bodies, research stations, trade associations.

Other suppliers and services will come to mind for particular organisations. Communications with these publics may be achieved through the external house journal, works visits, seminars, films and other PR media, but special efforts may be necessary in some cases. For instance, an organisation conducting a dangerous trade would be wise to keep doctors, hospitals, ambulance and fire brigades and the police aware of special hazards.

The maintenance of good relations with suppliers and services is one that can be overlooked, yet it is an example of the thoroughness which is necessary when a PRO is planning a comprehensive annual programme and is listing his objectives, publics and media. Remembering to put such people on the mailing list of the house journal, inviting them to social occasions, seminars and works visits, sending them copies of the annual reports and accounts may be very useful indeed. But by listing such people among the publics new communication tasks and difficulties may be highlighted. How does one communicate effectively with the Chief Constable, the hospital surgeon, the water board and even one's advertising agent and PR consultant? These are all part of the total communications of an organisation.

5. The Money Market

Public companies, and private companies 'going public' and being quoted on the stock exchange, depend on the money market being well informed about their history, performance and prospects. This will affect the take-up of new share issues and the maintenance of share prices, and the latter may be necessary to avoid a takeover. The money market begins with one's local bank manager, and extends through building societies and insurance companies to shareholders and investors. At the top end of the money market are investment analysts, stockbrokers, merchant banks and institutional buyers of large blocks of shares such as insurance companies, unit trusts and pension funds.

Financial and corporate PR has become a very important part of the overall PR programme, with many specialist financial PR consultancies. In fact, the City and Financial PR Group of the IPR is one of its most active and successful sections, having more than one hundred members.

6. Distributors

This is a very broad group and different organisations will obviously have different channels of distribution and use distributors best suited to their trade. Thus this very long list may include brokers, factors, wholesalers, cash and carry warehouses, rack-jobbers, supermarkets and chain stores, co-ops, neighbourhood shops, own shops, appointed dealers, clubs, hotels and holiday centres, mail order traders, direct salesmen, tally men (credit traders), exporters and overseas importers. To explain one or two of the less familiar terms, a factor is a wholesaler who takes over the collection of accounts while a rack-jobber is a wholesaler who specialises in stocking up supermarkets with non-perishable items such as toiletries and proprietary medicines.

Dealer relations is an aspect of public relations and marketing support which no manufacturer or supplier can afford to neglect, yet such neglect has been the cause of a number of product failures. Dealers are unlikely to sell a new product in which they have no confidence, no matter how beguiling the trade terms or massive the launch advertising. They have their own customer relations to consider.

7. Consumers and Users

Consumers may be described as the final customers, users who make use of the product whether it be a component for a product or an ingredient used by a hotel chef.

Some products (and services) are never known to the final consumer, and the PR operation is allied to the 'back-selling' operation of encouraging a user to adopt or continue to use a product. The PR effort will be aimed at the designer, formulator or specifier. But although an architect may be the essential specifier he could be influenced by the wishes of his client who may have a preference for brick, tile, timber, metal or glass. The 'Brick is Beautiful' campaign reached various customers and users.

Final customers are not necessarily those addressed by advertising. They could be young people who will be eventual customers, or junior customers such as those for whom the Abbey National Building Society issues its journal *Thumbs Up*. There can also be numerous minority groups, uneconomical from an advertising point of view, but approachable by PR. Moreover, the consumer public can be broken down into numerous demographic subdivisions of sex, age, marital status and so on which makes it possible for them to be reached by more specialised media.

Another comparison with advertising is that an advertising campaign may use different mass media from those used for PR purposes. For example the advertising may be in the *Radio Times* and *TV Times*, but the press stories may be in local weekly newspapers, national daily newspapers, special interest or women's magazines in which there is no advertising, so directing the PR information at certain sections of the consumer public.

Again, the PR effort may be aimed at educating new, potential customers, or at breaking down the prejudices of people not normally regarded as being within the target audience for advertising. The motorcycle market is rather like this.

8. Opinion Leaders

These can be any people who, whether well or ill informed, may express opinions and influence people because of their apparent authority. They may well be ignorant, hostile or prejudiced but certainly not apathetic. Or they could be knowledgeable, well disposed or at least tolerant. Their attitudes can be dangerous or helpful, according to the extent of their knowledge and understanding. Opinion leaders may be grouped like this:

(a) Parents, teachers, academics, doctors, clergymen.
(b) Central and local government politicians, political party politicians, trade union leaders.

(*c*) Civil servants and local government officers, officials of quangos.

(*d*) Commentators, presenters and other radio/television personalities.

(*e*) Journalists and authors.

(*f*) Authorities on specialised subjects, who may write, lecture or broadcast.

(*g*) Advisory services and information bureaux.

(*h*) Officials of societies, institutions, trade associations and professional bodies.

In this list an attempt has been made to group together certain kinds of opinion leaders. For some organisations there may be other individuals who may be regarded as relevant opinion leaders—for example, leaders of ethnic groups, the police or officers of the Armed Forces as might particularly be the case in some countries.

These people can be very important in a PR programme. They may have to be dealt with on a face-to-face basis, through the medium of the spoken word, at private meetings or over lunch. Or groups of them may be invited on a visit, tour or to a reception.

The Media

It is sometimes suggested that the media should be included as a public. The CAM syllabus for public relations gives a very odd list of publics: customers, distributors or agents, employees, government: national or local, management, media, shareholders, etc. This is a curious and inadequate list and the 'etc.' is an unnecessary mystery. The syllabus for the London Chamber of Commerce and Industry Public Relations examination gives a list of publics similar to that already discussed in this chapter, but does not include media.

If one thinks about it, it is illogical and contradictory to include media because they are the means of communicating with publics. However (and this is probably where the confusion arises), we can include among the opinion leaders people like Bernard Levin, David Dimbleby, Chapman Pincher, David Frost and similar personalities who may write in the press, publish books, appear on television or broadcast on radio. They are media personalities, not the media themselves. The distinction is perfectly clear.

From the analysis given in this chapter it is obvious that the range of publics applicable to any organisation is bound to be very large, and that it may not be possible to embrace them all in a PR programme. We shall return to this again in Part 3, but as an example let us consider at least some of the publics with which an organisation such as the Institute of Public Relations could be concerned with. (Due to lack of funds, staff and other resources a number of these publics have to be eliminated, or they are dealt with only occasionally as circumstances demand.)

Publics of the IPR

1. The general membership, including overseas members.
2. Officers and committee members, area groups, special interest groups.
3. The staff.
4. Prospective members.
5. Associated organisations, e.g. Public Relations Consultants Association, International Public Relations Association, Confédération Européen Des

Rélations Publiques (CERP), PR institutes in other countries, British Association of Industrial Editors, International Association of Business Communicators.

6. Other organisations, e.g. British Institute of Management, Confederation of British Industry, The Advertising Association, Incorporated Practitioners in Advertising, Institute of Marketing, Institute of Directors.

7. Educational bodies, e.g. CAM, Department of Education and Science, BEC, London Chamber of Commerce and Industry.

8. PR students.

9. Schools, colleges, universities regarding PR education.

10. Government departments, e.g. Department of Trade.

11. Careers advisers in schools, colleges, universities.

12. Opinion leaders, e.g. critics of PR such as teachers, politicians, media personalities.

13. Publishers of books, directories, etc., to achieve correct references.

Once again one could go on developing the list. It is an enlightening experience because it shows how extensive is the world of PR, and how very different it is from the blinkered view of PR as some sort of 'free advertising'.

4

FACTORS WHICH INFLUENCE PUBLIC ATTITUDES TOWARDS PUBLIC RELATIONS

Generally speaking, public relations is misunderstood by those who need to understand it better. Chief among these are those in management, marketing and advertising. As a result, they often misuse or abuse PR, and arouse the scepticism of others. Many people in the media are downright suspicious of PR, and are therefore antagonistic towards it. In books, plays and films the PRO is nearly always portrayed as a somewhat unscrupulous, contemptible parasite, next door to a shady lawyer, an unfrocked priest or a quack doctor. Teachers in schools pour contempt on PR. Journalists regard it as easy money and yearn for its greener pastures. Many young people fantasise about PR as a world of glamorous parties.

The general public regard it as some sort of twilight world, part of the unacceptable face of capitalism. They are not helped by the media which talk of 'tarnished' and 'dented images', associate PR with corruption exposés and the peculiarities of American presidential politics, or describe political initiatives as merely 'PR exercises'. Otherwise intelligent newspapers like *The Guardian* have a fetish about the unholiness of PR.

From these general observations seven specific factors deserve special analysis.

Bad Press Relations

The most visible area of public relations is press relations, largely because in literate industrial communities the press is the primary mass medium. It is a ready-made facility for PR messages. Unhappily, it is a PR medium which some PR people take for granted and they do not realise how much skill is required to write even a news release. Much of the criticism of PR comes from editors who are on the receiving end of bad PR. A love–hate relationship exists. The PR profession suffers because of its own mistakes and unprofessional work and behaviour. The principles of good press relations will be explained in Chapter 33.

Media/Art Misrepresentation

Partly as a result of bad press relations, those writing about PR, or using PR characters in creative works, tend to misrepresent the PRO. They do so because they are mostly aware of the bad PRO, the press agent, the glamorous hostess, the 'gin-and-tonic' PRO, the front man, the public apologist and so on, who do exist whether we like it or not. They may be the creations of management which does not understand PR, but there are also many fringe operators since anyone can call himself a PRO, and there are also many near-professionals—sometimes no more than press officers—who have not attained true professionalism. It may be that PR has yet to gain respectability, and we

27

have to recognise that other professions such as medicine and architecture had periods when they were not respected.

Behaviour of PROs

The image of the 'gin-and-tonic' PRO dies hard, and PROs of the past did overdo hospitality and so earned an unenviable reputation for buying too many drinks, giving lavish lunches, and running 'jollies' and 'junkets' instead of legitimate press receptions and serious facility visits. There are still clients who employ PR consultants because they think there will be lots of press parties, and there are still PROs who think you have to take editors to lunch to get an article published. The socialising rather than the hard-working PRO tends to be the general if false idea of a PRO.

Whitewashing

Again, there are people who want to abuse PR and others who expect PR to be an abuse of the truth. But effective PR is not about concealing the truth, pretending bad things have not happened or manipulating the media. Effective PR is a continuous process, and it will not work unless it is believed. The 'credibility factor' is supreme.

Advertising Attitudes

Because advertising people tend to regard PR as a sort of poor relation of advertising, instead of it being a different and more comprehensive range of communications concerning the non-commercial as well as the commercial sectors, misunderstandings exist. This is reflected in the attitude of CAM towards PR, and results in a CAM Certificate of Communication Studies which is primarily about advertising and has syllabus references to PR which reveal the misconceptions of PR held by examiners who are advertising practitioners. Some advertising agencies still think PR is no more than sending out news releases to augment advertising campaigns, or that sales promotion stunts are PR exercises. Other advertising agencies have wisely set up PR subsidiaries as independent consultancies which deal with PR in the broad-scale.

Marketing Attitudes

Marketing management tends to regard PR as an optional extra, instead of accepting PR as part of the job specification of a marketing manager. Many aspects of marketing such as branding, naming, packaging, market education, dealer relations, customer relations and after-sales service require an understanding of the PR implications of communication, understanding, goodwill and reputation. Consequently, PR takes a meagre place in the Institute of Marketing examinations and in marketing degree courses at universities. Unfortunately, there is antipathy towards PR by marketing people, and antipathy towards marketing by PR people. All this has the ultimate effect of encouraging ill-will (or anti-PR) towards marketing organisations. This is seen in articulate consumerism and other activist reactions to the business world.

Dislike of PROs and PR

The expression 'PRO' has unpleasant connotations in people's minds, often being associated with officialdom. The word 'officer' does not appeal to busi-

nessmen: it sounds like a civil servant. This may be why Conservative politicians are often antagonistic to PR, which they do not understand, whereas
they accept advertising which is a familiar part of business activities. Some
Conservative local authorities dislike PR and regard it as a waste of ratepayers' money.

Yet, in spite of it all, PR attracts many people of high calibre who work
very hard and accept high standards of professional behaviour. One of the
author's seminars was televised by BBC2, and the outstanding feature of this
programme was the impression of integrity and high calibre given by the
individual participants when they were interviewed by the television reporter.

There is obviously something very wrong with the image of PR in the
minds of countless people who need to know better. A difficulty is that too
many people want to believe PR is something which it is not. Sometimes this
is induced by those who expect PR to do things it cannot do, management
principally. Sometimes it results from the jealousy of marketing, advertising
and media people who see in PR a threat to their domains.

Somehow, the word has to be spread that PR is about developing knowledge
in order to create understanding, and that unless the information is credible it
will not be believed. This means disassociating PR from advertising, and establishing it quite clearly as an impartial communication practice, a profession
in its own right.

In this we have to start at the top. Management has to learn what PR is
and how it should be used, how its services should be bought and how cost
effective it can be. Management has to respect PR as it does any other professional service which it employs, but will do so only when it refrains from
treating PR as a means of 'conning the press', as a smokescreen or fire-
fighting exercise when there is trouble, or as a means of protecting itself from
the media. Management also has to learn that it has no divine right to expect
the media to do or say anything in its favour. But it can expect PR to achieve
results.

We also have to look very critically at the recruitment and training of PR
personnel. In Britain, the majority of PR practitioners have never had any
training in PR, except 'on the job'. We would be horrified if a doctor learned
his job after setting up in practice, but that is what happens in PR. When the
local authorities were reorganised a few years ago many of these new bodies
advertised for PROs. They offered low salaries and gave preference to journalists. Most of the appointees discovered that they knew nothing about PR
and were ineligible for membership of the IPR. This was scarcely anybody's
fault because there simply was no reservoir of trained let alone experienced
PROs to fill all those new jobs. At the time of writing, when consultancies are
showing that in a depression they are often excellent value for money, there is
a shortage of skilled consultancy staff.

The CAM Foundation has been operating for more than 10 years, yet very
few people hold the CAM Diploma in Public Relations. The main reason for
this is that CAM is chiefly concerned with training people in advertising, and
the CAM Certificate in Communication Studies is heavily advertising-
orientated. Consequently, it does not appeal to PR students, and only a small
number of PR students are proceeding to the third year of the CAM Diploma.
The majority of CAM's PR students are resident overseas, and lacking know-

ledge and experience of the British scene it is not surprising that three-quarters of them fail even the PR paper.

The situation is therefore serious and dangerous for the PR profession, its future and its image. The poor name of PR is likely to continue so long as staff have to be recruited at second or third career from somewhere else such as journalism, advertising, salesmanship, teaching or something vaguely connected with communication. Sometimes people are merely promoted sideways into PR to make way for another promotion. And in some large companies the PRO is a short-term passenger on his way up the ladder to higher things. This is not to say that many of the people holding PR jobs in spite of their lack of professional training are not working hard, doing their best, and may have learned the job the hard way. But it is not good enough, and it is at the heart of the antagonism which is so often directed at PR. It leads to management abusing PR and to the media and the public distrusting it.

The solution is obvious: there should be a recognised entry into PR via a standard training scheme either at further education or university degree level after which experienced practitioners can be admitted to the Institute of Public Relations. This would be similar to the entry routes, training and qualifications which apply in most other professions. Britain already has a GCE A Level in Communication Studies which could be part of the school-leaving entry to PR training courses.

Employers would then have a reservoir of recruits, and the public would be aware that a PR practitioner was a trained and qualified person. The whole process would begin at sixth-form level and proceed through the normal education channels of higher education. The media would be encouraged to feel that they were dealing with professionals instead of with tame or tamed ex-journalists.

This is not impossible. In small countries like Belgium there are PR schools such as the Hoger Instituut voor Bedrijfsopleiding which trains people for entry into PR. In Britain we have CAM courses for people *already working* in PR (at an age when they have already had enough of education), or polytechnics and universities offering diplomas and degrees in mass communication or communication studies which still leave their graduates needing to learn about PR. The practical need and solution is for a proper professional entry and training procedure. The effect of supply and demand will form the issue as the present CAM system collapses with the annual decline in Diploma finalists as it follows the pattern of the traditional product life cycle. But we have to be like motorcar manufacturers who have a new model ready when sales of the current model have fallen off. Fortunately the thinking has already begun along these lines. The Institute of Public Relations has produced an alternative, parallel CAM Certificate PR syllabus.

This is not a sermon but a statement of the inevitable. The result should be that it will become common professional practice to conduct PR according to the basic principles set out in this book. However, this book is only a beginning.

It will mean that management will expect PR to be planned to achieve specific objectives, and that it will be accountable both on a budgetary and a measurable basis. It will mean that the media, which are rapidly changing in this video age, will no longer have to reject at least 70 per cent of the material it receives from PR sources. It will mean that PR practitioners will become respected professionals, earning salaries like those enjoyed by accountants, company secretaries, architects, lawyers and other qualified people. It will mean that the wider public will be aware of the professional status and social usefulness of PR practitioners. And it will also mean that in the fast changing end of this century essential information necessary to the understanding, acceptance and enjoyment of entirely new life styles will be effectively disseminated. Such people will be skilled in the use of new communication technologies. No longer will it be possible to learn 'on the job' for that will be too late.

5

THE SERVICE NATURE OF PUBLIC RELATIONS

The service nature of public relations is threefold: service to the employer's or client's organisation, to the mass media, and to the organisation's publics.

Service to the Organisation—Feedback

Public relations is a two-way communication system, and while outward communication is necessary to extend knowledge and create understanding, inward communication is like an intelligence service. This may also be called feedback.

What is known and thought about the organisation? To what extent are people aware of it and correctly informed about it? Are there any misconceptions? Any complaints? Feedback can be a kind of insurance, forewarning those in the organisation about advance opinions and hostile attitudes which may or may not be justified. We shall discuss the image in Chapter 16, but we can anticipate this slightly by mentioning the current image (what outsiders think) compared with the mirror image (what insiders think outsiders think). In other words, feedback may show that management has a mistaken idea of how other people view the organisation.

Public relations can produce feedback by use of the following techniques:

(*a*) Research such as opinion or awareness polls, image studies, or discussion groups (which will be explained in Chapter 16).

(*b*) The monitoring of radio and television programmes.

(*c*) Questionnaires answered by customers, clients or patrons.

(*d*) Press cuttings.

(*e*) Evaluation of enquiries, visits to showrooms, attendance at exhibition stands, etc.

(*f*) Requests for literature.

(*g*) Showings of films and attendance figures.

(*h*) Educational requests.

(*i*) Complaints, suggestions and testimonials.

Let us examine each in turn.

Research

Quite apart from the marketing research normally conducted by the marketing department or advertising agency, the PR department or PR consultancy can engage research units to discover states of opinion, attitude or awareness and to define the current image.

Monitoring Broadcasts

Specialist agencies can be engaged to provide transcripts of radio and television programmes. Areas of interest will be similar to those described below about press cuttings.

Customer Questionnaires

Customers, clients and patrons can be issued with questionnaires to obtain information about services provided or product performance. This is a method much used by hotels, holiday tour operators and transportation companies, but questionnaires can also be included with products at the time of purchase to provide feedback on who buys what for whom.

Press Cuttings

Press cutting agencies can be subscribed to for several purposes:

(*a*) Cuttings can be obtained to discover the coverage gained by the distribution of press material. Methods of assessment will be found in Chapter 21, but briefly a tally of the volume of press coverage is less meaningful than an analysis of the coverage achieved.

(*b*) Cuttings can also be collected to learn what the media are saying about the organisation in addition to that initiated by press material. This can be allied to the research described above.

(*c*) It can also be important to collect cuttings which show what is being published about the total industry or subject, or about rival organisations. For instance, a British motorcar manufacturer should be aware of the road-test reports on imported motorcars.

Evaluation of Enquiries

The PR department can produce statistics on the interest aroused by PR activity and resulting in enquiries, callers and visitors, and this can take in sales offices, showrooms and exhibition stands.

Requests for Literature

This is a form of feedback which will indicate response to PR activity of value to the organisation. The literature could be recipe leaflets, advice on the use of products and other expressions of customer interest which can improve customer relations and influence sales.

Showings of Films and Attendance Figures

Again, this statistical information shows the extent to which expenditure on documentary films has been justified and so gives management a picture of the effectiveness of PR. But it can go further and show how, for instance, branch managers are taking advantage of back-up facilities and could be a guide to which managers are the most enterprising.

Educational Requests

Sometimes these are almost philanthropic (e.g. kits for school projects), others like poster displays and other visual aids could be important forms of pre-market education. Some educational material could be for product users, helping them to enjoy the benefits of the product and become more satisfied customers. This could then have a bearing on the next paragraph.

Complaints, Suggestions, Testimonials

Complaints should be welcomed if they help the management to know what people want and how the product could be improved. Similarly, suggestions may help the research and development department, while testimonials are always welcome and may be useful in advertising. Bringing customers into closer participation with the company can be a very useful form of feedback. This facet of PR demonstrates the 'mutual understanding' part of the IPR definition.

Service to the Mass Media

As will be stressed in Chapters 33 and 34, 'servicing the media' is an attitude of mind which the PR practitioner must adopt in media relations. Too often material is submitted to the press after it has been approved by some authority as if it is some official decree which must be published without alteration. Yet the only material that will be published is what the editor or journalist would write himself because it is likely to interest the readers. Put bluntly, an editor can afford to publish only what will sell papers. The circulation figures of newspapers reflect what certain numbers of people of certain types will buy and read. This explains why *The Guardian* sells so few copies and *The Sun* sells millions. If *The Guardian* printed *Sun* material and vice versa the circulation figures would be reversed.

The following are the requirements of servicing the press:

(*a*) Material submitted, in the words of Ivy Ledbetter Lee, should be 'of interest and value to the public'. It must not be puffery.

(*b*) Copy dates and times must be understood, and this implies knowing by which process the publication is printed.

(*c*) Photographs should be both good enough for reproduction, and sufficiently interesting to be worth printing. Photos must be captioned.

(*d*) Releases and articles should be written in a publishable style, not require extensive subediting and rewriting.

(*e*) Releases should be set out as manuscripts or printer's copy so that a minimum of alteration is necessary.

(*f*) The PRO should be a reliable source of information, taking the trouble to check facts before submitting stories, and being frank when asked questions.

(*g*) The PRO has to recognise that not every story can be favourable, and that there are times when it is sufficient to ensure that at least the facts in an unfavourable story are correct.

These are general principles which we shall go over in greater detail in the appropriate chapters, but here they help to illustrate the service nature of press relations in the larger format of public relations generally. We have concentrated on the press, but radio and television call for additional servicing to do with the requirements of their technologies.

Service to the Organisation's Publics

The Mexican Statement stressed that PR should be in the public interest, and this is repeated in the IPR Code of Conduct. It follows that all PR activity should be socially responsible, in no way deceptive, and, although as Henry James has said 'absolute truth is unattainable', it should be honest. It is not the place of PR to twist the truth or to pretend things are what they are not. Nor is it the place of PR to put the best or a better face on things. We are coming very near to saying that PR is neither advertising nor propaganda, in that its information must not be biased. This is sometimes rather hard for management, marketing and advertising people to swallow because naturally they want to boast about their product or service. But is an editor or a radio or television presenter likely to boast on our behalf? If he did so readers, listeners and viewers would think him insincere or in the pay of an advertiser.

Servicing the public therefore implies that we must provide people with information which makes them better informed, better able to judge for themselves, and therefore well equipped with information of value to them. The information may tell them about a new medicine, foodstuff, fashion design, holiday venue, insurance policy, birth control method, pension scheme, hospital service, educational service, savings scheme or whatever. Those who are interested or concerned should benefit from the knowledge they have gained.

After that, advertising can perform the commercial task of persuading people to actually buy, consume or use the product or service. The two are different functions. People may not be persuaded to buy unless they first know about the product or service and have confidence in it.

Computer manufacturers realise that management will not authorise large expenditures on hardware and software unless they first understand the use and value of computers. They cannot be taught through advertising and they are invited to attend courses. Insecticide manufacturers know that house-holders, gardeners and farmers first have to understand the nature of insects and how they can be controlled. Banks realise that customers will not use their services unless they are first shown the benefits of these services. In Third World countries, government departments have to teach millions of largely rural and illiterate people the benefits of public services which are being introduced. The public will not donate to charities unless they understand why funds are needed and what they are used for.

Servicing the public, whether by organisations in the private or public, commercial or non-commercial spheres, is therefore an essential part of effective PR. If the people are not serviced they will reject the information as 'mere advertising' or, worse still, as propaganda.

Particularly in our relations with the media and the public it is significant that a very important characteristic of PR is that we have to consider what people do not know and what they need to know. We have to put ourselves in other people's shoes. It does not matter what we would like to tell them, even what management and clients want us to say. Just as it is useless putting on a film or a play which no one wants to see, so it is useless and wasteful of time and money to try to foist on the media and the public information which is of no interest or value to them.

It is therefore practical to say that public relations will succeed in helping an organisation when it first of all succeeds in helping other people. This may seem a strange theory but it is the only one that works in PR. Every morning in editorial offices the world over large wastepaper bins are filled with news releases from non-believers in this theory. You cannot afford to be even an agnostic in PR.

6

QUALITIES NEEDED BY THE PR PRACTITIONER

There are five principal qualities which are essential to the public relations practitioner. These are:

1. Ability to communicate.
2. Ability to organise.
3. Ability to get on with people.
4. Personal integrity.
5. Imagination.

You may be surprised that the list does not specify that he or she should be a journalist, or a good social entertainer able to read a French menu and a wine list, and a member of good clubs, be good-looking or well-dressed, or able to buy centre court tickets at Wimbledon at a moment's notice. The professional PRO is a hard worker, not a miracle worker. So what do these basic qualities add up to?

Ability to Communicate

The art of communication means the ability to listen as well as to speak. Most people are thinking what they want to say next while they are pretending to listen. The expert communicator has to convey information so that it is easily understood and remembered. This is made difficult because the information is likely to be new and strange, and memories tend to be short.

We are also experiencing a visual age, as with television, when people watch rather than listen. So we have to be aware of the changing nature of communication. We are tending to become lazy communicators.

For years, many people have preferred to telephone rather than write letters. Teletext systems will soon make it unnecessary to hunt through directories, timetables and catalogues for information. Instructions are given better by means of diagrams and pictures than by words. Theories are expressed in models. Even serious newspapers use short paragraphs, and what book publisher today would accept a Henry James novel with paragraphs running to two pages of print? (This is *not* the Henry James quoted before!)

Whatever his medium of expression, the PR practitioner has to make his meaning as clearly and as quickly as possible. He may have to write his message, and a news release which is difficult to cut because it is so tightly written that every word is essential, is a blessing to a busy editor. That is why some of the best news releases are printed under the by-line of a journalist who never wrote a word of it. For the PRO that is absolute success.

Competence in the use of all communications media is important to the PR practitioner. Not only should he be able to write well, but he should be as familiar with a camera as he is with a typewriter or pen. How else can he instruct a photographer on the messages he wants photographs to convey? He does not have to be as expert a technician as the professional photographer,

36

but he should know how to *compose* a picture. Similarly, he should be able to speak well—that is, hold the attention of others and express himself clearly. He may have to do this in public, on the telephone, or in a radio or television studio. And he may have to instruct others in these techniques.

Ability to Organise

A favourite expression of the author's is that ability to organise means ability to anticipate disaster. One of the chief reasons why many women are good in PR is that they are meticulous over details. A good organiser is a born pessimist. He worries about all the things that could go wrong. He is not optimistic until he can guarantee success. A splendid example of this is the PRO who organises an annual press visit of some importance, and books both motor coaches and train tickets in case there is a rail strike.

Ability to organise means ability to take a scheme, start at the beginning and work it out right to the end. This requires planning a timetable of tasks to be performed and a budget covering every cost involved. It is a discipline, simple, methodical and purposeful.

Compare this with the interviews the author has frequently had with journalists seeking jobs as PROs. Their claim to experience was that because they had attended many press receptions they knew all about PR. They had no idea how to *organise* a press reception. Compare this again with the marketing director of a London advertising agency who scoffed at a PR consultant's careful planning, saying, 'All you have to do is ring up a hotel and they will do the rest.'

The ability to organise is a constant requirement. Client meetings, photographic sessions, press receptions, facility visits, support for exhibitions, film showings, private exhibitions, sponsorships, preparation of print, house journal editing, film production—the whole PR year is one of thinking, planning, costing, negotiating, executing, assessing, reporting. Hard work. Managerial responsibility. Especially if one is conducting tangible PR to achieve specific objectives.

This calls for a clear, objective mind. It won't necessarily be all right on the night. Even with the most brilliant planning, things do go wrong, and disaster has to be converted into success. The speaker fails to arrive, there is an air controllers' strike and no plane loads of press reporters arrive, there is a political crisis on the day of the press event, or there is a power cut in the middle of the film première, the ship breaks down on its maiden voyage with the press on board—every PRO has had his share of such disasters. And he has to overcome them and rescue the situation. If possible, the PRO has to anticipate such eventualities. The best way is to avoid complicated schemes and to plan simple events which are easily adapted if problems occur. The author once organised a press visit which was afterwards reported as going like clockwork, but the writer of that press report had no idea that behind the scenes arrangements were being revised all day because of unexpected difficulties. On another occasion he had a press reception well organised and attended except that at the vital moment the client failed to arrive with the product. The whole programme had to be turned round until the lost product could be found.

Ability to get on with People

This does not mean flattering people. The sycophant is no PRO. Getting on with people means liking people, tolerating them, understanding them. PROs have to work with all kinds of people with whom they cannot possibly always agree, let alone like very much. In an international organisation or export situation he will have to work with people of different nationalities, ethnic groups, languages, religions and politics. But even in the simplest, provincial situation there are numerous people to meet and coexist with. A resort publicity manager in a small coastal town has to live and work with scores of hoteliers, boarding-house keepers, entertainments proprietors, motor-coach operators, cafe and restaurant owners, shopkeepers, town councillors, reporters—a world of people in a world of its own. The author was once publicity manager of a Welsh holiday resort where he also had to contend with Welsh-speaking people. Perhaps it was significant that he invented the slogan 'come abroad without crossing the sea'.

Whatever the PRO's situation he is constantly dealing with people of every possible kind.

Wide-ranging tastes are also necessary. The wider the PRO's interests the easier it is to hold conversations with other people, and to be a sympathetic and interested listener. He will frequently have to subdue his own point of view and yet not feel compromised or hypocritical. A British Government department PRO—usually called a chief information officer—has, like any other civil servant, to serve any minister whatever his political party. Politicians come and go but civil servants stay for ever. It is also a theory of consultancy practice that not only should a good consultant be *able* to advise and service any client (since the PR principles are the same), but he should also be willing to advise and service *any* client whether he agrees with him or not. The simple explanation here is that PR is about information, not advocacy, and unlike the lawyer the PRO does not even have to present the best possible case, only the bare facts.

Personal Integrity

In spite of the contempt showered on public relations by its critics, in spite of the belief that he is a charlatan, parasite and master of the black arts, the PRO nevertheless has to be a person of integrity. This does earn its own rewards because the respected PRO has a deservedly high status in his company, has no difficulties over his relations with the media, and is honoured by his peers by being elected to offices, committees, and occasionally to Fellowship of the Institute of Public Relations.

Thus we have a contradictory state of affairs. No PRO can operate effectively unless he is accepted as a person of integrity—trusted for the reliability and impartiality of his information, respected for his professionalism. A few thousand British PR men and women do enjoy such recognition. Others may or may not deserve this respect, but by this basic quality more than anything else will they be judged. The three most serious cases to come before the Professional Practices and Disciplinary Committees of the IPR have revolved around integrity. The difficult question in such cases is whether a person has been evil or merely foolish, but many a foolish act can destroy integrity.

Imagination

The PR practitioner must be a person with *ideas*, capable of solving problems, able to produce original schemes, and use an imaginative approach to all creative work. This creativity will embrace press receptions, open days, house journal design, film scripts, feature articles, exhibits and displays, composition of photographs *and* the use of new technologies. The developing world of computers, video-discs, Viewdata and information technology all demand imagination.

Here we are not concerned with gimmicks and stunts but with a flair for mental perception and original thought and alertness in exploiting opportunities. This must be a form of communication, but it must not be done so 'cleverly' that understanding is obstructed.

7

PR ORGANISATIONS, UK AND INTERNATIONAL

The principal professional organisations of interest to the PR practitioner, and of which membership may be sought if the eligibility requirements can be fulfilled, are listed and described below. Election to membership is usually on the basis of experience or position of responsibility held. Addresses are given at the end of each section.

Institute of Public Relations (IPR)
Public Relations Consultants Association (PRCA)
British Association of Industrial Editors (BAIE)
International Public Relations Association (IPRA)
European Public Relations Federation (CERP)
International Association of Business Communicators (IABC)

In addition, many countries have their own PR institutes and associations, and their addresses are listed in *Hollis Press and Public Relations Annual*, the IPR *Register of Members* and the IPRA *Register of Members*.

Institute of Public Relations

The IPR was founded in 1948, and it has some 2500 elected members including members from 50 countries. It is the largest professional public relations organisation in Europe. Members are elected on an age and experience basis, and detailed application forms, duly sponsored, have to be submitted for approval by the Membership Committee whose recommendations are sent to Council for final acceptance.

The categories of membership are Honorary Fellow, Honorary Member, Fellow, Member, Associate, Affiliate and Student. Citations for Fellowship are voted on by the Council, and normally a candidate will have been a member for 10 years and have made an outstanding contribution to public relations. Just over 100 Fellows have been elected since 1948.

Objectives

The main objectives of the Institute are:

(*a*) To promote the development, recognition and understanding of public relations.

(*b*) To establish and prescribe standards of professional and ethical conduct and ensure the observance of such standards.

(*c*) To encourage the attainment of professional academic qualifications.

(*d*) To provide via meetings, conferences, seminars and printed material, information, discussion and comment on all aspects of the practice of public relations.

(*e*) To maintain two-way contact between the public relations profession in the UK and public relations practitioners throughout the world.

40

The Institute is governed by a Council, with an elected President, honorary treasurer and sometimes an assistant treasurer, a Council consisting of members elected nationally and also elected to represent area groups. There is a Board of Management, as well as Professional Practices, Membership, Disciplinary, Member Services, Education, Membership Development, Public Relations and International committees. A representative is appointed to the CAM Board of Governors.

There are vocational groups representing City and Financial, Local Government, and Consultant members and ten area groups.

The Code of Professional Conduct, which every member must undertake to uphold, is set out, with interpretations, in Chapter 8. The Institute publishes a Register of Members, guidance papers and a journal, and holds annual conferences, seminars and other functions.

The IPR is a constituent member of the Communication, Advertising and Marketing Education Foundation (CAM) which in 1969 took over the Institute's examinations (see Appendix 1). Today the Certificate in Communications Studies and the Diploma in Public Relations constitute the academic qualifications recognised by the IPR. Thus the IPR is the professional body, and CAM is the academic body. The designatory letters are MIPR and DipCAM, although graduates may join the CAM Society when they may use the designatory letters MCAM. The IPR makes its Institute CAM Diploma Award to the best student in the CAM Public Relations Examination.

Address: The Director, Institute of Public Relations, 1 Great James Street, London WC1N 3DA.

Author's comment

One does not *have* to be a member of the IPR to practice PR in the UK. There is no system of registration of PR practitioners. But there are two reasons why any eligible person should be a member. Membership provides recognition of a PR practitioner's professional status, and establishes that he is bound by a professional code of practice.

Public Relations Consultants Association

Whereas the IPR consists of individual members, the PRCA offers corporate membership to consultancies. Founded in 1969, it has about 100 UK members representing about 80 per cent of consultancy business in the UK, and 16 overseas associate members.

Objectives

To encourage and promote the advancement of companies and firms engaged in public relations consultancy. Its principal objectives are to raise and maintain professional standards in consultancy practice, to provide facilities for government, public bodies, associations representing industry, trade and others, to confer with public relations consultants as a body and to ascertain their collective views, to promote confidence in public relations consultancy, and, consequently, in public relations as a whole, and to act as 'spokesman' for the consultancy profession. The PRCA supports and maintains a close fraternal relationship with the Institute of Public Relations

Among its current main objectives are:

(*a*) The improved awareness and status of public relations consultants and the PRCA.

(*b*) Improving management capability in member consultancies.

(*c*) Extending the constituency from which consultancies draw their clients.

(*d*) Raising professional standards of practice at all levels.

The PRCA is governed by an elected Board of Management with an elected chairman, vice-chairman, honorary treasurer, and has Professional Practices and Consultancy Management committees. A representative is appointed to the CAM Board of Governors.

The PRCA Code of Professional Practice is similar to the IPR Code but has clauses specifically related to consultancy practice (see Chapter 8). The PRCA publishes a monthly Newsletter, guidance papers, case studies and *The Public Relations Yearbook* in conjunction with the *Financial Times*. The association has also conducted useful research into consultancy practice.

Address: The General Secretary, Public Relations Consultants Association, 37 Cadogan Street, Sloane Square, London SW3 2PR.

British Association of Industrial Editors

Perhaps because it has benefited from its singlemindedness, the BAIE is a lively and successful body of commercial and industrial house journal editors representing nearly two thousand sponsored or private journals, also being responsible for audio-visual communications. Founded in 1949, BAIE has more than 1000 members but, following a decision taken at its 1980 AGM, it has extended its constitutional basis to embrace communicators who use other than printed media, thus recognising the impact of audio-visual methods upon industrial editing.

BAIE's main objectives are:

(*a*) To develop the skills of members.

(*b*) To promote a regular exchange of ideas and experience between members on communication techniques.

(*c*) To provide education in all aspects of industrial editing and encourage other educational bodies to do so.

(*d*) To convince organisations that effective communication promotes good relationships and business efficiency.

(*e*) To improve standards of organisational communications and provide an expert consultancy service for members and managements.

(*f*) To cooperate with other organisations concerned in the work of organisational communications.

BAIE publishes the monthly *BAIE News*, sponsors and runs courses and seminars, holds luncheon meetings, publishes a directory of members and services, has an appointment bureau, offers consultancy services, holds an annual convention, and runs its well-known yearly house journal competition. Members are first admitted as Associates and may progress to full membership by examination or proof of suitability. Emphasis is placed on the Association's two-part examination for which there are day-release and correspondence courses.

Address: The Secretary General, British Association of Industrial Editors, 3 Locks Yard, High Street, Sevenoaks, Kent TN13 1LT.

International Public Relations Association

Founded in 1949, IPRA is a para-national society of experienced PR practitioners with international interests and has more than 600 members in some 60 countries. It has an International Code of Ethics (the *Code of Athens*), the Code's principles being inspired by the United Nations Declaration of Human Rights.

Since 1958, IPRA has held a series of World Congresses, including one in London in 1979 and one in Bombay in 1982. The IPRA Council meets in a different country each year. In 1975 IPRA sponsored the First All-Africa PR Conference in Nairobi.

The Association publishes the *IPRA Newsletter* and the quarterly *IPRA Review*, which provide an international forum of PR news and thought. The Register of Members is an exceptionally informative one with portraits of members.

Standing committees deal with Professional Standards, Education and Research, Membership, Conferences and Congresses, Services to Members and Finance. There are IPRA delegates to the United Nations.

Awards include a Gold Paper award and the President's Award which, in 1977, was accepted by the Nobel Foundation, in 1978 by the International Red Cross, and was made to Dr Edward Bernays for his outstanding contribution to better world understanding.

All members are elected in their individual capacity (minimum five years' international PR experience) and there is no corporate membership.

Address: The IPRA Secretariat, 49 Wellington Street, Covent Garden, London WC2E 8BN.

European Federation of Public Relations (CERP)
(Confédération Européen des Rélations Publiques)

This is a federation of the national professional PR bodies in 14 European countries (the British IPR being the largest) and it also has hundreds of individual members. Founded in 1959, it has a code of practice which harmonises the codes of its member bodies. Its main objectives are:

(a) To provide a means for public relations practitioners in Europe to exchange knowledge and experience and to develop PR techniques.

(b) To harmonise and raise professional standards on a Europe-wide basis.

(c) To support and promote public relations education to the highest standard.

There are three working sections:

1. CEDAN, the federal committee, in which the IPR is represented. This deals with matters of common concern to the national associations, especially on professional standards. A harmonisation programme is designed to ensure that every full member of every association will be 'guaranteed' to have an agreed minimum qualification of experience and observance of an enforceable code of professional conduct.

2. CEDAP, through which individual practitioners exchange knowledge of PR techniques and developments, through case studies, discussion meetings, etc. A model European contract for consultancy services has been issued. An award for social audit work has been launched.

3. CEDET, which is concerned with PR professional education. Sessions are given on PR educational developments in member countries.

CERP has a monthly newsletter, and publishes papers and reports, provides a scheme for exchange visits at no cost to participants other than their fares, and makes an international award for public relations, and an award for work on PR education. There is an active British section.

Address: The Secretary General, CERP, Avenue du Rond-Point 12, B-1330 Rixensart, Belgium.

International Association of Business Communicators

The IABC was formed out of a combination of US and Canadian house journal bodies and now has a large international membership with 93 chapters in North America, one in the UK and members in some 20 countries. In a short time it has gained a reputation for efficient organisation, impressive conferences, useful seminars, first class literature, its Gold Quill award for superior achievements and its annual directory.

The IABC publishes the monthly *IABC News* and the quarterly *Journal of Organisational Communication*. Seminars are announced in communication packages covering numerous topics. In the UK, the chapter issues a newsletter and also runs seminars. A special member service consists of idea files. Every two years an in-depth survey of trends and salaries is conducted. The international annual conference is a major event.

Membership is by application, but accreditation, based on examination and examples of accomplishments, is offered.

The IABC aims to establish the role and develop the expertise of the business communicator, especially in management–employee relations, raising the status of house journal editors to that of communications manager. This may be seen as a challenge to the older and often smaller, impecunious and precariously organised bodies such as the IPR, PRCA and PRSA, if not the BAIE. However, while it is not a national professional institute like the IPR, it is certainly an organisation of remarkable verve and authority which other organisations may have to emulate if they are to survive. Size of membership does provide the necessary funds to be efficient, and IABC has well over 7000 members.

Address: The Executive Director, International Association of Business Communicators, 870 Market Street, Suite 928, San Francisco, CA 94102, USA. UK Chapter: Nicholas P. Cutcliffe (Director), 130 Valley Road, Chorleywood, Rickmansworth, Herts WD3 4BN.

8

THE IPR CODE OF PROFESSIONAL CONDUCT
AND ITS INTERPRETATION

The following Code of Professional Conduct, and its interpretation, is reproduced by permission of the Institute of Public Relations.

Interpretation of the Code of Professional Conduct

Over the years the Institute's Code of Professional Conduct has often been revised and extended. This should be regarded as normal. No set of rules for the behaviour of members can afford to remain rigid in a fast-growing profession which is itself intricately involved with the changing standards of society.

Recent years have seen a number of important revisions, mostly based upon 'case law' experience gained in the Professional Practices Committee. To help IPR members to interpret and uphold the Code, the committee has prepared this pamphlet explaining the operation of the Code's 17 clauses.

No such brief commentary can hope to cover all the problems of interpretation which might arise under the Code. Members can always obtain advice from the Professional Practices Committee by writing to the Director of the Institute.

CLAUSE 1
Standards of professional conduct
A member, in the conduct of his professional activities, shall respect the public interest and the dignity of the individual. It is his personal responsibility at all times to deal fairly and honestly with his client or employer, past or present, with his fellow members, with the media of communication and with the public.

Clause 1 is intentionally drawn in broad terms. The expression 'the public interest' is used in statute law and the term 'the dignity of the individual' echoes wording used in the Universal Declaration of Human Rights. Both phrases have yet to be interpreted formally in a public relations context, but there are few members who would not in practice recognise any flagrant violation of the principles which they express.

'The public interest' can be assumed to mean the interest of the public as a whole, as opposed to the sectional interest of a public relations practitioner's employer or client, or indeed his own.

Which of us can claim to judge what is or is not in the interest of the public at large? It is, in theory, possible that the Institute might one day have to decide whether public relations action in support of some particular cause was promoting, say, immorality. In so unlikely a case, the Institute would certainly be guided by the climate of public opinion and the law in force at the time.

In practice, the more likely danger is the use of *methods* which are against the interests of the public. It is possible to envisage an unscrupulous practitioner lending himself to the fostering of ill-will between racial communities, or trying to conceal the future ill effects of an industrial process known to cause pollution. Such conduct would be contrary to Clause 1.

The 'dignity of the individual', if taken in its fullest sense, is equally a matter which can be judged only subjectively. Yet members in the National Health Service, for instance, will have no doubt of their obligation to respect the privacy and feelings of a patient or his relatives.

At a lesser level, perhaps, no member who respects the dignity of the individual would contrive a situation—perhaps in a press or radio interview—where a person was artificially held up to ridicule.

Dealing 'fairly and honestly' with clients, employers, fellow-members, the media of communication and the public is an all-embracing requirement. It applies particularly to consultants' public relations proposals, plans and reports.

In one example which attracted some publicity, a member was found to have represented to his client that he could arrange for his Scandinavian director secretly to edit an English language section of a foreign newspaper with a view to trying to place favourable articles. The statement was found to be incorrect; had it been proved correct, the member concerned would have been in breach of the Code in other ways!

Fairness and honesty must run through all public relations practice, from the way in which information is given to the financial world to the manner in which the employee communications aspects of redundancy are handled.

CLAUSE 2
Dissemination of information
A member shall not knowingly or recklessly disseminate false or misleading information, and shall use proper care to avoid doing so inadvertently. He has a positive duty to maintain integrity and accuracy.

The object of this clause is to make it plain that not only is it the member's moral duty to be honest and accurate, but that it must be his positive concern to ensure that all information issued, whether by himself or by those who work for him, is correct.

It forbids any form of deception in the issue of information and also lays upon the member the responsibility to ensure that no unchecked or unconfirmed material is released. This responsibility can range from avoiding misleading phraseology in financial documents to not stating as facts unproved claims for the performance of consumer goods.

CLAUSE 3
Media of communication
A member shall not engage in any practice which tends to corrupt the integrity of the media of communication.

This clause is aimed at protecting the freedom of the press, including radio and television, to publish news and views as they think fit. Any influence, or attempted influence, on the decision-making processes of the press is expressly forbidden. This is one of the most serious forms of professional misconduct, whether it takes the form of straight or disguised bribery or hints of 'advertising considerations'.

Commonsense should rule the provision of entertainment for the press, which can rarely be criticised as applying undue pressure. A meeting over drinks to get to know a specialist writer and his requirements is as acceptable as providing lunch during a press facility visit; on the other hand, a case of whisky for an editor before—or after—he has published a story is not permissible.

CLAUSE 4
Undisclosed interests
A member shall not be a party to any activity which deliberately seeks to dissemble or mislead by promoting a disguised or undisclosed interest, while appearing to further another. It is his duty to ensure that the actual interest of any organisation with which he may be professionally concerned is adequately declared.

The main purpose of this clause is to prevent the formation of 'front' organisations which appear to have a particular—and usually apparently laudable—objective, while in fact concealing vested interests of one kind or another.

An example would be the setting up of a body to campaign for more relaxed gaming laws on a social reform basis without revealing that the sponsors were running a chain of gambling casinos. A less extreme example would be an information bureau appearing to deal with a particular raw material, but which was covertly sponsored by one company and acted in its interests rather than those of the industry as a whole.

Actual cases of deception on similar lines have occurred and there are various situations in which the temptation to set up a 'front' organisation might exist.

Disclosure of interest is a necessity in any body which seeks to impose professional standards and perhaps particularly in public relations where accusations of misrepresentation are not unknown.

There are, of course, numerous promotional associations which set out quite openly to publicise a variety of products or services. Because the objects of these associations are clearly defined—often in the titles—and their sponsorship is made plain, there is no doubt about their aims and backing. The Professional Practices Committee would be happy to advise any member who might have doubts about the acceptability, under Clause 4, of forming a particular promotional body. Normally, the test is simple: is the interest which it is designed to further clearly and specifically identified?

CLAUSE 5
Confidential information
A member shall not disclose (except upon the order of a court of competent jurisdiction) or make use of information given or obtained in confidence from his employer or client, past, present or potential, for personal gain or otherwise, without express consent.

Any professional adviser, if his advice is to be of value, must receive the full confidence of his client. Public relations practitioners in the financial field are entrusted with figures and information which could make them a fortune on the Stock Exchange. Those concerned with marketing—and indeed almost all public relations practitioners in some degree—hold information which competitors of their employer or client would wish to obtain. It is not merely ethically right, but a practical necessity, for practitioners to respect these confidences if public relations is to hold the status the Institute believes it should.

It may well be that confidential information is obtained during the preliminary stages of negotiation with a client; the word 'potential' covers this phase. It is essential that confidential information obtained prior to there being a contract, or if no contract develops, must be subject to the same security.

In practice this means keeping a constant watch on security in the office. At least one financial public relations consultancy requires every executive and secretary to read and acknowledge a formal letter of warning regarding the buying or selling of personal shareholdings in client companies. If a practitioner changes employment, or takes on a new client whose business competes with that of a former client, great care must be taken to distinguish between what is useful experience in the field and what is information received in confidence by virtue of the public relations man's professional status. The bracketed phrase 'except upon the order of a court of competent jurisdiction' distinguishes the professional position of the public relations man from the position taken up by journalists, who have a traditional obligation—not, of course, recognised by the law—never to disclose their sources. The Institute does not ask or wish its members to defy the law, and their position in this matter is exactly the same as that of doctors or lawyers.

CLAUSE 6
Conflict of interests
A member shall not represent conflicting or competing interests without the express consent of the parties concerned after full disclosure of the facts.

The question of conflicting or competing interests is one which affects every consultant. Competition needs no clarification. Conflict is perhaps rather less obvious, but could arise if, for instance, a practitioner were to be retained by a local authority and by an organisation campaigning for improvement of amenities in the same area; or by a trade association of manufacturers and another of retailers in the same industry.

There is *no* rule that members may not represent conflicting or competing interests, only that they may not do so without the consent of those concerned, after full disclosure of the facts.

In some fields, clients often feel that the consultancy's special knowledge of their needs outweighs any danger caused by sharing its service with other organisations of the same type. This is so, for example, in the City, where merchant banks and others are themselves familiar with conflict situations, and where a highly confidential relationship between consultant and client is normal practice. In the context of consumer marketing, on the other hand, clients usually dislike their consultancy to represent a competitor.

Although the bigger the consultancy the more frequent are the possible clashes of interest, it is easier for a large consultancy to ensure that a different team works for each client. This, of course, is the way in which firms in other professions deal with this problem.

CLAUSE 7
Sources of payment
A member, in the course of his professional services to his employer or client, shall not accept payment either in cash or in kind in connection with those services from any other source without the express consent of his employer or client.

As a public relations man is paid by his client for writing and issuing a feature, it would be wrong for him to accept an author's fee from a paper which publishes it. That is the simplest example of the malpractice against which this clause is aimed.

However, it does not preclude a consultancy, for example, receiving a trade discount from a supplier, such as a printer or photographer, provided that acceptance of this discount is approved by the client. If it is not agreed by the client, then the discount must be passed on.

This clause, however, does forbid the member from receiving rewards from suppliers or others as an inducement to place his employer's or client's business with them.

In Clauses 5, 6 and 7 the words 'express consent' are used. To say 'I know my client would not mind' or 'he is aware of the situation and did not object' is not enough, either ethically or as a defence against any complaint that the Code has been breached in this respect. The practitioner's client or employer must be made aware of the facts and formally accept the situation.

CLAUSE 8
Disclosure of financial interests
A member having a financial interest in an organisation shall not recommend the use of that organisation, nor make use of its services on behalf of his client or employer, without declaring his interest.

This is an extension of Clause 7 to cover the situation in which, for instance, a consultant has an associated graphic design studio or photographic or model agency; or in which a staff public relations man is privately a partner in a printing or catering concern.

There is nothing wrong in the member having such an outside interest, but it is improper for him to use it or recommend its use without, firstly, disclosure of the interest and, secondly, the client's or employer's specific agreement.

CLAUSE 9
Payment contingent upon achievements
A member shall not negotiate or agree terms with a prospective employer or client on the basis of payment contingent upon specific future public relations achievements.

One of the most-discussed problems in the profession is the evaluation of the results of public relations activity. If there is any broad agreement on this it is that the basic need, in an ideal situation, is for sophisticated research to check regularly on changes in attitude among the audience concerned. The problem affects all practitioners, but only consultants are likely to face it in the context of payment.

Confusing the situation is the ghost of the old-time press agent, who often charged his clients per column inch of press mentions obtained on their behalf. Even today it is not unknown for some form of payment by results to be suggested. The basic argument against this is that the client is buying the professional skill and knowledge of the consultant. The success of the wide range of methods used to further the client's interests cannot fairly be judged by specific results over a given period; nor do corporate public relations campaigns, for example, depend for their success solely upon specific achievements. A further point is that many outside factors may be involved in determining whether the intended results are realised. Moreover a payment-by-results basis of operation is a potential inducement to corruption of the media.

Of course, at the end of the day the client has to decide whether he is getting value for money. This assessment is likely to depend upon the attainment of a variety of objectives ranging, perhaps, from improved employee relations to a defence against a takeover bid. The results which have been obtained need to be evaluated and management decisions made on future action and expenditure. This cannot sensibly be done on the basis of a prior agreement to pay a fixed amount for the achievement of such results as can be physically measured.

Members of the IPR are as much professionals in their own field as are accountants and solicitors. We do not pay a solicitor an agreed portion of the damages he might obtain in a court action; we pay for skilled work, having initially agreed what needs to be done. That this should also happen in public relations is the purpose of Clause 9.

CLAUSE 10
Supplanting another member

A member seeking employment or new business by direct and individual approach to a potential employer or client shall take all reasonable steps to ascertain whether that employment or business is already carried out by another member. If so, it shall be his duty to advise the other member in advance of any approach he proposes to make to the employer or client concerned. (Nothing in this clause shall be taken as inhibiting a member from the general advertisement of his services.)

The Institute does not want to rob the business of fair competition between its members, but professionalism, with all the sharing of knowledge and struggle for higher standards that the word implies, is essential. Members are hardly likely to behave as professionals if they are trying to steal the bread from each other's mouths. Hence Clause 10.

There is no harm in a member writing or telephoning to offer his services or capabilities to a potential client or employer, but he must first find out whether that employer or client is already using the professional services of a fellow member. If so, he must first advise the member of the approach he proposes to make.

In the case of employed fellow members this is not difficult to check from the Register of Members. In the case of consultants, however, it is not so simple for they do not always publish the names of their clients in the standard reference books. A check can be made with the Public Relations Consultants' Association provided, of course, that they are members of that association.

The blanket coverage circular—particularly if it contains a phrase inviting the recipient to disregard it if already satisfactorily served—is not prohibited by this clause: 'direct and individual' communication is its specific concern. Likewise, there is no restriction on press advertising or other public promotional activity. A general offer of services to a potential client by an IPR member who is a consultant—still provided that reasonable research is undertaken—does not constitute unfair competition.

CLAUSE 11
Rewards to holders of public office
A member shall not, with intent to further his interests (or those of his client or employer), offer or give any regard to a person holding public office if such action is inconsistent with the public interest.

Clause 11 simply reflects the fact that Institute members are citizens before they are public relations practitioners and must not improperly make use of the services of a public office-holder.

That does not mean that it is *never* proper to employ, or pay a fee to, a public office-holder; there are many respectable precedents for this both in and out of public relations.

For example, if an employer has premises which cause pollution or a consultant specialises in environmental problems, then to engage as an adviser an MP or a member of a local authority who has particular knowledge of such matters would not be improper, provided the public interest was not put at risk.

If, however, that adviser were then asked to be concerned with a specific issue with which he had to deal in the course of his public duties, there would be a clear risk of his acting in a manner inconsistent with his public responsibilities.

The moral problem facing both the Institute member and the office-holder may not be resolved by a simple declaration of the interests involved. It would clearly be wrong, for instance, to offer to pay the chairman of a planning committee for advice on a client's planning problems if eventually he were likely to hear an application from that client; nor would it be an adequate defence to say that it was the chairman's duty to declare his interest.

An Institute member does not breach the Code simply by employing or retaining a public office-holder, but he would do so if he tried to persuade that individual to act in his employer's or client's interests contrary to the public interest.

CLAUSE 12
Employment of Members of Parliament
A member who employs a Member of Parliament, of either House, whether in a consultative or executive capacity, shall disclose this fact, and also the object of the employment, to the Director of the Institute, who shall enter it in a register kept for the purpose. A member of the Institute who is himself a Member of Parliament shall be directly responsible for disclosing or causing to be disclosed to the Director any such information as may relate to himself. (The register referred to in this clause shall be open to public inspection at the offices of the Institute during office hours).

Clause 12 simply requires an Institute member who employs or retains a Member of Parliament, of either House, to register the fact formally with the Institute. If the member is himself an MP or peer, he has a personal responsibility for registering.

The Institute is thus provided with a register which reveals to the public the names of Members of Parliament involved directly or indirectly in public relations practice. In other words, professional conduct in this sphere must not only be good, but be seen to be good!

It is hardly necessary to add that this in no way diminishes the traditional responsibility of a Member of Parliament to declare any personal interest which may have a bearing on his public duties.

CLAUSE 13
Injury to other members
A member shall not maliciously injure the professional reputation or practice of another member.

Injury to the professional reputation or practice of a member is most likely to arise in practice under the temptation provided by competition between consultants: for instance, by informing a member's client of any real or imagined shortcomings in the member's practice of public relations.

It is probable that 'maliciously' in the context of Clause 13 could be proved by any such behaviour carried out with an improper motive; indeed, an improper motive could often be inferred from the circumstances.

CLAUSE 14
Instruction of others

A member who knowingly causes or permits another person or organisation to act in a manner inconsistent with this Code, or is party to such action, shall himself be deemed to be in breach of it.

Clause 14 is an important safeguard to professional standards. No member can excuse breaches of the Code by pleading that they were committed by, for instance, a member of his staff, who might not be a member and by reason of his subordinate position might in any case be under pressure to comply with his client's instructions.

A member must not be a 'party to' a breach of the Code. He must resist it and dissent from it. For example, a member who is a director of a consultancy must not acquiesce or join in any decision of the board which is in contravention of the Code.

If this were not so, a member would have the excuse that the breach was carried out by a corporate body which would not, of course, be amenable to the Institute's discipline.

CLAUSE 15
Reputation of the profession

A member shall not conduct himself in any manner detrimental to the reputation of the Institute or the profession of public relations.

Clause 15 applies to all forms of behaviour which could harm the reputation of the Institute or the profession.

Quite apart from the fact that certain jobs, possibly estimable in themselves, cannot easily be compatible with professional status, a member is unlikely to be able to hold a position on the staff of a newspaper or other medium without harming the reputation of public relations for professional detachment and the reputation of journalism for objective assessment.

However, there is no 'black list' and each case must be decided on its merits.

Many other circumstances are covered by the clause. A member who writes an article or makes a speech in which he seriously denigrates the profession, or the Institute which represents it, would be in breach of Clause 15. So would any member who was found guilty of a major criminal offence.

Clause 15, in fact is designed to protect the profession and Institute in all matters which, while not part of public relations practice, reflect on their collective good name.

CLAUSE 16
Upholding the Code

A member shall uphold this Code, shall cooperate with fellow members in so doing and in enforcing decisions on any matter arising from its application. If a member has reason to believe that another member has been engaged in practices which may be in breach of this Code, it shall be his duty to inform the Institute. It is the duty of all members to assist the Institute to implement this Code, and the Institute will support any member so doing.

Clause 16 requires members to uphold the Code, and—as a duty—to help the Institute to deal with possible breaches. The Institute has an effective procedure on disciplinary matters, but in the last resort it is helpless without members' cooperation. The Professional Practices Committee can often give guidance to members which—if they follow it—will ensure they keep within the Code.

Where disciplinary proceedings have to be taken, the Institute must depend on the cooperation of everyone concerned: it does not possess the powers of a court of law to compel witnesses, and without evidence the Institute may be rendered powerless against an individual who has harmed the profession by his conduct.

CLAUSE 17
Other Professions
A member shall, when acting for a client or employer who belongs to a profession, respect the code of ethics of that other profession and shall not knowingly be party to any breach of such a code.

This most recent clause to be added to the Code recognises the public relations practitioner's responsibility for understanding and respecting the code of ethics applicable to a client or employer who is a member of one of the established professions.

It is specifically aimed at ensuring that members of the professions are not aided or persuaded to act in breach of their own ethical codes by the application of public relations techniques. The restraint laid upon doctors, architects and others over the use of publicity to attract business is an example of a likely area of difficulty.

If in doubt about the interpretation of this—or any other—clause, members may seek the guidance of the Professional Practices Committee, writing first to the Director.

November 1977

9

COMMON AND STATUTE LAW AFFECTING PUBLIC RELATIONS

There are two kinds of law with which the PR practitioner needs to be familiar, although the advice of a solicitor may be required if legal matters are encountered. Broadly speaking, there is **common law** which concerns contracts and torts or civil wrongs and by which an aggrieved party can seek damages through suing in the civil courts, and **statute law** (Acts of Parliament and Regulations) which makes offenders liable to prosecution, fine and/or imprisonment as a result of criminal proceedings between the Crown and the wrongdoer.

Contract

This is probably the most common legal experience of the PR practitioner. A consultant has a contract with a client to perform agreed services for an agreed fee. If print or photographs are ordered, there is a contract between the two parties. It is therefore important that both sides are clear about the conditions and requirements of such contracts, and that they avoid breaches of contract. Ideally, a contract should be in writing, but many contracts are entered into on the telephone when, say, a photographer is asked to carry out an assignment, or a hotel room is booked for a function, and this agreement is not necessarily confirmed in writing. Contracts may be effected in conversation on a 'my word is my bond' basis, and hands are shaken as a sign of trust.

But what makes a contract? Three things are necessary. There must be an **offer**, an **acceptance** and a **consideration**. If the acceptance is not unconditional but introduces conditions different from the original offer the acceptance becomes an offer which now has to be accepted. In this situation there must be a definite intention to create a legal situation. It is no use one side offering goods or a service, and supplying them, unless the other side has clearly agreed to accept the offer. Moreover, there is the third element—consideration— which means that both sides must make a sacrifice or give value to the other. In other words, one side may supply goods while the other side makes payment. A one-sided bargain, such as a gift, is not a contract. Both sides must surrender something of value to the other, although the fairness of the exchange is immaterial.

So it is vital, if a contract is to be enforced, that both sides are absolutely clear about what they are offering, accepting and using as consideration. There must be no **mistake** or **misrepresentation** which could render the contract invalid in the event of a dispute.

Let us take two typical examples.

1. If a PR consultant makes an offer of service to a potential client, and this offer is accepted, the letter of contract should specify all the special con-

ditions of the contract such as its duration, the required period of cancellation, and the method by which remuneration shall be paid, such as three months' fee in advance. If the consultant is to engage in creative work such as photography or print design, it is wise to state in the letter of contract whether or not the copyright of original work is to remain the consultant's property or whether this copyright is to be assigned to the client automatically or on the final payment of all monies due.

2. If a PR practitioner is buying print his acceptance should be in the form of a letter which either repeats exactly the terms of the printer's quotation, or refers specifically to the quotation by some clear identification such as its date or number.

This also implies that if a strictly legal relationship is required with a supplier, so that a remedy may be sought if the order is not properly fulfilled, a quotation should first be obtained. This could apply to much business conducted by a PR practitioner such as when holding a press reception, printing a house journal, having an exhibition stand designed, ordering photography and so on. A quotation is an offer and a good basis for a clearly understood contract. But if one orders print, and there has been no definite agreement about, say, the weight or quality of the paper there are no grounds for dispute if the job is printed on a paper which the PR practitioner (or a consultant's client) dislikes after the job has been printed. The PR practitioner has to be businesslike!

Defamation

Care must be taken not to bring another person, organisation or perhaps product into disrepute. Although unintentionally committed, the offence could result in an action for damages or an injunction to prevent further reference. English law contains two forms of defamation: the spoken or transitory kind called **slander**, or the permanent kind (not only written or published but also broadcast statements) which are known as **libel**.

To be scandalous or libellous, a statement must be:

(*a*) Defamatory.
(*b*) False, unless proved contrary.
(*c*) Understood to refer to the person claiming to be defamed.
(*d*) Made known to at least one person other than the plaintiff.

For instance, in giving a reference one has to be careful not to defame the person written about, which is why many references are written in very diplomatic terms. Some employers will state no more than the facts of employment, and make no comment, favourable or unfavourable!

Here is an actual example of an innocent PR act which resulted in an embarrassing injunction.

A PRO wrote and published an article about a repair service. Without seeking permission, the make of product repaired was named. The makers interpreted this to mean that their product was faulty. As a result of an injunction all copies of the magazine and all printing materials concerned with it were seized on a court order. This concerned **slander of goods**.

One also has to be careful about the use of pictures in which people are featured. Normally, people in a crowd scene cannot claim damages because they were present of their own volition (even if the disclosed presence is unfortunate!), but if some comment is added which could be held to be defamatory action may be possible. This occurred once in a pamphlet when a comment was 'ballooned' to a person in a queue outside a shop, and this person sued successfully because the comment was false and could have been held to hold the plaintiff in disrepute.

Copyright

Copyright subsists in any original work, although not in an idea, and is subject to the Copyright Act, 1956. Generally, it covers very broadly 'literary, dramatic, musical or artistic, work'. This covers written or printed material, photographs, pictures, charts and other artwork, gramophone records, tape recordings and broadcast material.

There are certain exceptions known as '**fair dealing**' such as if the material is not a substantial part, or the use is educational, or if it is not used commercially or for profit, but one still has to be careful, and due acknowledgement is desirable as well as courteous.

Copyright is automatic and does not have to be applied for, although it should be declared wherever possible. The author's copyright is stated at the front of this book. Normally, copyright exists for 50 years. Copyright can be assigned to someone else who then owns the copyright.

A typical PR copyright problem occurs when a photograph is taken by a newspaper photographer, and it may be so useful to the PRO that he wishes to use it perhaps to illustrate a house journal. He will usually be expected to pay a reproduction fee. But he cannot issue it with a news release because the editors will be unable to print it without paying the copyright owner a fee. Editors expect PR pictures to be the copyright of the sender, and therefore supplied 'free of copyright' so that they may be printed free of charge. It is therefore nonsense to state on a PR picture that it is the copyright of the sender and cannot be printed without permission since this is self-defeating.

Consequently, a **news release** is not copyright since it is issued widely to anyone who wishes to use it, even change or rewrite it. A **PR feature article**, however, is different because it is usually written by agreement (virtually commissioned even though not paid for) and is exclusive to the publisher under a 'first served rights' agreement. In other words, it would be an offence to publish the article in another publication without the first editor's permission. However, another kind of PR article is the **syndicated** article, meaning that it may be offered and published in a number of publications, but such articles should be clearly offered as syndicated material, and it is sensible and courteous to state that they are offered to editors with non-competing circulations since editors will not wish to print the same feature articles as their competitors. The PR practitioner should be aware of the distinction between a news release or news story, and an exclusive or syndicated feature article.

Passing Off

This offence may occur by (i) misuse of a trading name; (ii) misuse of the trade name of the goods; and (iii) imitation of the get-up of the goods. 'Get-up' could include the container, label or package. For example, if a product was packed in a specially shaped bottle with which people were familiar (e.g. Coca-Cola, Bovril, Marmite) and was given a very similar name, people might buy it because they thought it was the well-known product and not a substitute. This practice has become a big problem in Nigeria, while pirated books in Asia present a similar problem.

For a case to be brought under English law, the plaintiff must show that:

1. The trade name or get-up is associated with his goods in the public mind.

2. That the acts objected to have interfered or are calculated to interfere with the conduct of business or sale of goods in the sense that there is confusion in the public mind.

The two products must be in a common area of trade. If operating in different trades—e.g. Colt beer, Colt gun, Colt motorcar—no legal action can be taken.

It is not necessary to prove a fraudulent motive or that the public has been confused: only that confusion was likely to occur, although proof of actual confusion will strengthen a case. It is not necessary to show actual damage, but again it helps if damage can be shown to have been suffered.

This situation may be encountered by a PRO if the reputation of his original product is suffering because an inferior substitute is assumed to be the original, and confusion, complaints or loss of sales are occurring.

Lotteries

Competitions should contain an element of skill otherwise they are liable to be illegal under the Betting, Gaming and Lotteries Act, 1963, and subsequent amending Lotteries Acts. Correct answers must not be pre-judged. For non-commercial purposes, lucky draws are usually acceptable. If a competition is to be published in the press, editors usually require to see the rules and to check that there is adequate time for the submission of rules, that contestants are required to use their judgement and that entries will be fairly and competently judged. It is not sufficient that in a two-stage contest only the tie-breaker calls for skill: skill is required in both parts.

Statute Law

There are many Acts, apart from those already mentioned which may concern the PR practitioner in his work, chief among these being:

Fair Trading Act, 1973
Misrepresentation Act, 1967
Race Relations Act, 1968
Trade Descriptions Acts, 1968 and 1978
Sex Discrimination Act, 1975

Of these, the Trade Descriptions Acts are particularly significant because PR material could contain false descriptions even inadvertently. For instance, the place of origin can be misunderstood or misleading if a product is normally thought to have a special place of origin. Sherry is a good example: is it 'genuine' Spanish sherry or is it Cyprus or South African? When writing product publicity stories one needs to read labels, packages and other product material to see that correct descriptions are given in releases, photo captions, feature articles and elsewhere. It is all too easy to refer to something as being of, say, Scandinavian design when in fact it is actually made in the Far East.

The Fair Trading Act is concerned with consumer trade practices, and if such practices are held to be unfair and the related PR activities could be construed to be some form of advertising, marketing or canvassing, the Director General of Fair Trading could refer the matter to the Consumer Protection Advisory Committee.

For fuller information the reader is referred to the legislation itself, copies being obtainable from HM Stationery Office, while useful books are the latest edition of Philip S. James' popular *Introduction to English Law* (Butterworth), *Advertising Law Handbook* by Diana Woolley (Business Books), R. G. Lawson's *Advertising Law* (Macdonald & Evans) or *Law Made Simple* by C. F. Padfield and F. E. Smith (Heinemann). The Institute of Public Relations publishes a guidance booklet *Public Relations and the Law*.

PART 2

PUBLIC RELATIONS PRACTICE IN ORGANISATIONAL FRAMEWORKS

10

IN-HOUSE PR DEPARTMENTS AND PR CONSULTANCIES

A PR consultancy is not a PR agency. The misleading and incorrect term 'PR agency' is borrowed from advertising, and is another example of the confusion that exists about PR and advertising.

Historically and strictly speaking, an advertising agent is an agent of the media from whom he gains most of his income in the form of commission on the space and airtime he buys. He is 'recognised' or 'accredited' by the media owners' organisations (e.g. the Newspaper Publishers' Association and the Independent Television Contractors' Association) for the purposes of the 'commission system'. He is a kind of commission agent: *the PR consultant is not.*

Commission and recognition are irrelevant to the PR consultant, who cannot therefore be termed an 'agent'. His income is derived from professional fees based on man-hours and expertise. Some advertising agents have rejected the commission system in favour of being paid for what they do and how skilled they are at doing it, but however more professional and admirable this advance may be it has been adopted by only a few. The commission system favours the advertiser (who gets free services) and the media owner (who has to deal with fewer accounts and can depend on prompt payment).

From this it will be seen that one reason why advertisers use agencies is that they get free services. So why use a PR consultancy whose services have to be paid for? Why not handle PR yourself? While most organisations do, the question is not quite as simple as that because the situations are not identical. For this reason, it will be best if PR consultancies are discussed before we deal with in-house or internal PR departments.

Let us consider the different reasons why an organisation may use an advertising agency and a PR consultancy.

Reasons for Using an Advertising Agency

1. Because the organisation has reached a level of expenditure on advertising when it has become economical to use the services of an agency rather than employ expensive specialist staff who may not be required full-time.

2. When it becomes economical for an agency to accept the account under the commission system although agencies do accept accounts with little commission income on a service fee basis, e.g. industrial advertisers.

3. Because the advertiser requires expert media planning and space/air time buying services.

4. Because the advertiser needs clever, original creative services such as design, copywriting and the production of television and radio commercials.

5. Because the advertiser needs advice on marketing and market research.

6. Because the advertiser needs an all-round service incorporating all the above plus other services covering print production, exhibitions, sales promotion and merchandising.

7. Because the advertiser is situated out of town and needs services which are city-based.

8. To handle recruitment advertising through agencies specialising in this field.

Reasons for Using a PR Consultancy

1. Because the organisation has not reached a level of expenditure on public relations when it would be justified in setting up its own PR Department. *This is the opposite to the advertising situation.*

2. Because the organisation needs counselling services on communication problems.

3. To supply a press relations service.

4. To provide an information service.

5. To plan and execute a complete PR programme.

6. If the organisation is out of town, to use city-based or media-centre services for organising press functions such as press conferences, press receptions and facility visits.

7. To handle *ad hoc* assignments such as PR in connection with participation in an exhibition.

8. To provide specialist services such as house journal production, corporate and financial PR, Parliamentary liaison or sponsorship or fund raising, or because the consultancy specialises in a certain interest such as motoring, travel, fashion or entertainment.

Kinds of PR Consultancies

In the UK there are some 600 PR consultancies, most of them small but there are many quite large ones which offer a variety of specialised services comparable with the divisions of labour to be found in service advertising agencies. About seventy of those doing about three quarters of consultancy business in the UK are members of the Public Relations Consultants Association. Nevertheless, because large back-up services such as media, creative and production departments are not required, the PR consultant can be an all-rounder and one-man consultancies can operate as efficiently as, say, a doctor or a solicitor does.

Nevertheless, outside PR services do fall into the following categories:

1. *PR department of an advertising agency.* The value of an advertising agency PR department depends on how well the agency understands PR, and how independently the PR manager can operate. But the risk is that the PR service could be limited and inhibited by its connections with advertising. No more than a product publicity support to advertising campaigns may be offered, and if the PR plays merely a supportive role, it will be a negligible PR exercise. But there could be the advantage that PR was integrated into the total marketing strategy so that it could influence marketing thinking.

2. *PR subsidiary of an advertising agency.* In this case the PR subsidiary is a separate consultancy in its own right, having its own clients (which may or may not be agency clients) and being responsible for its own profitability. There will be linking directorships or partnerships with the agency. It will probably operate under a different name, e.g. Lexington PR (J. Walter Thompson), Welbeck PR (Foote, Cone & Belding), Planned Public Relations (Young & Rubicam) and Leedex (Brunnings). An advantage of this type of

consultancy is that it has the on-the-spot back-up services of the agency's studio, print production, library and other services. An occasional problem, however, is that clients do not always appreciate why they have to deal with two account executives from what, to them, is the same organisation.

3. *Independent PR consultancy.* Here we have the typical PR consultancy which has no parental agency ties. It may, however, have a working arrangement with an agency, or with clients' agencies, and—like Burson-Marsteller—it may operate the other way round and have its own advertising service. Some of its clients may not be involved in advertising and require only PR services, while PR programmes may not be related to advertising campaigns, e.g. house journal design, editing and production, or financial PR as when a private company goes 'public' and sells shares on the stock market for the first time.

4. *PR counsellor.* This is the truest form of PR consultancy in that it offers no more than a consultancy or counsellor service, advising clients and perhaps proposing the setting up of a PR department or the appointment of a service PR consultancy to carry out its recommendations. A PR counsellor may be called in to give advice, or to give an independent outside opinion of internal PR activities. Some of the larger PR consultancies in category 3 above also offer purely counselling services.

Advantages of PR Consultancy Services

1. *It can offer independent advice.* In this, its role can be very different from that of an advertising agency. While an advertising agency may seek to please a client, a PR consultancy may be paid to criticise. These somewhat contradictory roles can be embarrassing if both account executives are present at a client meeting, especially if the PR consultancy is owned by the agency! It may even be necessary for the consultancy to criticise the advertising if it is considered to be in bad taste or in any way damaging to the client's image or likely to provoke ill-will. The agency may be the herald of a company's sales, but the consultancy is the guardian of its reputation.

This is not to suggest that the agency is unethical but it could be overzealous, and it does have to contend with more than 100 legal acts and regulations and an increasingly complex Code of Practice. Nowadays the British public are invited through advertisements issued by the Advertising Standards Authority to submit written complaints about advertisements which they consider to be misleading. The results of investigations, stating which complaints have been upheld or dismissed, are published in a monthly report. It is obviously unfortunate PR to be included in a report, and bad PR if the advertisement is found to be in breach of the Code. The system is, of course, subject to abuse by cranks and critics of advertising. Thus, the PR consultancy applies vigilance to see that its clients' advertising does not invite public complaints to the ASA. This is not easy since a teetotaller may object to every alcoholic drink advertisement! One such complainant made 150 complaints in a year.

'Advice' can cover scores of communication topics concerning the entire range of an organisation's activities, internally and externally. A possible change of company name, how to deal with a proposed relocation, how to conduct PR overseas, the effects of new legislation, what sort of video system to use for internal communications, how to distribute a documentary film—these and countless other problems may be presented to the consultancy.

2. *It has long and varied experience.* This is implied by the previous paragraph, and it is a professional service arising from having trained staff who have undertaken many forms of PR for a variety of clients. In choosing a consultancy it is therefore important to check whether the account executive is well trained and experienced, the hallmarks being whether he or she (and women are very good at PR) holds the CAM Diploma in PR and is a member of the Institute of Public Relations (or holds equivalent qualifications in other countries). Membership of the IPR implies five years' comprehensive experience.

Such checks are important because the profession is not subject to registration, and anyone can call himself or herself a PR consultant, perhaps transferring from some other calling such as journalism, advertising or something even less remotely to do with communications. Until they have undertaken training and gained considerable practical experience, they remain fringe operators, a liability to the PR profession, and of doubtful service to their clients. These 'cowboys' have to be avoided.

What exactly do we mean by 'comprehensive'? It applies just as much to PR practitioners in general as to PR consultants in particular, and the best explanation may be taken from the IPR membership application form. To be accepted by the Membership Committee and Council, an applicant has to show that he has a good spread of experience in most of the following areas:

1. Writing/journalism (e.g. articles, press releases, pamphlets, booklets, brochures, speeches, scripts for visual productions).
2. Print production/distribution/promotion.
3. Film or audio-visual production/distribution/promotion.
4. Exhibition and displays production/promotion.
5. Advertising.
6. Communication and liaison with: (*a*) press; (*b*) radio; (*c*) television.
7. Conferences and meetings: (*a*) public; (*b*) otherwise.
8. Parliamentary liaison.
9. Government or local government liaison.
10. Relations with special interest groups (including voluntary bodies).
11. Industry or commerce liaison.
12. Community relations (race or otherwise).
13. International relations.
14. Employee relations.
15. Consumer/dealer relations.
16. Financial/shareholder relations.
17. Market research/attitude surveys.
18. Communication from and about the public to your employing organisations.
19. Planning, budgeting and managing public relations programmes.
20. Formulating public relations policies.

A consultant, it might be expected, should be able to offer experience in the majority of areas, but some might be especially experienced in certain areas. For instance, financial PR consultants, with their expert knowledge of corporate affairs and the workings of the money market, and probably having an economics or City Page background, may well have less or little experience in the broader fields of PR. Similarly, a house journal expert would be especially professional at journalism, page layout design, typography and printing, including the buying of print and working with printers.

The buying of PR consultancy services therefore calls for understanding of what is required and what can be supplied. It is an unhappy fault of business management that it is often ill-equipped to buy such services; it is something which is often lacking from management studies. This can sometimes result in clients not appreciating the range of services available, expecting things that cannot be provided, and perhaps misunderstanding the role of PR in the affairs of their organisation.

3. Having worked for a number of clients over a period of years, *the consultant is experienced in the use of all the media of communication*, both existing like the press and created like video-cassettes. He will be constantly familiarising himself with new media and techniques which can be used for different clients' programmes. Media are also constantly changing. In his day-to-day work he will get to know a lot of media personalities. This should not be misunderstood under that old misnomer of 'good Fleet Street contacts'. Knowing people in the media means knowing who they are, what they want and when they want it, not how to manipulate favours in a Fleet Street bar or a West End club.

Disadvantages of PR Consultancy Services

In spite of the glamour that surrounds the consultancy world—perhaps because of its independent, proprietorial nature compared with working inside a big organisation—there are some disadvantages both from the client's and the consultancy point of view. Taking the latter first, it can be a precarious business. Accounts come and go, and if one does not have a good business head it is easy to lose money—very easy if clients are given more service than they are paying for. The creative mind is not always given to strict budgets and the careful keeping of time-sheets. The PR consultancy is not cushioned by commissions on large expenditures on space and airtime. The consultant has only his time to sell and it has to be rationed in proportion to the varying fees paid by different clients.

The disadvantages from the client's point of view are these:

1. The client will receive only what he pays for—a certain number of hours' work—but PR goes on all the time and is threaded into the entire fabric of an organisation. It does not have office hours. Consequently, a PR consultancy can provide only a partial service.

2. Since PR concerns the communications of the total organisation, and lines of communication are needed with directors, managers and others in responsible positions, there is a lack of intimacy in the client-consultancy relationship, which is usually based on one main contact in the client organisation. The consultancy can be too remote. Public relations is like an intelligence service with numerous informants. Advertising is more like a flow chart.

How to Appoint a Consultant

When appointing an advertising agency it is common to invite a number of agencies to make competitive presentations, paying for any creative work involved. This is perhaps natural and sensible because the client needs to judge ideas and media proposals. Being familiar with this procedure, clients tend to approach the appointment of a PR consultant in the same way. But would you ask a number of doctors to present competitive cures for an illness? Would you invite alternative diagnoses? Similarly, would you invite competitive prosecutions or defences before appointing a lawyer? Hardly, and the same applies to PR. The service provided by a PR consultant should be based on a preliminary study of the situation, which may involve some form of research. Unless it is merely a product publicity or press relations assignment, a PR programme cannot be based on the client's view of the situation, nor is it like giving an advertising agency a product or service to promote. The PR consultant also needs far more confidential information than is possible when rival firms are asked to make competitive presentations.

Once again we see how advertising and PR differ.

To achieve a practical proposition from a consultant it is therefore best for the client to draw up a short list of likely consultancies. Addresses (and client lists) can be found in *Advertiser's Annual*, the *Hollis Press and Public Relations Annual*, and the PRCA *Public Relations Year Book*.

The selected firms can then be visited by appointment for initial discussions. Advice can also be sought from business friends who use consultancy services, consultants can be met socially at PR events, or seen 'in action' as speakers at conferences, and their publications can be read. By a process of 'shopping around' it is possible to decide on final discussions and the appointment of a consultant who will be invited to study the problem and put up a proposition, acceptance of which will result in a contract of service. Ideally, the consultant should conduct an intensive survey, at the client's expense, before presenting a proposition on which the final contract will depend.

This professional approach to the engagement of a professional service is fair to both sides, and if it is not adopted often enough it is because of the confusion which still exists regarding advertising and public relations. Moreover, under the competitive proposition method the consultant is obliged to spend hundreds of pounds in time alone on the preparations of schemes, with no recompense if he does not win the contract. PR consultancies are rarely large firms, nothing like advertising agencies in manpower, resources and income, so that they can survive only if the maximum amount of their time is devoted to producing income. Like many other professionals, the PR consultant's income is based on the value of his time.

As a PR consultant, the author refused on several occasions to accept an invitation to produce a competitive proposition, simply because of the cost involved. How else does a consultant get business? He has to promote himself, and unlike some professionals who are debarred from advertising, he can do so provided he does not poach clients from other consultants. Mostly, however, he will gain new accounts on the strength of his reputation, just as a barrister receives briefs. Successful new consultancies are usually started with a nucleus of clients who want his services, meaning of course that he was a well-known PRO in the first place and not a beginner such as a journalist who thinks he would like to be a PR consultant. But even here it does happen that an experienced journalist will be known to a number of organisations who would be happy to use his services if he set up a consultancy. This has happened, for instance, in the case of motoring journalists who understood the industry, were familiar with the specialised media, and really had something professional to offer.

The In-house or Internal PR Department

Most advertising people work in agencies, but most PR people do not work in consultancies. The clientèle of consultancies are mostly business concerns plus a sprinkling of non-commercial organisations. Outside this minority of users of PR are Government and local government, state enterprises and quangos, the health authorities, education, fire services, police, Armed Forces, charities and other voluntary bodies, churches, institutions and societies, sport, trade unions—a vast world outside that of the market place. All have to communicate and have spokesmen. Public relations is their life-blood. It may be part of the job specification of a chief executive, but many of them employ a PRO. But even in the world of industry and commerce, the staff PRO is well established.

He may have only a secretary, or he may command a department. He may double his duties with advertising. Sometimes he will be found in the market-ing department. More sensibly, he may work independently of other depart-ments and be responsible to the chief executive. In some of our larger, more successful companies he may be an adviser to the board of directors, or be a board director. He will be decorated with any one of more than a hundred titles from the lowly information officer to the fanciful public affairs director. His efforts may be augmented by those of a consultancy. Each has his special merits and there is no reason why in-house PRO and outside consultant cannot work together without one being threatened by the menace of a takeover by the other.

Having looked at the reasons for employing a consultancy, and also at the strengths and weaknesses of outside PR services, let us look at the in-house or internal PR department in the same way.

Advantages of In-house PR Department

1. It offers a full-time service, which can mean a 24-hour service which is not subject to the limitations of a fee. In Part 3 we shall emphasise that the staff PRO is also required to plan his time, for while he is doing one thing he cannot do another, but nevertheless it is true that the company PRO does not have to share his time between clients and give each according to his due. His entire time, and much of his 'spare' time, is devoted to his organisation.

2. He is part of the organisation, known to his fellow employees, easily able to establish lines of communication throughout the organisation. An outsider cannot have this advantage.

3. Company personnel tend to stay longer, growing up with the company, whereas consultancy staff are less permanent. This helps the PRO to know the organisation intimately.

4. He can often work very economically, dove-tailing various jobs such as researching material for feature articles while working on the house journal, or finding material for house journals, documentary films, the photographic library and so on while engaged in other activities, all of which mean mixing with his colleagues and knowing what is going on.

5. He is on the spot when the organisation is in the news, often able to act spontaneously, or at least having immediate access to information and authority. This can be important in disaster or controversial situations.

Disadvantages of In-house PR Department

1. A serious disadvantage can be the tendency for the PRO to be uncritical

and biased, partly out of loyalty or enthusiasm, partly because of pressure from management. The consultancy can enjoy the oracle role and be treated rather like a Harley Street specialist. It depends on the professional status which the PRO has achieved, and perhaps the title PR adviser is a good one. The PRO who is merely management's dogsbody is in a hopeless position. But he can assert his proper status only by his proved competence and value, so that he is respected and needed by management.

2. An inherent weakness may be the narrowness of the industry or business he is in so that he does not enjoy the broad span of PR activity and experience which is characteristic of the consultancy. He may be in, say, food or textiles or engineering which brings him into contact with a limited section of the media. He may be out of his depth if the company diversifies or acquires other interests.

3. He may have been transferred to PR from another job in the company and have no training in PR, and being perhaps a senior person he may be reluctant to undergo professional training. Some very odd appointments are made by management which does not appreciate that much has to be learned before one can practise PR. Sometimes, a sideways promotion can put a totally unskilled person behind the PR desk. The PR profession is not helped by such appointments which encourage the cynicism of the media.

4. Similarly, PR duties may be assigned to an existing executive such as a marketing manager, personnel manager, or commercial manager who knows nothing about PR, may well treat it as some form of 'free advertising', have no time to become proficient in PR, and will probably do more harm than good. Even if he is aided by a PR consultant, he will not be speaking the same language.

5. In some large organisations—multinationals, for example—an executive who is being groomed for top management is put in charge of PR for perhaps three years. While it is excellent that top management should be trained and experienced in PR it is nonsense to place an unskilled and unqualified person in *control* of the PR function. The place for his training is in business school.

6. He may be appointed for the wrong reasons. Management may misunderstand PR to the extent that it employs a PRO for protective reasons, either to shield top management from the media, or to act as an apologist for management inadequacies. This is an abuse of PR but has been known where management is nervous of criticism. Unhappily, it is a view of PR almost universally held by writers of novels, plays and films.

In the above two sections we have shown a mixture of in-house situations which suggest that while the PRO can perform a valuable function it is necessary for the job specification to be right. Some calamitous situations have arisen from the recommendations of management consultants who have shown woeful misunderstanding of the role of the PRO. On the other hand, many of our most successful companies are the ones where the PRO occupies an important position and has been able to contribute much to his company's success.

The question, however, is not which is best—a PR department or a PR consultancy, or being a staff PRO or a consultant. They are different and they each serve different purposes. They do not compete. The staff PRO may be happier in the more permanent, secure and singleminded organisation role, the consultant may prefer his independence, variety and precariousness.

11

PUBLIC RELATIONS IN INDUSTRY AND COMMERCE

There are three functions in a business undertaking: production, finance and marketing. The PR function falls thus:

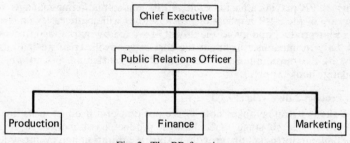

Fig. 2. The PR function.

Responsible to the chief executive, the PR services production, finance and marketing, and also handles corporate PR through the chief executive and the board. This is an oversimplified chart which may suit a manufacturing company but needs modification to suit other businesses such as servicing or retail organisations. It is true of enlightened companies or rather ones with enlightened management which recognises that PR concerns the total organisation. However, few companies are organised logically. They grow up as a result of circumstances and personalities, and PR may be positioned according to who thought of it first. Since management is not always the initiator of a PR appointment, and marketing is, it often happens that PR is responsible to the marketing director. In conglomerates it may happen that because there is a group headquarters, and a central spokesman is required, a Group PRO may be appointed.

PR in the Marketing Department

There are two ways of looking at PR in relation to marketing—and again this can be influenced by the nature of the company. First, the PRO may be one of the marketing team. Second, whether or not a PRO (or a PR consultant) is employed, PR should be part of the marketing manager's philosophy.

Marketing and public relations have much in common since both are to do with human relations and communications. In practice there is frequently an unwarranted antipathy between marketing and PR when in fact PR can be marketing's third arm. We find marketing people sceptical about PR as if it was either an optional extra or something inferior to advertising. This sort of misunderstanding is seen when marketers think a new release should read like an advertisement and do not appreciate the vast difference between persuasive copywriting and informative editorial writing. A PRO employed in a marketing department may be the victim of demands and commands which destine his work to editorial waste bins. But it also has to be said that many PROs are antipathetic towards marketing which they regard as a dirty word, failing to realise that marketing is a necessary function of a trading company. Ideally, the PRO should understand marketing and be able to contribute to the many PR aspects of the marketing mix.

The following distinction is perhaps apt in this chapter: public relations is telling, advertising is selling. While advertising brings the product to the customer, PR brings the customer to the product.

In another book, *Public Relations for Marketing Management*, the author has presented an extended chronological marketing mix comprising twenty elements, PR playing a part in each. A PR-minded marketing manager should be aware of these PR implications because they will create easier understanding of his product and avoid the ill-will provoked by marketing efforts which seek only to maximise profits at the cost of goodwill. Here we shall look at some of the most important elements of the marketing mix to which PR thinking should apply.

The Product Life Cycle (PLC)

Marketing strategy takes note of the position of a product in its life cycle. The traditional six-stage PLC shows a product passing through stages of development, introduction, growth, maturity, saturation and eventual decline. Different kinds of PR activity will be required at these different stages, e.g. to educate the market, to coincide with advertising, to maintain sales and so on. Some products may be designed to have a certain life cycle. Fashion goods may live for a few months but a car (with minor modifications) for ten years. This does not refer to the life expectancy of individual products but to the selling life of the total production. In the case of a motorcar a replacement model will be designed to replace the old model when sales fall below a given level. Products like Guinness or Coca-Cola may have an indefinite life cycle.

There are variations on the traditional life cycle which are also significant in PR terms. There is the recycled PLC which applies to projects pulled out of decline by improvements or other changes such as re-packaging or price-cutting. Then there is the leapfrog effect when one model is replaced by another, and the staircase effect when new product uses or new services are introduced. The classic example of the staircase effect PLC is nylon, but it can also be applied to shipping, insurance and banking which have diversified their services over the years. Changes in the behaviour of the life cycle provide special opportunities for PR activity, an example in the continuous story of nylon being the introduction of motorcycle wheels made of nylon.

The four types of PLC are shown in Figs. 3–6.

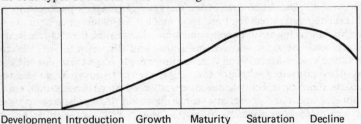

Development Introduction Growth Maturity Saturation Decline

Fig. 3. Traditional product life cycle.

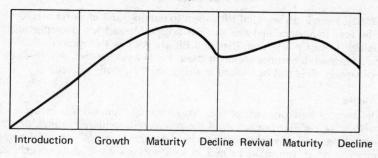

Fig. 4. Recycled product life cycle.

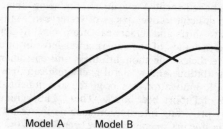

Fig. 5. Leapfrog effect product life cycle.

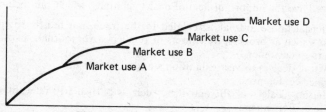

Fig. 6. Staircase effect product life cycle.

Company Names and Product Brands

In days gone by it was sufficient to use a family name for the company: today a name has to be easily pronounced and remembered and this calls for the invention of a name which can quickly win corporate identity. For example, S. Smith & Sons (England) Ltd derived from the name of a watchmaker's shop, but Smiths Industries is more appropriate for a company with diversified interests.

Some complicated names (especially of international companies) communicate better as shortened versions, sets of initials, or acronyms based on initials, examples being P & O for Peninsular and Orient, IBM for International Business Machines and Toshiba for Tokyo Shibaura Electrical Company. In some cases it is not always realised by customers that a name such as Fiat or Sabena is an acronym, while the words represented by initials are unimportant when the name represents a product as synonymous as IBM is with computers.

Clearly, there is an essential PR aspect to naming, and in world markets it can be very important that the name is acceptable and has no unfortunate meanings. Coca-Cola, Volvo, Esso and Elf are good in this respect.

Good memorable names are often short, but in any case they gain from the use of vowels. This will be noticed in the examples already quoted.

Packaging

The type of container, its shape, size, material, convenience in use and possibly after use and protection of the product; its colour, wording, design and labelling; and any instructions which it carries, are all forms of communication which can make or mar its sale, successful use and re-purchase. Both dealer and customer relations are involved here.

Modern packs such as sachets, blister packs, dispensers, aerosols, flip tops and plastic bottles have benefited consumers, replacing clumsy, heavy, breakable, dangerous or difficult to open packs of yesteryear. Many products, from cakes and biscuits to shirts and underwear, are packed hygienically or clearly in cellophane. The demands of the supermarket have inspired some modern packaging but nevertheless the thoughtfulness and customer satisfaction are PR attributes. Ostentatious and wasteful packaging can provoke ill-will.

An interesting PR innovation has been the attachment of topical 'news' labels on the necks of Tuborg beer bottles. These 'Tuborgrams' provide topics of conversation by providing information such as the result of an American presidential election, and in Copenhagen have been dubbed the 'people's library'.

Distribution

Here we have the important field of dealer relations, which can include:

(a) External house journals circulated to the trade, but mostly to special distributors such as brokers, franchisers or retailers. (*Not* journals distributed by retailers to customers.)

(b) Inviting dealers to visit exhibition stands.

(c) Dealer conferences.

(d) Advising dealers of PR activities, such as particularly relevant press, radio or television coverage.

(e) Training dealer staff.

(f) Trade press relations.

(g) Works visits to see the product being made.

(h) Dealer contests, e.g. window display contests, or awards based on sales successes. Prizes are often holiday trips for two.

Sales Force

Field salesmen often feel neglected. They need a strong, regular link with headquarters, help to understand what the company is doing, to be educated about new products, and encouraged to feel part of a team and not to feel isolated individuals. Some of the PR techniques which may be employed are:

(a) A special newsletter or house journal, rather than a general staff newspaper mainly intended for factory employees they do not know.

(b) Audio-cassettes which can be played in representative's cars.

(c) Regional and national conferences.

(d) Incentive schemes and sales contests.

(*e*) Supply of reproductions of press cuttings and reprints of PR feature articles.

(*f*) Explanations of annual reports and financial results, using media such as the house journal, audio or video tapes.

(*g*) Advance notice of advertising campaigns, with copies of press ads and advice on dates and times of new television or radio commercials.

(*h*) Similarly, advance notice of television or radio programmes featuring the company.

(*i*) Supply of documentary films, slide presentations and video-cassettes for showing to clients at local receptions, with synopsis notes for handing out afterwards.

(*j*) Speaker's notes so that salesmen can address local organisations.

(*k*) Information forms or pads so that salesmen can report newsworthy items, or suggestions for articles.

Market education

Some products and services, especially technical ones, benefit from PR efforts to educate the market so that salesmen and distributors can sell more effectively, and advertising can work. Typical methods are:

(*a*) External house journals aimed at customers or users.

(*b*) Conferences and seminars with lectures, exhibits and visual aids such as films and slide presentations.

(*c*) Educational literature and print such as books, pamphlets, folders, wall charts.

(*d*) Training schools.

(*e*) Showrooms, display and information centres.

(*f*) Participation in trade and public exhibitions—educational rather than sales stands.

(*g*) Taped interviews for distribution to radio stations.

(*h*) Television coverage in programmes devoted to, say, new ideas or dealing with the company's subject.

(*i*) Physical demonstration of products.

An example of a physical demonstration has been the Acrilan acrylic fibre carpet installed at Brussels National Airport. An average of 2.3 million passengers per year fly into the airport and have walked over this long length of carpet which covers one of the corridors leading from the arrival point. Both Monsanto and VTW/Prado, makers of the carpet, have earned recognition by this practical demonstration. The first carpet was installed in 1973, since when there have been replacements.

The timing of some of these activities could be either before the launch of the product in order to create a favourable marketing situation, or continuously as a marketing support.

Sales Promotion and Merchandising

The mistake is sometimes made of expecting the PR department or consultancy to organise sales promotion and merchandising, probably because they call for special organisational abilities, but this is a misuse of PR. However, there can be a considerable PR element in these special sales activities, and this is where the PRO can advise the marketing manager.

Some promotional schemes can provoke ill-will if extra sales are gained but, due to bad planning, customers are disappointed. The typical example is the premium offer, an item being offered at a privilege price on receipt of packet tops or labels plus cash. The volume of demand may be so under-estimated that the supplier is unable to cope and there is a long delay in delivery of the item to the customer.

The After-Market

This is where many a marketing strategy has come unstuck. What happens after the product has been purchased, when it breaks down, when the customer is in trouble? The philosophy that it is cheaper to replace rather than repair may not always apply. Japanese car makers probably learned the lesson from British indifference: Toyota even supply nuts in protective packages. One can understand Japanese supremacy in world markets when an advertisement for the Mitsubishi Sigma, inserted by the Cycle and Carriage Group in the Malaysian *New Straits Times*, can state: 'All Mitsubishi car owners can enjoy the full benefits of Cycle and Carriage Back-up Service and a ready availability of spare parts at 42 centres throughout Malaysia.'

Care of the after-market is the most effective PR aspect of the entire mar-keting strategy. It breeds satisfaction, admiration, recommendation and above all repeat purchase. It creates trust, confidence and reputation—the objectives of PR. It is expressed in the simple abundant promise rather than the guarantee with the miserly clauses, in the efficient after-sales and spare parts service, in the explicit, well-illustrated instruction manual, in follow-ups to ensure that the product is cared for, and in PR activities to maintain interest (e.g. customer magazines, feature articles in the press) and to extend enjoyment of the product's benefits.

A feature of the after-market which can reflect credit or discredit on a company is the manner in which it treats the recall of a defective product. Sometimes the frankness and helpfulness with which a recall is handled can turn an apparently bad situation into one of respect and appreciation from customers whose safety has been preserved.

Employee Relations

Here we have one of the most important developments in PR, and something which helps to justify the contention that PR should not be restricted to the marketing department but should operate independently and be responsible to top management. This is advisable because it has become increasingly necessary for management to explain itself to employees, and for employees to have the means of speaking up to management. We have here an example of PR as two-way communication. In the absence of the works councils and worker directors to be found in some countries, it is imperative that manage-ment–employee relations should be stimulated by PR techniques. These tech-niques include:

(*a*) **House journals** which can report what management is doing and how the company is performing, including interpretations of financial matters such as the annual report and accounts, *and which provide a platform or forum for employees' ideas and views*. A number of British employee newspapers do this very well, and it is a form of industrial democracy which helps to harmonise industrial relations. Even the inclusion of readers' sales and wants advertisements contributes to reader interest.

(*b*) **Notice-boards** can be designed, provided and controlled by the PR department. 'Control' can mean the orderly positioning of news items so that all notice boards are uniform, the PR department producing the items in a distinctive way, and being responsible for attachment to the boards. This is particularly valuable when the company has numerous staff activities and societies. It makes the board more attractive and intelligible than the kind where anyone can pin something on so that there is an untidy mess of notices pinned at random by anyone who wishes to make an announcement. Shell do this very well.

(*c*) **Audio-visuals.** Documentary films, slide presentations, closed circuit television and video-tapes all provide the means of presenting visual information to employees. The familiar television screeen and the taped or live telecast can bring management face to face with staff, creating personal relationships which overcome the normal remoteness of management.

(*d*) **Speak-up schemes.** Encouragement to communicate with management comes in many forms such as phone-in facilities, 'speak-up' forms and collection boxes placed at strategic points throughout the premises and managerial 'open doors'.

(*e*) **Shop-floor talks.** More effective than the one-way media of visual aids are face-to-face talks by management which invite questions and provide feedback. Shop-floor talks can be organised by PR as part of the employee-relations programme.

(*f*) **Staff conferences and other get-togethers.** Gatherings of staff, preferably off the premises and sometimes out of hours, can be another organisational responsibility of the PRO. They can include conferences, visits, socials, sports events and dinners serving either business or pleasure purposes. Such events are very useful when staff are not confined to one location and do not see each other frequently.

Community Relations

It is an old PR saying that PR begins on the doorstep: a company should take its place in the community adjacent to its location, playing a responsible role, and making itself known to and understood by members of the community. In the long run this can be helpful when recruiting staff, dealing with local services and the local authority, or when problems arise as they may over noise, pollution, accidents or strikes. The cooperation of works managers, personnel managers and other executives will be needed when there are many locations. Some of the methods of conducting community relations are:

(*a*) **Local press relations.** There should be contact with the local press which should be supplied with relevant news stories, and local journalists should be known to location managers, be welcome to visit and be invited to attend company activities.

(*b*) **Works visits** should be arranged for local people, such as members of local organisations.

(*c*) **Participation** should be made in local events, perhaps sponsoring them or awarding prizes.

(*d*) **Talks, film shows and slide presentations** may be given to local societies.

(*e*) **The local MP for the constituency** should be familiarised with the company's activities.

(*f*) **Community leaders** such as church leaders, headmasters of schools, officials of the local Chamber of Trade, etc., should be similarly familiarised.

(*g*) **Assistance** (where possible or relevant) should be given to educational establishments, hospitals, clubs and so forth.

The expression 'works' has been used, but the company location might be a retail store, research laboratory, mine, office, or some other business or industrial centre.

Corporate and Financial Relations

Corporate identity will be dealt with in Chapter 26, but here let us consider other PR duties which are separate from the marketing function, although they could be undertaken by a PR consultancy specialising in this work.

Corporate PR aims to establish and maintain a correct image or impression of the organisation as a whole. The organisation will be judged by its behaviour and what is known and understood about it. The corporate image can have a halo effect on the company's recruitment, trading, financial and other activities. It is bound up in the 'good name' of the company.

However, one has to be careful not to divert PR into the pursuit of 'favourable images' as if PR can create a world in which there are no misfortunes. For most companies there are good days and bad days which have to be accepted philosophically, and the bad news has to be dealt with as frankly and impartially as the good—even though the media find that it pays to report mainly the bad news.

Management can be oversensitive to apparently unfavourable comments. When a basic English primer for French 11-year-olds contained an English husband's remark 'My cigarette, please, dear', but added 'It's horrible', and his wife's reply 'It's a Gauloise. It's French. These cigarettes are strong. Here's your Dunhill', the French state-owned tobacco company Seita was not amused. It sought legal action to stop Fernand Nathan from distributing the book. The publishers' defence was that the sketch merely implied that the Englishwoman preferred a strong French cigarette, while Englishmen preferred a mild one. In France, apparently, the smoking habits of schoolchildren are vital to the French tobacco industry. At the time of this incident sales of foreign cigarettes in France had nearly doubled over the previous three years. A survey had shown that 46 per cent of children between 12 and 18 smoked, but only 40 per cent of adults were smokers.

All the methods of conducting PR can be applied to corporate PR, but overall the activities of top people, the reliability of products, industrial relations and other public evidence of the company's behaviour and performance will affect the corporate image.

Much of corporate and financial PR will be conducted in the more serious newspapers such as *The Times, Financial Times, Daily Telegraph, Guardian, Scotsman, Sunday Times, The Observer* and *Sunday Telegraph* and in business magazines such as *The Economist, Financial Weekly* and *Investors' Chronicle*. The importance of this coverage may be seen when there is a new share issue or debenture issue, a takeover, or in the movement of share prices on the Stock Exchange. Usually, it will be less easy to take over a successful company which maintains a good share price, while new issues will succeed if the market is well informed about a company's performance and prospects.

The significance of financial PR may be seen in the 200-strong membership of the IPR City and Financial Group. It is a highly successful vocational group holding regular and well attended meetings.

Such PR activities would be less expensive and more effective than a fatalistic 'tender offer defence expense insurance policy' to compensate a company for 80 per cent of legal, banking, consultancy and other costs incurred in opposing a takeover bid. The insurance would not prevent the bid from succeeding whereas good PR could prevent it from being contemplated.

Financial relations can also begin 'on the doorstep' with the company's own bankers, and any other financial relations it may have with brokers, insurers and merchant bankers. Its external relations will be with the institutional investors—insurance companies, pension funds, investment trusts and unit trusts who buy or hold large blocks of shares—and the analysts who advise investors.

In recent years corporate PR has sometimes been separated from the general run of PR and given fancy names like 'public affairs', 'external affairs' and 'corporate affairs', as if boardroom communications need to be given an aura of respectability. Such management fails to understand that public relations is a perfectly respectable name: it does not require a *nom-de-plume*.

So-called 'public affairs' sometimes deals with the company's conscience and its concern for the public interest. It is that area of PR which has become prominent as a result of challenge by articulate activists or pressure groups—called 'the people factor' by Philip Lesly, the American PR counsellor—which may represent consumerists, environmentalists and the anti-smoking, noise-abatement and other lobbies created to protect the public interest.

Some companies have made considerable PR capital out of their concern for combating the energy crisis or dealing with environmental problems. Esso have used corporate PR television commercials to publicise their search for new forms of energy. The 3M Company has run its 'Pollution Prevention Pays' campaign in 15 countries, and in the first nine months of this campaign it eliminated 70,000 tons of air pollutants and 500 million gallons of waste waters. The clean-up actually *saved* 3M 11 million dollars a year in operating costs. North British Distillers, accused of polluting the local salmon river, recovered its reputation by installing evaporators and driers and actually sold over £1 million of dried pollution as animal feed. English Clays converted Cornish china clay wastes into prefabricated houses, while several companies (such as Ready Mixed Concrete) have turned excavation pits into aquatic sports centres. Out of very bad PR situations famous firms have turned bad news into good news for both the public and their shareholders. On the other hand, the 1980s have seen a spate of 'issue' advertising (e.g. about oil prices) which is mostly negative PR seeking to prevent trouble or protect interests.

'*Social Responsibility*' was the paragraph heading in a recent Marks and Spencer annual report from the chairman, the Honorable Sir Marcus Sieff, who said: 'We are concerned with the shopping and social environment in the areas we serve and support the national policy to protect viable city centres and to rehabilitate inner urban areas. Businesses such as ours have some experience which could be helpful in dealing in a practical way with these problems, and we are considering how best to help. We donated this year

£638,000 to national and local charities with the emphasis on social well-being, the arts, education and health. We encourage our management and staff to take part in communal activities since local personal involvement and help are important and valuable.'

At the 1978 Annual General Meeting of Unilever, Sir Donald Orr, chairman of Unilever Ltd, delivered a notable speech on *Unilever and The Third World Food Problem*, a digest of which appeared in press advertisements, while the speech was reproduced in booklet form. It was an effort to encourage the Green Revolution in the Third World, and so reduce malnutrition in the developing world.

Yet another example of responsible corporate action and its PR implications is shown by the development of contingency planning for disasters, something which very much concerns the PROs of companies which are engaged in dangerous industries that can create immense public ill-will, mistrust and antagonism. These situations are not easy to deal with when the media want the facts, but public statements could jeopardise legal relations with suppliers, insurers and even victims. The Thalidomide tragedy was a case in point, and so have been mine, rail and air disasters. Increasingly, this becomes a critical area of corporate PR.

In the years to come the two areas which are likely to engage public relations more than any are **management–employee relations** and the handling of **activist pressures.** We have to be careful not to be misled by the one being termed *business communication* and the other *public affairs*: they are best recognised as the modern face of *public relations*.

International Marketing

Neglect of PR in overseas trading has produced some very bad PR for all kinds of firms. The promotion of unsuitable products or ones which would be banned in the manufacturer's own country, the failure to provide spare parts and after-sales service and carelessness about modifying products to suit overseas conditions have provoked ill-will for many famous companies, especially in the Third World. Most of this bad PR is caused by indifference, ignorance and carelessness by some of the world's leading companies. There is no excuse for it, and in the end it will have serious consequences for the Western World. The motorcar, pharmaceutical, tobacco and powdered milk industries are among the worst offenders.

The baby milk scandal persists in spite of international exposure. In 1979 the Zurich-based International Council of Infant Food Industries (ICIFI), representing 14 European, Japanese and American companies responsible for supplying 85 per cent of infant feed to the Third World, agreed to voluntary guidelines. A year later, at a conference sponsored by the World Health Organisation (WHO) and the United Nations Children's Fund (UNICEF), the International Baby Food Action Network (IBF-AN) condemned 200 sales campaigns by 19 companies in 33 countries which violated the agreed recommendations. But in the 1980s some milk-powder companies are using PR methods to teach mothers how to use the products safely and beneficially.

12

PUBLIC RELATIONS IN CENTRAL GOVERNMENT

The history of British Government PR was well covered by Freddie Gillman in the paper he presented to the IPR Annual Conference at Bournemouth in 1977, and subsequently published in an extended form in the *IPRA Review* and *PR Bulletin*. The following is an interesting and revealing extract from the *IPRA Review* (April 1978):

The first Government department to concern itself with making its services known was the Post Office, once described as a pioneer of Big Business. In its first annual report, published in 1854, the Postmaster-General commented on the public's inadequate knowledge of the Post Office's activities and said: 'It could not be otherwise than satisfactory to Parliament if by means of a periodical report the general scope and extent of the progress made by the department were brought under its notice.'

A section of the report contained Suggestions to the Public which are familiar today— for example, that people should post early in the day, write addresses legibly and equip their houses with a suitable letter-box. The Post Office was also the first Government department to embark on a mass advertising campaign when in 1876 its staff distributed a million handbills explaining the services offered by the Post Office Savings Bank.

The distinction must be made between Government propaganda which aims to seek support for the Government and information services which provide information of benefit to the people. This information may be to do with education, housing, health, road safety, pensions and national events such as a census.

This chapter embraces both Government ministries and departments and the hundreds of quangos (quasi-autonomous national government organisations), plus the Central Office of Information. The principal PRO in the Government service is usually called a Chief Information Officer (CIO). His duties include a mixture of propaganda, advertising and public relations. When he requires advertising the COI will arrange this for him with the appointed advertising agency.

Government information services vary from country to country. In some countries there will be a Ministry of Information, but not in Britain. In Nigeria there is a Department of Public Enlightenment. Other countries are quite forthright about having a Ministry of Propaganda. It depends on whether there is a democratic, one-party or military government, and in the newer independencies it is not always easy to convince people that there is any difference between propaganda and public relations. Their universities teach mass communications in which the words 'public relations' and 'propaganda' are interchangeable. To them the British approach to PR may seem pedantic.

But the distinction is necessary here since we are not dealing with propaganda—that is, biased information in favour of a cause, opinion or belief which can include a government: we are dealing with impartial information, public relations. In war and peace all countries use propaganda, and it would be naive to pretend that only the enemy or foreigners tell lies or, at worst, exaggerate or put the best face on things. The sun always shines in tourist pictures and films.

In a democratic country, propaganda belongs to the political parties. Consequently, government leaders and ministers will indulge in propaganda for the purpose of remaining in power and winning the next election. But it is necessary to explain policies, legislation and public services to the people, and this calls for public relations.

Ministers will call press conferences, arranged by their CIOs. Statements may be official, but sometimes information is given 'off the record', meaning that the minister shall not be quoted. Material from a 'non-attributable source' may be reported as coming 'from a usually reliable source'. Information may also be 'leaked' by ministers, civil servants or departmental CIOs. 'Leaked' information enables journalists to write authentically about a government's intentions before they are officially announced, a system not all journalists like when they feel they are being used to prepare the public for some government action.

The most striking and perhaps reprehensible example of this was the 1980 Conservative Government budget. Normally, the budget is printed in the press, bit by bit as the Chancellor makes his budget speech in the House of Commons. In 1980, most of the important (and unpalatable) proposals had been leaked days before so that the media were able to forecast and comment with unprecedented accuracy. When the Chancellor made his speech on budget day the electorate were more or less reconciled to their fate. This may be regarded as government by public relations, a new usage which may be yet another expression of the Conservative Party's attitude to public relations.

The last comment calls for explanation. It is a curious fact that the Labour Party dislikes advertising (it even produced a Green Paper to control it) but likes PR and, when in power, makes great use of Government information services to familiarise the public with ministers and Government services. The Conservatives tend to cut back on Government information services, being great advocates of advertising (e.g. their support for commercial television in the 1950s), but generally disliking PR. This view also extends to local government (e.g. investigation of the GLC information services and the refusal of the Conservative London Borough of Croydon to appoint a PRO as this would be 'a waste of ratepayers' money!')

The media are often contemptuous of government spokesmen, and this view is not confined to Britain. Addressing the Journalists' Club in Sydney, Australia, Tom Farrell delivered the old chestnut: 'We want our facts first and from the person who knows the facts and is prepared to stand by them, but it is often very difficult to achieve this. The main reason is that a barrier lies between the community's leaders and the press—in the form of the mouthpiece.' This is the perennial plea of journalists who regard journalists turned PRO as turncoats. Perhaps this is a good argument for not recruiting journalists as PROs and for training entrants to PR as in other professions.

However, any government has to explain itself and do its best to see that legislation is acted upon. For this purpose it needs the services of professional PR practitioners. Legislation will range over hundreds of regulations and services of which a few may be:

(*a*) New contributions to be paid by employees, employers and the self-employed in respect of pension, sickness, accident and social security benefits.

(*b*) Schemes regarding education and training.

(*c*) Safety regulations regarding workplaces or products which may be hazardous.

(*d*) Traffic, driving and road safety regulations.

(*e*) Changes in passport or exchange control regulations.

These are matters which have to be given maximum publicity, and use will be made of advertising, leaflets, posters and press relations.

Meanwhile there will be the day-to-day press liaison work, partly to do with announcements of policy, and partly to do with answering questions from the press about current topics requiring ministerial, Cabinet office or the prime minister's office views or decisions.

On very important issues, senior ministers or the prime minister will be invited to give television interviews, or may ask for television time to make important announcements to the nation. These appearances are not to be confused with party political broadcasts which are purely propaganda. The difference is understood by viewers.

Three kinds of journalist are involved in political reporting. There are the Parliamentary correspondents who sit in the Press Gallery and report on sittings of MPs; lobby correspondents who attend the Houses of Parliament and interview the Members; and political correspondents who attend Government press conferences and deal with the ministries and departments.

The Third World

In developing countries, the government information services are closely associated with the development of the country. Often, life styles (especially of rural communities) will be changing and the government will be engaged in educating people about planned parenthood, child welfare, hygiene, education, modern farming, pest control, public health, nutrition, road safety, energy conservation and census-taking. Most governments are concerned with international trade and tourism, and some with attracting investment and immigrants.

Census-taking is a good example of the need for PR techniques. The government cannot plan the future infrastructure unless it has accurate statistics on population. While censuses have been held in Western countries for upwards of 200 years, they are a very recent innovation in independent states where colonial governments seldom succeeded in making more than estimates. People in such countries may misunderstand the purpose of head counting. They may fear it is connected with tax collecting. They may resist giving information because of tribal taboos, or they may give false figures out of pride in virility or because there are benefits to be gained. In Nigeria, the figures for small or little-populated states were inflated because of the promise of shares of oil revenues according to size of population. There can also be corruption if enumerators are paid according to numbers of people counted. A census can fail if it is announced too late, reliance being placed on advertising and public notices. A sustained PR educational programme is necessary, and trained, responsible enumerators are necessary.

Writing in the Nigerian daily, *The Punch* (August 25, 1978), Godwin Mzeaka said: 'It is believed here in Nigeria that population determines not only bargaining strength but also the amount of "national cake" that should accrue to any section or state. It is also believed that numerical strength presupposes the number of constituencies into which any given area should be broken for representation at national level. These and other factors combine to mitigate against the genuine need to produce accurate census figures in Nigeria.'

In Malaysia, the 1980 census was preceded by information such as the following which appeared in the *New Straits Times* on May 8:

PLAYING YOUR PART ON CENSUS DAY
LEAFLETS TELL WHAT IT'S ALL ABOUT

Kuala Lumpur, Wed.—Thousands of leaflets have been distributed throughout the country to explain to the people the forthcoming population and housing census.

The leaflets, in Bahasa Malaysia, English, Chinese and Tamil, state that the population census would be carried out from May 17 to 26 and the housing census from June 11 to 28.

The census is being taken to get a detailed picture of the situation to help the Government plan the future needs of the country in education, employment, housing, social welfare and other facilities.

During these periods, enumerators with special badges and identification cards will be calling on households.

The leaflets state that June 11 will be Census Day and urge households to note down the names of people who spend the night of June 10/11 in their homes. This information should be given to the enumerator.

The people are given the assurance that personal information would be treated as confidential.

Enumerators are sworn to secrecy and information given would only be used for compiling statistics and not for any other purpose, say the leaflets.

At the same time, Singaporeans were preparing for their census. On May 14, 1980, for instance, the *Straits Times* carried a census story on the front page, and on page 6 carried a feature headed:

FIRST STAGE OF
THE CENSUS IS
ON NEXT WEEK

This included a reproduction of a poster bearing the slogan:

Help Plan A
Better Future

The first story concluded by saying:

Singaporeans are thus asked to help in these ways:

SUPPLY the census officer accurate information of themselves and their households.
LEAVE their particulars with an adult member of the household who is usually at home if they will be out at work.
DO NOT remove or deface the identification label placed at the entrance or doorway of the house.
INFORM and give the required particulars to the census officers when they come this month to label their houses if they plan to go abroad for holiday or other purposes during the period from May 30 to June 23.
CHAIN up their dogs, if any, when the census officers call on them.

Information given will be treated as strictly confidential and will be used strictly for statistical purposes.

Particulars of individual persons or households will not be published or disclosed in any form to anyone, not even to the tax men, Mr Goh said. The information collected will be processed by computer and will be published only in aggregate form.

Central Office of Information

The COI operates home and overseas information services. In the UK it is the intermediary between Government ministries and suppliers of services such as advertising agencies and printers, while its news distribution service provides the media with official news. Overseas it publicises British events and achievements, distributing news stories, articles and photographs to the world press; documentary films and specially commissioned films for overseas television; and radio tapes for overseas radio. It publishes a catalogue of films which may be borrowed through British Embassies and High Commissions abroad. Mainly, it works through British Government information officers attached to diplomatic missions overseas. This is a service which is available to any British organisation which has news or films (free of advertising content) of international interest and in the interest of Britain. Any exporter who has a new product, invention or achievement should take advantage of this free service.

According to an article in *Export Direction* (January 1980), the *News In North America* service—'Nina' as it is known in the British Information Services in New York—has been remarkably successful in making known the achievements of British industry. A survey of its work showed that 31 product stories published in the USA generated 2400 reader enquiries. The British Information Service vets all stories and will issue only those which have 'some edge to sell in this market. It must be better, cheaper, lighter, in some way more desirable. We want this substantiated.'

The COI has the following divisions: Advertising, Exhibitions, Films and Television, Overseas Press and Radio, Photographs, Publications and Design Services, and Reference, together with the Tours and Facilities Section, a Regional Organisation (with regional offices) and news distribution service, a research unit, an Establishment and Organisation Division and a Finance and Accounts Division. These are shown in the following Fig. 7.

British Overseas Trade Board

The BOTB has an active Publicity Unit which deals specifically with planning and coordinating international news coverage for the Board's overseas trade promotions such as joint ventures, British pavilions at trade fairs, the annual All-British Exhibition at a foreign centre, store promotions and seminars. In support of participants in these events, the London-based Publicity Unit provides a free service.

Nationalised Industries

In Britain, nationalised industries such as coal, water, electricity, gas, railways, buses, airways, the Post Office, British Telecom and so on operate like commercial firms and have PR departments, usually extensive ones since they have large publics to deal with. Some of these enterprises, e.g. the Post Office, serve the majority of the general public and are vulnerable to constant criticism if services fail to satisfy. It is impossible to satisfy everyone, and it is therefore essential to have an efficient PR department which can issue information and deal with customer enquiries and complaints, and deal with the media which are regularly reporting topics concerning national industries in the public interest.

In the Third World there are also parastatals (corporations financed by the

84

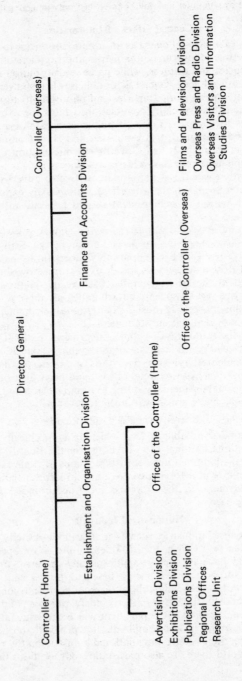

Fig. 7. The organisation of the COI.

Controller (Home)

Establishment and Organisation Division

Office of the Controller (Home)

Director General

Finance and Accounts Division

Controller (Overseas)

Office of the Controller (Overseas)

Films and Television Division
Overseas Press and Radio Division
Overseas Visitors and Information
Studies Division

Advertising Division
Exhibitions Division
Publications Division
Regional Offices
Research Unit

government but managed independently) which run industries such as copper, cotton, rubber, rice—mainly primary industries—in countries such as Indonesia, Malaysia, Tanzania and Zambia. In developing countries, as in most countries except perhaps the USA, there are nationalised public service enterprises such as posts and telecommunications, railways, airlines, gas and electricity. The nationalised industry is by no means a peculiarity of British Labour governments, and many countries, however capitalist, nationalised essential industries long before the British. State railways are a good example: it was mostly in Britain and the USA that railways were developed under almost racket conditions by railway kings and robber barons.

Quangos

Quangos have somewhat unfairly gained a bad name as 'jobs for the boys' organisations, to quote a typical editorial view. They have been attacked by the press, by MPs, and by the Conservative Party prior to the 1979 Government's election, but the majority have survived, presumably because pragmatic government finds that they are useful after all.

According to one arch-critic, Philip Holland, MP, there are 900 quangos with 20,000 members costing £12 million a year in salaries alone. But a Whitehall report claims there are only 252. Perhaps it depends on what you class as a quango. It is an unfortunate name which embraces bodies as eminent as the BBC, IBA, National Economic Development Office and the Police Complaints Board.

Initiated and funded by ministries and departments, quangos cover a multitude of interests and represent the complexity of modern industrial society. Very often their activity is in itself a PR operation, or a form of liaison between the Government and special interests (e.g. the Schools Council, the Commission for Racial Equality, the Equal Opportunities Commission and the Sports Council). Once again, the PRO is an important officer.

From this brief survey of Government and Government-sponsored services, it will be appreciated that several thousand PROs are employed, adding considerably to the majority of PROs who are employed outside the private sector of industry and commerce.

13

PUBLIC RELATIONS IN LOCAL GOVERNMENT

Most British local authorities employ a PRO if not a PR team, and the Local Government group is a large and important section of the IPR, well-known for its annual conferences. From time to time there has been criticism of these PROs by the press, who would like to by-pass them and have direct contact with councillors and officials. On the other hand, some local authorities publish civic newspapers because they find local press coverage inadequate, wishing to inform the ratepayers fully and not rely on what the commercial press sees fit to print. The tug-of-war between media and PROs exists here just as it does in every other sphere.

The work of the local authority PRO is largely to communicate the proceedings, decisions and work of the authority, not to promote the political ideas of Councillors or party groups or the controlling party. Party political information is for the parties or individual local politicians to issue, for it is propaganda.

Not all authorities are the same and according to whether they are County Councils, Metropolitan Borough Councils, or Borough Councils under the 1974 reorganisation they will have different responsibilities. Some councils have special trading interests, a few have airports, others have sports, conference or exhibition centres, spas or resorts. A number are anxious to attract industry or shoppers. Still others are university or cathedral cities, or are of historic or tourist interest. Some will contain a mixture of these interests and attractions.

As a result, the local authority PRO can be responsible for communicating a rich variety of information, not always just locally, but nationally and sometimes internationally.

In most cases the PRO will be responsible to the chief executive (e.g. the Town Clerk or Clerk to the Council), but in the case of authorities with holiday or tourist attractions the PRO will report to a publicity or publicity and entertainments committee. He may be responsible for entertainments as well, although in a large resort a separate officer will deal with entertainments.

For convenience, two other forms of 'local government' or 'public service' PR may be included in this chapter, although we have included the water authorities under nationalised industries along with other public utilities.

Regional Hospital Boards

Regional hospital boards have PR departments providing spokesmen for the hospitals in their area. In recent years the hospital service has been very much in the news, some hospitals being famous for their treatment of motoring accident victims, others for heart transplants and some for gynaecology.

Development Corporations

Throughout Britain there are new towns which often offer special facilities and advantages to companies which are encouraged to relocate their offices or factories or start new businesses there. Overseas companies are also encouraged to establish themselves in these development areas. Once again, this calls for the services of PROs.

Qualities of a Local Government PRO

In his book *Public Relations For Local Government* (Business Books) Geoffrey A. H. Lewis, a past president of the IPR, sets out the following qualities and experience required by a local government PRO:

1. An ability to communicate, clearly and concisely, both orally and in writing.
2. An ability quickly to understand complicated situations and to explain them in simple terms.
3. An ability to appreciate the council's objectives and a desire to explain them.
4. An ability to handle several subjects without exasperation.
5. An alertness to political situations.
6. An even temper and an acceptance, without bitterness, of rejected advice, yet a determination to press home a sincerely held opinion.
7. A knowledge of what the media want and how they 'tick' and how to make use, where appropriate, of the tools of the trade.
8. A knowledge of local government and what makes it 'tick', or the ability to learn this quickly.
9. An understanding of people and sympathy with their problems—including members and fellow officers.
10. Experience in the tools of communication of one sort or another and preferably several sorts.
11. An inborn ability to act as a full-time organiser and a part-time manager.
12. An appropriate qualification, preferably membership of the Institute of Public Relations.
13. A sincere belief that democratic government, for all its faults, is worthwhile government.

Range of Local Government PR Work

Taking all these authorities together, the range of PR activities may include:

1. Relations with local, regional, national and sometimes international press, radio and television. This will include press attendance at meetings, or the issuing of news releases about decisions taken at meetings of councils, boards and committees. News about the authority's activities will also be issued at press conferences or by news release. Feature articles may be written for newspapers and magazines.
2. Liaison with colleague officials responsible for other activities which require PR services or provide sources of material for PR purposes, e.g. entertainments, parks and recreation grounds, civic transport, etc.
3. Liaison with relevant local organisations (e.g. tourist boards, chambers of trade, hotels and restaurants associations, sports, entertainments, transportation operators, local societies, etc.).
4. Provide a public information centre for townspeople and visitors.

Sometimes this is done in cooperation with the public library.

5. Publish an official guide book, which will also include selling advertisement space, obtaining photographs, advertising and distributing it. Also, accommodation lists, maps, leaflets, showcards and other material may be produced.

6. Invite and assist conference organisers, especially large bodies which organise annual events and require conference hall and sometimes exhibition hall facilities plus hotel accommodation for delegates. Brighton, for example, publishes a regular magazine which is mailed to prospective organisers.

7. Organise visits by appropriate people such as editors, businessmen, travel agents and foreign delegations.

8. Deal with numerous unsolicited enquiries from people requiring information on numerous subjects such as residential facilities, schools, camping and caravan sites, business opportunities, sales conference facilities, sports such as fishing or golf—all of which have to be dealt with quickly and courteously. This may be handled by the information centre, which will be stocked with every kind of local information that will have to be invited or collected, a major task in itself.

9. Organise external publicity such as travelling exhibitions and film shows, store promotions, exhibition stands and in some cases, maintain information bureaux in, say, London.

10. Cooperate with package tour operators who require pictures and write-ups for their holiday brochures.

11. Advertise as appropriate to the authority. This may include holiday advertising in the popular press or on poster sites, overseas advertising to attract tourists or shoppers (people from the Continent come on shopping trips to places like Sheffield), business paper advertising to attract industry, or financial column advertising to attract investors in civic bonds.

12. Publish a civic newspaper for the ratepayers.

13. Organise a variety of events to produce PR for the authority, some requiring much time, effort and expertise as when a town is involved in a programme such as the BBC's *Down Your Way*, or *It's A Knockout* when the town is twinned with an overseas town. He may also be concerned with the organising of local events such as regattas, golf tournaments, *concours d'élégance*, flower shows, musical festivals, drama festivals and the like.

14. In some authorities he may act as the mayor's secretary and be responsible for organising civic receptions and other functions, together with writing speeches for the mayor (or chairman of the council or board, according to the type of authority).

15. He may also have to handle PR aspects of the council's legislation, as when a private bill is placed before Parliament or new by-laws are introduced.

16. Liaise with advertising agents who will produce and place press advertisements and posters, and design guide-books and other print.

According to the specialised nature of the authority, there will be other duties not listed above. In this sphere the PRO has to be competent to deal with media relations, printing and publishing, events organising, advertising and considerable cooperation with numerous people who either rely on him for support or on whom he relies for cooperation.

As an example of the unusual demands on a local government PRO's expertise, Ronnie Sampson (when chief PRO of South Yorkshire County Council) was involved in a campaign to obtain EEC funds for a £10 million rebuilding project for a 23-mile stretch of the South Yorkshire Navigation Canal. The British Government had refused finance: it finally approved an application to the EEC's European Regional Development Fund for up to 30 per cent of the cost. A well organised PR campaign proved the SYCC's case that the project was worthy of financial support because the canal could be a magnet for new industry.

In local government, PROs are subject to trade union conditions (e.g. membership of NALGO), something which can clash with professionalism and cause dual loyalties, a situation which rarely applies in industry when PROs have management status and have no need to belong to a trade union.

Once again, we have a large section of several hundred PROs who are outside the private sector. Although a few engage in advertising, and it has become fashionable for some authorities to appoint marketing officers, these PROs swell the numbers of those engaged outside normal industry and commerce.

14

PUBLIC RELATIONS IN NON-COMMERCIAL ORGANISATIONS

In this chapter we shall discuss PR on behalf of the multitude of other organisations which have been omitted so far. Some are public services, others are voluntary bodies, several are uniformed services, all are non-profit-making and so add yet more PROs to the large numbers which inevitably exceed those in industry, commerce and the consultancies. However, some of them may employ PR consultancy services, although not advertising agency services. Before going into detail about a few of them let us list the non-commercial organisations which are engaged in PR.

1. The Police.
2. The Fire Brigade.
3. The Armed Forces.
4. Charities and voluntary bodies.
5. Special interest societies.
6. Religious organisations.
7. Trade associations.
8. Employee associations.
9. Trade unions.
10. Political parties.
11. Sports organisations.
12. Professional institutes.
13. Educational establishments and organisations.
14. Friendly societies.
15. Private hospitals and clinics.
16. Youth organisations.

The list could no doubt be extended. Many other organisations such as industry training boards can be regarded as quangos, while most of the social services come within either central or local government. Let us look more closely at the PR work of some of these sixteen non-commercial groups.

The Police

Police PR has been an interesting development of recent decades, the psychology being to win the cooperation of the public in either preventing or detecting crime. The panda car largely having replaced the friendly Bobby on the beat, there has been need to keep the public sympathetic by other means. Fortunately, the police in the UK are rarely armed and violent police action is not expected. The rare occasions are when criminals are known to be armed, or when police are engaged in diplomatic duties such as guarding embassies. Constabularies have their PROs but, as is seen on television when investigations are being conducted, senior officers have to be capable of handling interviews with reporters. They also have to be careful that they do not reveal information which would lead to crime or help a suspect to evade arrest.

Police activity can often be of the kind that is welcomed by the media. The crime story is all the more exciting and readable if it is true and actually happening. This means that the police can expect a heavier press coverage than it always wants, but generally it has many opportunities to enjoy a good press.

Nevertheless, there are occasions when the opposite is true as in cases of police corruption, brutality or inefficiency. The police are therefore both fortunate and vulnerable, exposed to both good and bad publicity.

Some of the PR techniques used by the police are:

1. Press liaison information services.
2. Internal house magazines.
3. Documentary films such as the splendid ones produced by the Metropolitan Police.
4. Exhibitions at local events when demonstrations are given of police work.
5. Open days at police stations.
6. Television interviews. A number of chief constables have become television personalities as spokesmen on law and order.
7. Road safety visits to schools.
8. Daily broadcasts on local radio, describing robberies and inviting assistance, or giving advice on traffic conditions.

The Armed Forces

In addition to the PR work of the Ministry of Defence, individual units of the Army, Royal Navy and Royal Air Force have their full-time PROs and other officers have short-term PR assignments. In peacetime the Armed Forces are frequently engaged in activities which bring them in contact with the civilian public, or are involved in duties which are of local, national or international public interest. Officers commanding units are highly capable at being interviewed. Instances in recent years have been NATO exercises, the military presence in Northern Ireland, and the British forces sent to Rhodesia prior to the 1980 elections and the creation of Zimbabwe. They also provide valuable air, sea and mountain rescue units which are a community service, while RAF transports carry supplies to distant parts of the world when there are flood, earthquake or famine disasters.

Open days at Army, Royal Navy and Royal Air Force establishments have been major PR exercises for many years. Even as long ago as the 1930s, Portsmouth Navy Week and the Hendon Air Display were famous events, while today the Red Arrows' flying display is familiar at shows such as the Biggin Hill Air Show.

In *Planned Press and Public Relations* (Intertext), the author gives the example of the special Directorate of Military Public Relations Corps in Nigeria which was of special relevance before the military government handed over to a civilian democratic government in 1979. The Corps dealt with internal PR—e.g. a road safety campaign for Army transport drivers—and an external campaign to develop good relations with the public. This Nigerian PR Corps published an interesting *Public Relations Officers Handbook*, and the following quotation is universally applicable:

'Your first objective, always within bounds of security, is full and timely disclosure of the facts as they are known. The Army should be open and unafraid to admit its occasional blemishes, as well as its many accomplishments. This policy enhances the Army's credibility.'

The Armed Forces are often involved in propaganda, and the Northern Ireland situation is one in which Army spokesmen, having to explain ugly events, have been tested to the full in endeavouring to win, let alone enhance, credibility.

Charities and Voluntary Bodies

Ever since the concept of the Welfare State confusion and misunderstanding has surrounded some charities, while others have become well-known for their work to relieve the distress and sufferings of refugees, famine and flood victims or simply the underprivileged in many parts of the world.

Charities need funds and other resources, including voluntary help. In Britain, misunderstandings surround organisations which are thought to be financed by Government agencies. When disasters occur in far-off places it is sometimes difficult for people to associate themselves with people and places they know little about. To some extent, modern mass media help to familiarise readers and audiences with scenes from disaster areas. But there can be 'overkill', and people can become inured to suffering.

In December 1979 we had the curious contradiction of an appeal for toys for Vietnam refugees who had won the sympathy of the British public through the coverage of the boat people tragedy—but a long respected British charity, Dr Barnardo's Homes, found that the inflow of toys for its Christmas distribution was far below the usual supply. A spokesman for Dr Barnardo's appeared on television, telling viewers about the shortfall of gifts, and the toys flowed in again.

Every year the Royal National Lifeboat Institution holds a flag day to raise funds for the purchase, maintenance and operation of lifeboats which are strategically stationed round the coast of Britain. The fact that it is an independent service manned by voluntary crews is something which is not always appreciated, and it has to be reinforced by special PR efforts. Television has been a primary means, a good example being the retired lifeboat coxswain who told his story on the popular BBC 1 Parkinson programme.

Some of these voluntary bodies have full-time PROs but in others PR is part of the duties of the director or appeals organiser. Others use the services of a PR consultancy which specialises in fund-raising techniques. A typical technique is to find a distinguished donor to head the list with a generous donation.

However, PR is a continuous process and it does not rely solely on a dramatic piece of nation-wide publicity like an appearance on the Parkinson programme. The day-to-day work may consist of:

1. Regular liaison with the press, radio and television.
2. Publication of journals for friends, supporters and donors such as Oxfam's *World of Children*.
3. Publication of critical reports like those of War On Want on the baby milk scandal and the export of cigarettes with high tar content to developing countries.
4. Exhibitions, such as those at lifeboat stations.
5. Use of advertisements with challenging copy such as Save the Children Fund's *Save the Children. Please.*

6. Finding commercial sponsors of documentary films, and distributing these films.

7. Giving talks about the work of the society, including organising a panel of voluntary speakers who will address local organisations.

8. Getting schools to assist with collections of silver paper, milk-bottle tops and other saleable salvage to provide funds for, among other things, guide dogs for the blind.

Associated with much charity PR are special commercial ventures such as Oxfam shops, charity Christmas cards and mail order gift catalogues which all help to make known the cause while enabling people to contribute through purchases.

Religious Organisations

Whether or not one believes in a particular religion or supports a certain denomination, tolerance and understanding can be achieved in a world in which religious beliefs provoke more conflict than almost anything else. A great social problem with religion is that the believers of one faith seldom know anything about other faiths. Jerusalem is perhaps an example of the meeting together of many faiths and denominations, and yet the tragedy of Israel is that Jews and Arabs are racially the same Semitic people. In Singapore, Buddhists, Hindus, Muslims and Westerners worship in their temples, mosques and churches in 'The Land of Prayers' as Singapore was described in the April 1980 issue of *Check In*, a visitors' magazine issued by the Singapore Hotel and Restaurant Association. 'Singapore is one of the few countries,' stated the editorial, 'where various religions coexist peacefully.'

An interesting example of PR for a religion is the Buddhist Promoting Foundation of Tokyo which places copies of its book *The Teaching of Buddhism* in hotel bedrooms in South-East Asia, much as The Gideons of the USA (with national associations in 110 countries) place copies of *The Holy Bible* in hotel bedrooms throughout the world. The Buddhist Promoting Society prints *The Teaching of Buddhism* in English so that Westerners may understand this Asiatic faith when otherwise they might merely wonder at exotic Buddhist temples as tourist sights.

The Catholic church, the Society of Friends and other religious organisations place advertisements in the press inviting members of the public to write and find out what they stand for. Perhaps the study of comparative religions and denominations is a PR exercise which could promote considerable community relations in some troubled parts of the world. The journeys of the Polish Pope John Paul certainly earn much respect among non-Catholics.

Tolerance is therefore a major feature of religious PR, and this is quite distinct from the more propagandist nature of seeking converts. To spread knowledge and seek understanding for its own sake is a basic PR concept. It follows the PR transfer process, and emphasises the role of PR in achieving tolerance and understanding of things with which people do not necessarily agree, and appreciation of the truth that few things are wholly good or bad. It breaks down bigotry and prejudice, and it is the sort of PR which could help to solve the problems of Northern Ireland and Belgium where the conflict between Calvinists and Catholics produces such misery and chaos. As people migrate about the world as never before, religious leaders have a great PR responsibility.

Educational Establishments and Organisations

A great many universities, polytechnics, colleges and educational organisations make use of PR and employ PROs. The need is to inform potential students and all associated with education about the facilities and activities of these establishments and organisations, and to deal with the media when they are in the news.

For more than ten years the Open University in the UK has been engaged in PR on several fronts, establishing understanding of a new venture in higher education, seeking acceptance of the academic status of its courses and degrees, and overcoming the prejudices of many hostile politicians. The OU has had to bear the cross of being Harold Wilson's best idea, the misunderstanding that degrees from a university without conventional entry requirements must be inferior and general confusion about the name 'Open'. There has also been some prejudice about distance learning, although this has been highly successful in countries as different as Russia and South Africa. How to attract the right applicants, how to win the approval of employers and other institutions, how to justify government grants—these have been among its many PR objectives.

Something of the success of the OU's campaign is shown in the year-by-year record of its opinion polls which showed that public understanding of the Open University rose from a negligible percentage in 1969 to around 60 per cent in 1979, the year when Her Majesty the Queen awarded the degrees and there were some 60 000 part-time students. The OU is now regarded as Britain's greatest educational achievement. Moreover, lecturers in traditional universities respect the OU teaching material and often use it themselves, and with the OU's degrees being won by dedicated adults they have gained a new place among academic qualifications.

But educational PR is not confined to large establishments like universities. It also concerns schools in their local environment and it is significant that a local school can contribute to community affairs and win the respect of townspeople as well as parents. A wise headmaster or headmistress does not ignore the local media, and will use the opportunities which exist to enhance the reputation of the school. We have seen some excellent examples of schools performing valuable community services and gaining reputations for social responsibility. Among them have been raising funds for charity, organising visits to old people's homes and distributing food parcels to old people at Christmas. The community relations efforts of college PROs are also important in those areas where there are racial frictions.

Friendly Societies

Before the National Health Service came into being friendly societies acted as agencies for the existing contributory medical system, but when they lost this sickness benefit service to members the societies lost much of their attraction. Over the past thirty years they have had to introduce new benefits of their own and show that they can compensate for the financial inadequacies of the National Health Service. With an appeal mainly to the working classes it has not always been easy to sell additional health insurance to those who expect to be cared for by the State, and who are not particularly insurance minded. Recruitment of members is usually dependent on enthusiastic voluntary workers.

The Manchester Unity of Oddfellows is one society which employs a PR consultancy at national level and has voluntary PROs at lodge level. The PR work is not easy, and some societies are not helped by having archaic names. Yet these societies offer remarkable value to the thrifty. For example, the cost of a funeral can run into hundreds of pounds, a shock to those who are left with the responsibility and find that unless a substantial funeral benefit is due the cost has to come out of their pockets. This has been an important PR message from the Oddfellows.

Another friendly society, the Tunbridge Wells Equitable, makes good use of a quarterly house journal which links together its branches and keeps its members aware of privilege rates for life, household and motor insurance apart from its normal sickness benefit scheme.

PART 3

OPERATIONAL PUBLIC RELATIONS

15

PLANNING PR PROGRAMMES

This is a good point to remind ourselves of the essentials of the three definitions discussed in Chapter 2. The first spoke of 'deliberate, planned and sustained effort', the second brought in 'objectives' and the third added 'analysing trends'. With these concepts in mind we can apply the discipline of planning PR programmes in order to achieve definite results.

We are not concerned with haphazard efforts, short-term 'fire-fighting' exercises or intangible PR. To be successful, a PR programme has to be organised like a marketing strategy, an advertising campaign or a production schedule. The campaign should cover a reasonable length of time such as a financial year, and some large organisations prepare three-year PR programmes. It also needs to be planned well in advance, at least three months ahead.

It may well be argued that PR often has to deal with the unpredictable. A few things may be unpredictable but no business can operate on a day-to-day basis. Allowance can be made for the unexpected: there can be a contingency fund, the programme can be reviewed at monthly meetings with management, and flexibility can be observed. But certain things will be known. If a house journal is to be published it has to be edited, designed, printed and distributed regularly. The launching of new products will be expected. The PR programme may have to dovetail with many already planned events such as participation in an exhibition, the announcement of company results, sponsorship of sports fixtures, an opening ceremony and so on.

If the year's work is not planned the likelihood is that a muddle of unconnected things will be attempted so that in the end nothing is done properly and it is difficult to assess any results. But if there is a definite programme it is possible to tailor the supply of manpower, resources and money to achieve the best results. This will call for priorities and constraints. You cannot build a four-storey house if you only have labour, materials and money for a bungalow. In PR the money largely represents salaries or fees (which in turn mean time, the primary expenditure). Unless there are major costs such as making a film or publishing a large-circulation, frequently-published house journal, material costs will be comparatively small. Similarly, hospitality and expenses should be a modest proportion of the budget. For PR is mostly labour-intensive, mostly hard work, not gin and tonics and lavish lunches.

Submission of a PR Programme

1. In efficiently run organisations, the staff PRO will be expected to present his programme and budget for the forthcoming year.

2. When making a presentation to a client, a consultant should present a detailed programme of proposals supported by a fully calculated budget so that the client knows what he can expect for his money and the consultant knows what he may expect to be paid. This should form the basis of the contract of service.

3. Even when management does not expect a programme and budget, it will enhance the professional status of the PRO if he initiates a businesslike approach by voluntarily presenting his programme and budget. This will then enable him to control his expenditure of time and money and establish what he is capable of doing with given staff and resources. It will establish priorities and make clear what can or cannot be done, helping to deter management from imposing extra work on the PRO unless he cancels other work, is given extra staff or funds, or is permitted to augment the PR department with the outside services of a consultant.

Charting a PR Programme

A PR programme for, say, a year will be a complex undertaking, and many things will be happening simultaneously. For instance, a typical day's work might be something like this:

9.00 a.m. Read incoming post, which includes a quotation for printing an educational booklet. Compare quotation with others received.

9.30 a.m. Dictate letters in reply, including acceptance of quotation.

10.00 a.m. Read draft of article typed the previous day. Give revised draft to secretary for re-typing.

10.30 a.m. Phone photographer and arrange photographic session for illustrating a forthcoming news release.

10.45 a.m. Visit hotel and agree plans with banqueting manager for a press reception.

12.30 p.m. Take lunch while out of office.

1.30 p.m. On way back to office collect proofs of invitation cards from printer.

2.00 p.m. Read and correct proofs and give to secretary to return to printer.

2.15 p.m. Answer phone call from radio producer wanting information.

2.30 p.m. Write speech for managing director at press reception.

3.30 p.m. Give speech to secretary for typing.

3.45 p.m. Phone printer to make sure of delivery date of invitation cards.

4.00 p.m. Sign letters.

4.30 p.m. Receive telephone call from editor requesting photographs.

4.45 p.m. Select pictures, make sure captions are correct and give to secretary to despatch.

5.00 p.m. End of day—but he may take typed draft of speech to read overnight.

This day in the life of a staff PRO shows that he deals with ongoing work, is preparing for a press reception, deals with unpredictable phone calls, relies very much on an efficient secretary, and that his work may not be confined to office hours. But many of his actions are slotted into an overall plan of operations, and unless he does them on this day they will be too late on another day. Unless the flow of contributory actions is maintained, deadlines will not be met. It will be perceived that three jobs are in progress and two unexpected ones emerge for which he must be prepared with existing information and a photographic library.

The overall plan may be presented by a critical path analysis which could look something like Fig. 8, which is reproduced from the author's *Effective PR Planning*.

But for a separate job or event, such as the press reception mentioned above, a D-Day planning timetable could be plotted, working back from the event to the first action. This diary of events or responsibilities will help the PRO to check things to do and progress made on a day-to-day basis. In practice, actual dates are replaced by the numbers so that the following example, quoted from the author's *Effective Press Relations*, covers a period of three months. This will provide detail for one of the items shown on the critical path analysis.

D-DAY PLANNING TIMETABLE FOR A PRESS RECEPTION

D-90	Decide date
D-85	Plan programme for press reception
D-85	Shortlist venues
D-85	Invite quotations, menus, from prospective venues
D-80	Complete compilation of invitation list: check names
D-75	Compare received hotel quotations and menus
D-70	Visit prospective venues
D-65	Select and appoint venue
D-50	Design invitation card: agree wording
D-50	Seek printer's quotation for card
D-42	Receive printer's quotation: order cards and envelopes
D-35	Photograph subject
D-32	Receive, check and return proof of invitation card
D-30	Write managing director's speech
D-30	Order self-addressing lapel badges, press kit wallets, visitors' book
D-30	Book projector, projectionist, microphones
D-25	See contact prints: order photographs
D-24	Obtain approval of managing director's speech
D-22	Send special invitations to radio/television producers' news/programmes
D-20	Write news release
D-14	Delivery of invitation cards and envelopes
D-13	Address envelopes and invitations
D-12	Despatch invitations; order studio artwork—tent cards for speakers, displays, directional signs
D-10	Record acceptances/refusals
D-9	Follow-up non-replies, important refusals
D-8	Photographs supplied; items at D-30 delivered
D-4	Collect 16 mm film
D-3	Give hotel numbers for catering, seating, together with plan of the room
D-2	Run off news releases, MD's speech
D-2	Assemble press kits
D-1	Deliver materials, equipment to venue
D-1	Prepare room
D-1	Rehearsal: run through film
D-Day	Press reception

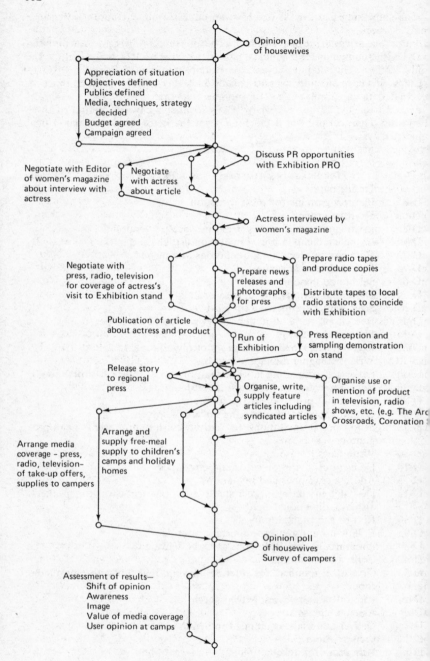

Opinion poll of housewives

Appreciation of situation
Objectives defined
Publics defined
Media, techniques, strategy
    decided
Budget agreed
Campaign agreed

Discuss PR opportunities with Exhibition PRO

Negotiate with Editor of women's magazine about interview with actress

Negotiate with actress about article

Actress interviewed by women's magazine

Negotiate with press, radio, television for coverage of actress's visit to Exhibition stand

Prepare news releases and photographs for press

Prepare radio tapes and produce copies

Distribute tapes to local radio stations to coincide with Exhibition

Publication of article about actress and product

Run of Exhibition

Press Reception and sampling demonstration on stand

Release story to regional press

Organise, write, supply feature articles including syndicated articles

Organise use or mention of product in television, radio shows, etc. (e.g. The Arc Crossroads, Coronation

Arrange media coverage – press, radio, television– of take-up offers, supplies to campers

Arrange and supply free-meal supply to children's camps and holiday homes

Opinion poll of housewives Survey of campers

Assessment of results–
Shift of opinion
Awareness
Image
Value of media coverage
User opinion at camps

Fig. 8. Critical path analysis of a PR programme.

The point to be observed is that most of the PRO's time is devoted to self-initiated work—it is 'deliberate, planned and sustained'—and does not derive from unexpected instructions. He is nobody's dogsbody. Logically, this should be because top management understands PR, knows what it wants from PR, and values the PRO's time and expertise. The same should apply if the programme has been submitted by a PR consultant engaged in executing it.

Controls

The best way to control time is to use a simple daily or weekly **time sheet** on which the PRO (or PR consultant) records how his time is taken up. This will provide a check on the amount of time spent on particular jobs, and can be a warning if more time is being spent on a job than was originally estimated in the agreed programme. In the case of first-time jobs it will be a guide to future planning. Time sheets will help a consultant to ration his time according to the different fees paid by different clients. It is easy to allow a given amount of time to, say, the organising of a press reception, but in practice it will be scattered in small portions over a period of perhaps three months as shown by the D-Day timetable. If too much time is spent on one job it means that less time can be given to another. The solution may not lie in working late, or taking work home, because some jobs can only be done when other people are available during their working hours. The PRO's secretary can collect time sheets, keep running totals of time expended, and compare them with target totals for the job. Without such a control, a consultancy could go out of business.

Another valuable control is the use of **job numbers** so that all orders and invoices from suppliers are identified. This will be discussed again in budgeting. It helps to isolate items so that the costs of photography, print, out-of-pocket expenses and so on can be allocated to the respective tasks which have been budgeted. It also makes easy the approval of suppliers' accounts.

Six-point PR Planning Model

The planning of a PR programme should follow a systematic pattern, and the following model covers the whole operation:

1. Appreciation of the situation
2. Definition of objectives
3. Definition of publics
4. Selection of media and techniques
5. Budget
6. Assessment of results

Publics have already been covered in Chapter 3, but publics must be seen in relation to objectives, while media and techniques will be the means of communicating with these publics. Constraints have to be applied so that the number of objectives and publics, the availability of media and the kinds used conform to the restrictions of the budget. And the budget is chiefly concerned with man-hours, which control the workload that can be accepted.

Items 1, 2, 4, 5 and 6 above, together with preparing the proposition, will be the subjects of the next six chapters. The proposition is the document setting out the proposed scheme for consideration, approval or amendment by the PRO's superiors or the consultancy's client.

16

APPRECIATION OF THE SITUATION

The Image

'Appreciation of the situation' is a military expression. The story is told of Field Marshal Montgomery, during the Second World War, calling for such a report, but when he was given a sheaf of papers full of information he retorted 'put it on a postcard'. Admirable though this was, in PR we are more likely to be greedy enough to want the sheaf of papers.

A PR programme cannot be planned without detailed knowledge of the situation, for PR is a problem-solving business. Assumptions are not enough. We need to be very cautious of management's convictions about external knowledge or opinions. Management could be entertaining illusions.

The **mirror image** is how management thinks outsiders see the organisation. The **current image** is that held by outsiders, and this could conflict with the mirror image.

The **multiple image** is that produced by salesmen and others with whom people have contact, each individual producing a separate and personal image which may not be a uniform image of the organisation.

It is important, therefore, to understand these different images. This can be done by conducting an **image study** which seeks a comparison between the images held of the sponsor and his rivals. A graph can be produced to show how respondents rate the qualities of each organisation. Topics such as delivery, prices, service, research facilities, performance or instructions could be tested. Such a study will show the organisation's strengths and weaknesses in the eyes of customers.

Or we may need to know the extent of knowledge, awareness and understanding, and an opinion survey can measure these attitudes. Before Cornhill Insurance decided to sponsor test cricket it conducted such a survey and discovered that awareness of the company was small compared to that of other large insurance companies.

Sources of Information

An inexpensive way of obtaining such information is by piggy-backing a set of questions on an **omnibus survey**—questionnaires with sets of questions sponsored by different organisations and submitted to a consumer panel for answering.

Inexpensive research can be undertaken by organisations which have close contact with their customers, patrons or clients. Questionnaires can be circulated and a simple means such as reply paid or Freepost envelopes, or personal collection, can secure return of the completed forms. This is frequently done by airlines, hotels and tour operators and it can also be applied to readers of house journals or members of a voluntary organisation.

Many forms of research are available for this quest for information to reveal the true situation.

The survey of the situation should not ignore existing information which may be found within the organisation, or in published information which may be available elsewhere in independent reports, Government reports, or in journals whose back-numbers may be searched. The PRO may also interview people within and outside the organisation. These sources may be summarised as follows:

1. Press cuttings, including feature articles and readers' letters, will show the attitudes of journalists and readers towards the organisation. Is it accurate, biased, ill-informed, hostile or sympathetic?

2. Sales figures and salesmen's reports will show whether sales are stable, fluctuating, falling or rising and also indicate the attitude of the trade towards the company.

3. If it is a voluntary body, the state of membership, funds and other statistics will have their implications.

4. Economic and political trends will be important: what are the effects of Government measures such as taxation and legislation, competition, imports and so on?

5. Industrial relations could be significant, and information could be gained from the personnel manager, trade union leaders, and through efforts by management such as systems of internal communications, benefit and in-centive schemes, social services and the extent to which worker participation is encouraged.

6. The financial front could also be important. What is the stock market situation? How are the shares performing?

7. Community relations should not be forgotten. How is the organisation regarded by local people? Does the company participate in local affairs?

8. Research surveys may have been conducted for various purposes, especi-ally by the marketing department, and they may well contain relevant in-formation about the situation.

9. Many people employed by the organisation or in some way associated with it such as suppliers of services and materials and distributors of all kinds may be helpful. Spending time in the field with representatives, visiting branch offices and observing activities in the field can be instructive.

From such investigations, according to the nature of the organisation, it will be possible to write a report which will form a basis for defining objectives and publics and preparing proposals.

In North America different terminology is used, and what has been de-scribed here will be called a **PR Audit.** As David Scott-Atkinson has written in the Canadian *Marketing*: 'The public relations audit determines what an organisation thinks of itself, its strengths and weaknesses. Those conducting such audits cross-check and validate with external publics—set the story to be told to paper . . . focus on changes that need to be made if objectives are to be met . . . and make a deliberate and sustained plan to create greater under-standing of that organisation's activities and objectives. A greater demand for goods and services traditionally follows. . . .'

Later in his article Scott-Atkinson sounded a warning: 'If the results of audits become known without accompanying plans of action to improve what they reveal, they may do more harm than good. If on the other hand they go hand in hand with a good workable plan under strong leadership, confidence in the association or organisation will be greatly enhanced.'

In other words, it is no use flunking the consequences of appreciating the situation or undertaking a PR audit. As the Mexican Statement says: you have to *analyse trends, predict consequences, counsel leaders,* and *implement planned programmes of action.*

17

DETERMINING OBJECTIVES

The review of the situation, the directives of management and the needs of departments will combine to provide objectives. We cannot plan without objectives and without objectives results cannot be assessed. This is tangible PR. So what do we want to achieve? Have we the means of coping with all these objectives? The process of deciding priorities and applying constraints has begun. The plan may be for six months or one, two or three years. Some objectives will be short-term, others will require continuous endeavour. Together they will form the jigsaw of the complete scheme, time, money and resources permitting.

Let us consider some lists of potential objectives for some of the organisations we looked at in Part 2.

A Manufacturing Company

1. Organise a community relations programme to promote understanding of the company among local community leaders who would act as innovators and spread their knowledge of the company.

2. Organise a programme of dealer activities to improve trade understanding of the company.

3. Develop international public relations in those overseas markets where the company aims to set up agents or licensing agreements for manufacture, familiarising these markets with the company and its products.

4. Improve the flow of corporate and financial news to city editors and the financial press, in readiness for a share issue.

5. Make a 16 mm film of a sporting event which the company has agreed to sponsor, and distribute this to organisations which arrange film shows in order to perpetuate the PR value of the sponsorship.

6. Increase reader participation in the employee newspaper in order to improve management–employee relations.

7. Develop more in-depth understanding of the company by relevant journalists by organising a series of individual visits for them.

A Local Authority

1. Organise a programme of talks and slide-presentations to schools and youth organisations to combat vandalism of parks, recreation grounds and public buildings.

2. Cooperate with local history society to organise a town history exhibition, organising visits by school parties and seeking coverage by press, radio and television.

3. Edit and distribute a civic newspaper in order to make ratepayers better aware of the authority's services on their behalf.

4. Organise a team of councillors and officials to act as spokesmen about local affairs on local radio.

5. By acting as PRO to, say, a music festival, use this event as a vehicle for increased media coverage for the town and, for the first time, seek to gain television coverage of the finalists' concert at the end of the event.

6. Organise both local and national coverage of the opening of the town's new leisure centre which has won an international architectural award.

A Charity

1. Increase public awareness of the charity's independence and that it is supported by voluntary contributions.

2. Make known the continuous story of the charity's work in under-developed countries.

3. Seek a sponsor for and make a 16 mm film about the charity's work for people in disaster situations.

4. Organise a series of magazine interviews for the director following his return from an overseas fact-finding mission, in order to make known the charity's relief appeal.

5. Obtain maximum coverage of the air-freighting of relief supplies when these take place.

6. Seek industrial donors of advertising space in the press and on poster sites.

A Trade Association

1. Make better known the association's code of practice.

2. Revamp the association's newsletter for members, and issue it monthly instead of quarterly.

3. Obtain maximum coverage of the association's campaigns to amend a law which is detrimental to members' interests.

4. Write, publish, publicise and distribute a pamphlet on this legal question.

5. Organise seminars for members.

6. Participate in the annual trade exhibition at a National Exhibition Centre.

In each case the list of possible objectives could be much longer, and the above are given merely as examples. The final choice of objectives will depend on the budget and how they fit into the available man-hours. Time has to be allowed for general day-to-day affairs and administration, and the possibility of unpredictable calls on the PRO's time.

Here is how the European Economic Commission defined the objectives of its information policy in 1960:

'The immediate objective of the information policy of the Community is to make known the activities of the institutions of the Community to the public and to stimulate a public interest and comprehension. But there is more. The final objective is a political community in Europe in which citizens can live with greater security and prosperity and in this way better develop their personalities. To realise this objective it will be necessary to develop a new European public opinion which will replace the same autonomous, democratic function as national public opinion inside the frontiers of different countries.'

18

SELECTING MEDIA

A thorough understanding of communication media is one of the most important assets a PRO can possess. The media scene is a constantly changing one. It is not limited to mass communications, and so-called mass communications studies are only of partial value to the PRO. For this reason, it is unfortunate that mass communications courses are confused with PR training.

A great deal of PR media are by no means addressed to the mass public, the 'admass' as it is sometimes rather cynically dubbed. Effective PR may depend on addressing messages to small groups, or face-to-face communication with individuals, or on the use of video-tapes and the small screen watched by small audiences. The media may have to be specially created, and may include documentary films, video-tapes, audio- and video-cassettes, video-discs, slides, notice boards, internal and external house journals. In developing countries media may have to be mobile, and innovators and folk media ranging from puppet shows to gong men may be required. The range of PR media is as endless as the human imagination and extends far beyond the normally accepted mass media of the press, radio, television, cinema and poster or sign. It is also more diversified than advertising media. Micro (or information) technology promises to bring to the post-industrial society of the future new and individualistic media such as demand publishing in place of supplied publications.

Media will be discussed more analytically in Part 4, but here let us consider the task of selection. Unlike advertising, we do not have to buy space or air-time, but the mistake should not be made of thinking that no cost is involved. Media are the vehicles of communication and the PR cost lies in the time spent in working with them and the materials required.

Some media and some techniques take up a lot of time: researching articles, photographic sessions, working with television producers, editing house journals, cooperating with documentary film producers, or organising press receptions, seminars, film shows and exhibitions are all very time consuming. A story may appear in the press, and it may be only a paragraph, but considerable time was spent in its preparation and distribution. The question is: how much time have we got and how can it be divided up most economically and effectively?

The choice of media will be derived from our decision regarding publics. Which media will best convey our message to our chosen publics? If no media exist, what private media should we create? This can be an urgent question in developing countries. But even in a sophisticated republic like Singapore it could be a problem when the major newspaper, the bulky *Straits Times*, is all things to all men where most of those born post-war speak English, and the only other newspapers are the *Business Times*, *New Nation*, four Chinese dailies, the *Sunday Times*, plus a handful of magazines. In most African states there are few newspapers, some of them devoting a great deal of space to political news. Britain is unusual in having large-circulation and, in the case of *The Sun* and the *Daily Mirror*, multimillion circulation newspapers (rivalled only by Japanese dailies) which have national distribution. The British PRO is spoilt by having the ability to put a story on the nation's breakfast table by means of a few London-produced national morning newspapers. And if the story is big enough he can reach maybe twenty million people by networked television.

Cost-benefit Method

Where costs are incurred in producing private media, the decision needs more than a value judgement, and the cost-benefit method of selection, which the author first introduced in *Marketing and PR Media Planning* (Pergamon Press, 1974), can be helpful. In the following revised version, an arithmetical answer is found which could be especially useful if the costs were similar. Values from 1 to 10 are given to the attributes of each.

Factor	House journal rating	Documentary film rating
Reaches desired public	10	8
Lasting effect	7	8
Regular impact	8	2
Colour	6	10
Sound	0	10
Action	0	10
Involves little manpower	0	7
Score	31	Score 55

Obviously, the ratings will be influenced by the importance of the factors to the person making the evaluation, but the difference of 14 points is largely to do with audio-visual values and time consumption. If sound and action are unimportant, and time is not a problem, the calculation can be interpreted differently. But if the PRO is biased towards editing a journal and has little experience of films, the cost-benefit analysis method could show that his personal preference was wrong. Thus he could be guided by a more independent assessment. The method is also useful when other people are trying to impose their prejudiced judgements.

From this it will be seen that an essential element when selecting media is the time factor, but it should not be overlooked that although this represents money and the budget, it could be a very rewarding expenditure. Although Lord Leverhulme's famous assertion that half of the amount he spent on advertising was a waste of money, but he did not know which half it was, suggested a very uneconomical approach to advertising, far less money needs to be spent on PR with far less uncertainty about the results. This is because we are not operating on such a hit or miss basis as mass communication encourages since we are addressing messages to more well-defined and often smaller audiences. If some firms spent double their normal expenditure on PR they would still not be spending an enormous amount of money.

19

BUDGETING

Budgeting is not only a means of finding out costs and controlling them: it also identifies work to be done so that the D-Day timetable and the critical path analysis aids to planning and control, as explained in Chapter 3, can be drawn up in parallel. A budget is similar to the shopping list which a housewife prepares before going shopping, reminding her of what she has to buy which in turn is controlled by the amount of money in her purse or her credit limit.

The three principal PR costs are **time**, **materials** and **expenses**.

Time

Time represents man-hours, which can be looked at in two ways: the amount of time it will take to carry out a particular task (such as editing a house journal, handling a news release, or organising a PR event), *or* the amount of time that is represented by a PRO's salary or a PR consultant's fee. The value of the time will be the hourly rate.

To find out the PRO's hourly rate his annual salary has to be divided by the total of his working days—that is, the total after statutory holidays, weekends and annual holidays have been deducted. The same has to be calculated for the members of his staff. We now have a **time bank** which can be allocated to the tasks in the programme. If this fails to agree with the estimated man-hours for the programme it will be necessary to do one of three things: make cuts in the proposed campaign, engage extra staff or augment the PR staff with freelance or consultancy services.

A more complicated calculation is required to arrive at the consultant's hourly rate because this rate has to recover the costs of running the business and produce a profit. The consultant's hourly rate will take into consideration salaries and all overheads such as light, heat, air-conditioning, rent, rates and so on, plus the percentage desired for profit. There are variations in the method, some consultancies basing the hourly rate on the salaries of the account executive and his secretary only, others working out hourly rates (salary plus oncost) for every member of the consultancy staff so that their work is both estimated and charged out according to its usage. A rough rule-of-thumb method is to treble the salaries of the account executive and his secretary.

In the case of an account executive, if the fee is £20,000 and the hourly rate is £40, the total number of hours available is 500, or about 1½ days' work a week. It is important that the client should understand this for he may well imagine that a certain fee is worth more service than it really is. But the client can expect only what he pays for, and if the counsellor exceeds the paid-for workload he does so at his own loss unless a supplementary fee is agreed. Correct calculations and expectations are therefore critical on both sides.

The consultant's hourly rate could at first sight seem to be high, and the false impression may be given that his earnings are exorbitantly high. The truth is that the consultant does not sell 100 per cent of his working time. A considerable proportion of his time is taken up by the administration of his business, including efforts to secure new business. This could absorb perhaps 50 per cent of his time.

Materials

Materials consist of all goods which have to be purchased on the client's or company's behalf. Stationery, postage, photographs, print, slides, films, cassettes, exhibits and displays come under this heading. The consultant has to be careful to recover all such costs, otherwise they will come out of his profits. Unless there are very expensive items such as house journals or documentary films, material costs will make up only a small proportion of the total budget.

Expenses

These are the costs of fares, taxis, hotel expenses and hospitality, and will also include catering, transportation and other costs for press events. Again, this should not be a large item in the budget in spite of myths about PR entertainment.

Three Examples of Budgets

In this section three kinds of budget will be demonstrated with dummy figures. The first is the kind which the consultant should include in a proposition to a client. The second is a budget for a press reception. The third is an estimate of the cost of running a PR department. These are freely adapted from similar examples which have appeared in the author's other books.

PR Consultancy Budget

This calls for a little preliminary explanation. It differs from an advertising appropriation because no free services are covered by commission on media purchases. All time has to be paid for, including talking to the client. You will notice that progress meetings—regular monthly meetings—are chargeable, whether held on the client's or the consultant's premises. The calculations should be interpreted as the number of items multiplied by the number of hours multiplied by the hourly rate, which in reality might be 1×10 hours $\times$ £40 per hour equals £400. However, since from the reader's point of view the hourly rate may be different and he may not be thinking in sterling, dummy noughts are used.

		£
12 Progress meetings	12 × 00 hrs × £00 =	0,000.00
PR coverage of exhibition	1 × 00 hrs × £00 =	0,000.00
25 news releases	25 × 00 hrs × £00 =	0,000.00
Organising 3 seminars	3 × 00 hrs × £00 =	0,000.00
Press visit to factory	1 × 00 hrs × £00 =	0,000.00
3 Photographic sessions	3 × 00 hrs × £00 =	0,000.00
Editing, designing, quarterly house journal	4 × 00 hrs × £00 =	0,000.00
General information services	00 hrs × £00 =	0,000.00
Contingency 10%	00 hrs × £00 =	000.00
		00,000.00
Estimated material costs	News releases	000.00
	Photography	0,000.00
	Printing house journal	00,000.00

	Postages, stationery	000.00
	Press cuttings	000.00
Expenses	Travelling expenses	000.00
	Transportation	000.00
	Seminars	0,000.00
Contingency 10%		000.00
	Total	00,000.00

Budget for a Press Reception

This is a very useful standard budget because press receptions are common PR exercises. But it is very easy to forget things, make mistakes and miscalculate. A press reception may seem such a familar event that the PRO may be tempted to be careless. He may leave too much to others, especially the caterers, and then be faced with unexpectedly high bills. He must beware of management, who sometimes introduce their own last-minute and sometimes overgenerous ideas, and of company staff who are apt to stay behind after the guests have gone and so run up an unnecessary bar bill. It is sensible to control such expenditures by giving the barman a stop figure, and closing the bar by serving coffee.

Normally, journalists are not there 'for the beer', but want a good story. Hangers-on are usually freelance writers, and every PRO knows the saying 'first to arrive, last to leave'. It is also possible to control the volume of drinks consumed by guests. Never have a waiter walking round with a tray of drinks unless this is the easiest way of serving a large party. If the event is merely one of those old-fashioned cocktail parties where people stand around, and eventually someone makes a speech, the drinks will flow because there is nothing better to do. But if there is an organised programme, and for most of the time journalists are seated, listening or watching, the only time for drinking is on being received and following the business.

In recent years there have been changes in drinking habits. Journalists tend to prefer coffee on arrival, and tomato juice and dry white wine have tended to replace spirits. Nevertheless, one has always to be prepared to meet all tastes and one should allow for the occasional brandy addict.

	£
Printed invitation cards, reply cards, white envelopes	00.00
Postage on invitations	00.00
Telephone: checking names on invitation list, following up non-replies	00.00
Hire of room	00.00
Hire of projector	00.00
Projectionist's fee	00.00
Hire of microphones	00.00
Average 3 drinks at £0.00 per head	000.00
00 buffets at £00.00 per head	000.00
00 coffees at £0.00 per head	00.00
Gratuities	00.00
Press kit wallets	00.00
News releases, copies of speech	00.00
Display panels for photographs	00.00
Photography and prints	000.00
Captions	00.00

Order forms for photographs	00.00
Visitors' book	0.00
Samples/Souvenirs for guests	000.00
Lapel badges	00.00
Artwork for tent cards, displays, notices	00.00
Taxi fares transporting materials, staff	00.00
Special effects: costume hire, decorations, musicians, lighting, etc.	000.00
Incidentals	00.00
Contingency fund	000.00

Total   £0,000.00

Budget for a PR Department

PR departments will vary in size and duties according to the type of organisation so the budget given here is aimed to show a comprehensive range of activities and it can be adapted as required.

It covers everything included in the consultancy budget except profit. Overheads are identified instead of being calculated in the hourly rate. The variety of activities is likely to be greater than that of a consultancy budget because we are now dealing with full-time staff—not a share of a consultancy team—and the work will entail internal as well as external PR responsibilities.

	£
Salaries: PR manager, his assistants, secretaries	00,000.00
Overheads: Rent, rates, lighting, heating, air-conditioning, cleaning, share of telephone switchboard, etc.	00,000.00
Depreciation: Furniture and equipment	00,000.00
Insurances: Car, all risks on equipment, travel, pensions, health	00,000.00
Press events: Materials, catering, hire/rental charges	00,000.00
Visual aids: Preparation, production, distribution and maintenance films, slides, cassettes	00,000.00
News releases: Preparation and distribution	00,000.00
Press cutting service, television, radio monitoring services	00,000.00
Feature articles: Preparation and publication	00,000.00
Information Service: Staffing and equipping	00,000.00
House journals: Editing and production	00,000.00
Educational literature: Creation, printing and production	00,000.00
Sponsorship: Awards and coverage	00,000.00
Seminars: Materials, catering, hire/rental charges	00,000.00
Photography: Shooting, prints	00,000.00
Vehicles: Car, van	00,000.00
Equipment: Camera, projector, TV set, tape recorder, etc.	00,000.00
Stationery: Letterheadings, news release headings, photo caption headings, envelopes, etc.	00,000.00
Telephone, Telex, Prestel	00,000.00
Postage:	00,000.00
Travelling expenses: car expenses, taxis, rail/air fares, hotels, hospitality	00,000.00
Contingency: say 10%	00,000.00

Total   £000,000.00

It will be seen that several of the figures are totals and require detailed individual budgets, an example of which has already been demonstrated in the budget for a press reception.

Budgets can be produced in conjunction with D-Day charts or a critical path analysis chart. The one depends on the other.

Management is used to dealing in this businesslike way, and the proper planning of programmes, forecasting of results and budgeting of costs is the sort of accountable professionalism which will enhance the PRO in management's estimation. It will greatly diminish management's often false idea that PR is something which happens on a day-to-day basis, perhaps subject to the whims of management, so that it could be regarded as intangible and dispensable. Of all things in an organisation, PR should be indispensable.

In some organisations, especially in less sophisticated countries, management sometimes does not know what to do with PR. Thrust upon PR are all sorts of irrelevant tasks such as servicing other departments by arranging travel requirements, 'protocol' (which in developing countries means the arrangements for social occasions), and even personnel management which is another job altogether. Budgets bring out the real responsibilities of PR.

From experience, the PR practitioner will know roughly what most things cost (in time or money or both) so that even in a meeting or during an interview he should be able to produce a tentative budget at short notice. He can always confirm this afterwards with a more accurate calculation based on real figures.

20

PREPARING REPORTS AND PROPOSITIONS

Reports and propositions are necessary in order to spell out what the PRO or consultant recommends. Again, it is businesslike, and something management understands and appreciates. It shows logical, responsible thinking.

It is no use making suggestions or recommendations verbally. They will probably be met by a response of 'No!' or 'What will it cost?' Armed with a written scheme and calculated costs, the PR practitioner is in a strong position to argue his case. Never say, 'Wouldn't it be a good idea if . . .' *unless* you have done your homework first and can back up your proposal with facts and figures.

A written report or proposition needs to be set out in an acceptable and readily understood fashion. It should be written in an objective, factual style, the information should be presented in a logical sequence, and different kinds of information must be easily located.

The report should be preceded by the **brief**—that is, a statement of the purpose, scope and limitations of the report. If initiated by someone other than the writer, it will be on instruction. In order to understand the report it is necessary for the reader to understand the brief. The reader will also require a **summary** so that he has a quick, simple impression of the proposals.

The writer should consider how, when and by whom the report will be read. These considerations may be as follows:

1. The reader is likely to be busy and have to read many documents. For him the report has to be both concise and comprehensive.

2. He may have to deal with it at a board or committee meeting, may not have studied it beforehand, and so needs to be able to find his way about the report in the midst of a discussion.

3. The report should be capable of easy reference and understanding by anyone reading it in the future.

4. Those reading it may not have detailed knowledge of the subject. It should not be too jargonised and essential terms should be explained.

The above remarks should emphasise that writing a report or proposition is very different from writing advertisements, news releases or feature articles, all of which have their special literary styles. They are as different as a map, a poster, a telegram and a book. The skilled communicator has to be able to change his writing style according to the job. The proposition also has to sell.

Three things are therefore essential to the preparation of these documents:

1. Adequate research, as discussed in Chapter 16.
2. Concise, precise writing.
3. Methodical lay-out of the information.

Here, then, are the outlines for two reports, first an internal report to management, second a business proposition from a consultant (or any other out-

116

side service). While a good consultant should automatically produce such a report, the PRO should also expect one. Two extremes do occur: some consultants are poor businessmen and think a letter is sufficient, while others indulge in showmanship and dress up propositions in too-fancy binders.

The plan of an internal report could follow the following pattern:

Internal Report

Title page—perhaps stating the purpose of the report and for whom it is intended.
List of contents, giving chapter or section headings and page numbers.
The brief—purpose, extent and limitations of the study.
Summary of findings or proposals.
Methodology—if there has been research, a statement of the methods used. If a questionnaire has been used, this should be reproduced in the appendices.
Appreciation of the situation.
Solution or recommendations.
Techniques or plan of action with perhaps a timetable.
Budget.
Appendices containing specific supporting items.

The plan of a consultancy proposition will be slightly different because (*a*) the client has to be convinced of the consultant's ability to perform, and (*b*) the client has to understand how the costs are arrived at and how the consultant will be remunerated. This proposition may well have to compete with other propositions.

Consultancy Proposition

Title page—stating for whom the document is prepared, and by whom.
List of contents, giving section headings, and page numbers.
The brief—as instructed by the client.
Summary of recommendations.
Statement of experience setting out consultant's relevant experience with other clients.
Personnel—identification of account executive who will handle the account, plus names of any specialists who may be used.
Appreciation of the situation as researched by the consultant, resulting in certain problems or needs which the recommendations will be designed to resolve.
Recommendations and programme—an outline of the consultant's plan of action.
Budget—allocation of man-hours on an hourly rate basis, arriving at the fee, plus estimates for materials and expenses.
Payment—method of payment, e.g. quarterly in advance.
'Brag list'—list of clients, past and present, serviced by the consultant.
Appendices—supporting material such as samples of work done.

The production of the report should be neat and orderly, but not flamboyant. All pages should be numbered and a contents list or index is essential. The document should be presented in a convenient form, say A4 size, printed on one side of the paper only, and bound in stiff covers with perhaps a spiral or comb (wire or plastic) binding. Thus the report will be easy to read and easy to keep flat and clean.

21

ASSESSMENT OF RESULTS

The final element in the six-point PR planning model given at the end of Chapter 15 is *Assessment of Results*, and as was stated at the beginning of Chapter 17, *'We cannot plan without objectives, and without objectives results cannot be assessed.'* This is the logic of PR which belies the nonsense about its supposed intangibility. In that chapter we listed no fewer than 24 potential PR objectives for different kinds of organisations—a manufacturing company, a local authority, a charity and a trade association.

If PR is conducted without objectives, results cannot be assessed, or at least they are less easy to measure. Unfortunately, a lot of PR *is* conducted haphazardly, and this leads to the complaint that its effectiveness cannot be proved.

In Chapter 28 examples are given of corporate advertising campaigns which were assessed, perhaps because they were created by advertising agencies for whom research is second nature. To be fair, PR consultancies tend to be less familiar with research because much less is spent on PR than on advertising, and budgets rarely allow for research. But things are changing and image studies, opinion polls and the piggybacking of questions on regular omnibus surveys are being adopted by PR practitioners.

Users of PR are beginning to (*a*) want to know what they are getting for their money and (*b*) realise that results are assessable.

The trouble in the past has been that both employers and clients have had too little understanding of PR, and hardly ever any wish to use PR for specific purposes. If PR is used merely to get favourable mentions in or on the media; to attempt to whitewash an unfortunate incident; to provide a bulwark between the media and top management; suddenly to start providing an information service without defined purpose; or merely to back up an advertising campaign, there is little if any positive objectivity to measure against. Such PR is trivial, anyway.

Management are sometimes blamed by PR practitioners for their poor understanding of PR, and for their misuse or trivialisation of PR so that perhaps it is restricted to comparatively minor activities such as product publicity and media relations, the only record of achievement being a collection of press cuttings. It is true that on the whole a good deal of management is ignorant about PR. It is possible to have a management expert who has no idea how to write a job specification for a staff PRO or how to buy the services of a PR consultancy, nor for what purposes.

But it is also true to say that our most dynamic and successful management has a very shrewd comprehension of PR, and without always calling it PR they practise PR very efficiently as a business technique. The world's finest example of this has been Marks and Spencer during the past fifty years. There are also companies, such as Rentokil, where top management personalities like Bob Westphal have had an inherent appreciation of PR, have known

118

precisely what they wanted PR to do for them, and have achieved spectacular results. One very obviously assessable result has been Rentokil's share price. Between December 1979 and December 1980, in spite of recession and growing mass unemployment, Rentokil's share price rose from 98p to 180p. Very interesting is the fact that neither Marks and Spencer nor Rentokil spend much on advertising, but their PR is superb, their reputations are impeccable, and top management has for decades been thoroughly objective about its public relations. A lot of that PR has been inspired by management, has been conducted at all levels of and by the staff, and has often had little to do with press cuttings.

There are three main ways of evaluating the results of PR programmes:

1. By observation and experience.
2. By feedback and its assessment.
3. By research.

Observation and Experience

Some objectives will be seen to be achieved. This is clearly the easiest and most inexpensive form of assessment. The following are some typical examples:

(*a*) We may wish to stem a trend in staff instability, particularly if money is spent on training staff only to lose them to rival employers. The PR programme may aim to inform employees better about company policies and prospects. If this succeeds, the reduction in resignations will be a measure of the PR programme's success.

(*b*) The need may be to employ the right calibre of staff. Has a campaign to educate prospective recruits produced the desired result?

(*c*) The company may have had a poor reputation locally, resulting in a bad local press, public criticism, letters of complaint and poor response to vacancy advertisements. Has this situation been turned round as a result of a PR programme to achieve a more deserved image?

(*d*) As a result of good communications with the financial media, has a new share issue been successful, or has the stock market price been improved?

(*e*) Are distributors better disposed towards the company, stocking lines, permitting displays, receiving salesmen more favourably, as a result of a trade relations campaign?

(*f*) Have industrial relations improved as a result of franker or more personal management–employee communications?

(*g*) Are the media better informed, more accurate, less hostile, more sympathetic or more interested as a result of a media relations programme?

The above are seven possibilities. It may be disappointing to note that we have not mentioned sales and profits. This is because PR is not only, perhaps not at all, concerned with the marketing and advertising aspects of business. There *are* other aspects of business (e.g. to do with production and finance), and if PR did not pay attention to these there would be no marketing or advertising.

Of course, too much should not be claimed for PR and in making such assessments it is always sensible to consider whether other factors have influenced the result. Economic, political and other influences may affect the situation. It would be silly to claim that PR had been totally responsible for improved trade relations if one's principal rival had declined in popularity!

Feedback and its Assessment

Since PR is a two-way process, and the PRO provides the eyes and ears of the organisation as well as the voice, part of the PR task is to initiate and receive a constant inflow of information. This may arrive in many forms, both internally and externally. It may take the form of complaints, ideas, suggestions, reports and recommendations, or it may consist of press cuttings, monitored broadcast materials, books containing comments on the organisation, Parliamentary reports, independent research survey reports and so forth. Some of this may have been inspired by the PR practitioner, but much of it will be outside his direct control. Some of it may be provoked for good or ill by other people in the organisation.

One of the PR practitioner's jobs will be to examine such feedback, and perhaps comment on it and report to those whom it concerns within the organisation. He may have to act on it by correcting false reports or making sure that people such as journalists and broadcasters are better informed next time they deal with the subject. It is often poor policy to 'keep a low profile', which can be worse than making 'no comment'. Negative PR is sometimes advocated when organisations are in trouble, but there is the adage that 'the best form of defence is attack', and this can be true of unfortunate PR situations.

Among this feedback will be the material for which the PR practitioner has been directly responsible, e.g. press cuttings and the monitored scripts of broadcasts with which he has been involved.

Not entirely dead, though it should be even if it is still favoured by those Americans who have a dollar measure for everything, is the evaluation of media coverage by its advertisement rate-card value. It is a nonsensical yardstick for the logical reason that editorial space and programme time is priceless, at least in most countries where editors and producers cannot be bribed. Equating column-centimetres or air-time with advertisement rates is also false because an advertising campaign would not have used similar publications or air-time, or have been booked for the same positions, dates or quantities. There is no sensible comparison between the two.

So, when someone says 'that two-page article would have cost so much if we had bought the space', or 'that hour's programme on networked ITV about our sponsored golf tournament would have cost x million pounds if we had bought air-time', they have not made a realistic comparison. For one thing, had they bought the space, and if they could have bought all that air-time (which is impossible in the UK where there is no sponsored TV), they could have said what they liked as favourably as they liked, provided it was ethical and legal. But they have no control over what is said or not said by editors, journalists, producers and commentators.

There are, however, genuine and better ways of evaluating media coverage, for example:

(*a*) One can note which papers or programmes have covered the story. This can be important. Were they influential media? Half an inch in a multi-million circulation women's weekly magazine could be much more valuable than a page in a small circulation business monthly. A story in *The Sun* could be more valuable than one in the *Financial Times*, and vice versa. The *volume* of coverage could be immaterial. Coming nearer home, a PR story in *PR Bulletin* (with its penetration of the PR world) could be much more useful than one in

Campaign (even if it would publish it!), which has little penetration let alone understanding of the PR world. Thus, it is valid to evaluate *where* a story has appeared. This can be represented on a value scale like this:

Publication	Rating	Story 1	Story 2	Story 3
Daily Blower	4	X		X
Daily Sizzle	2		X	
Sunday Scandal	2		X	X
Sunday Bore	4	X		
Weekly Gloom	4	X		
Weekly Hope	2		X	X
Score		12	6	8

The ratings would obviously be different for different organisations.

(b) One can also evaluate the **potential readership** or **audience** by multiplying each appearance of the story by the published circulation or readership figure of each journal or, in the case of broadcasting, by the published audience figures.

Thus one could say that if a story appeared in journals with estimated readerships of 500,000, 750,000, 1 million and 4 million, $6\frac{1}{4}$ million people had the *opportunity* of seeing or reading the story. This is called an **OTS rating**. Or a television programme may have a recorded audience figure of, say, 15 million.

(c) Picture usage can also be counted, and this may be a good indication of which publications should be sent pictures and which not, or whether it is better to *offer* pictures, perhaps submitting miniatures from which editors can choose and request pictures. Again, this exercise might suggest the wisdom of reproducing pictures on the news release with the offer to supply prints if required. Money is often wasted on sending expensive photographs to journals which are never likely to use them.

Research

Marketing research techniques can be used when the objective of the PR programme is to effect a change or improvement in awareness, attitude or image. A base percentage of awareness or attitude is necessary, and this would have been obtained initially when the appreciation of the situation study or the image study was undertaken before planning the PR programme. There are two ways of going about this. A piece of primary research may be set up independently, or—very economically as described in Chapter 28—questions may be inserted in the questionnaire of an already set up omnibus survey with its already recruited panel of respondents.

Suppose, in the case of an attitude study or opinion poll, it had been found that only *5 per cent* of respondents had heard of the organisation, or knew what it did, or liked what it did, and the objective of the PR programme was to increase this figure to *20 per cent*. A post-PR programme survey would reveal the degree to which this had been achieved. Similarly, with an image study, the effectiveness of the PR programme in achieving a more accurate image would be revealed by a later survey to measure what changes had been brought about.

Thus, tangible quantitative results could be recorded because this type of research measures changes in trends over time, and this can be represented in the form of graphs, bar charts or pie charts.

It is also possible to apply research techniques to news releases *before* they are despatched and after they have been published. James B. Strenski (*IPRA Review*, September 1980) says:

'Pretesting and post-testing specific communications campaigns of a random audience sample can be as helpful in public relations program planning as it is in advertising campaign planning. Pretesting is particularly effective in avoiding needless, poor impressions. Post-testing can help avoid repeating mistakes.'

The problem, however, is how to induce management to accept the results of a pre-test when they have probably rewritten and 'approved' what they are adamant shall be issued! On the other hand, submission to pre-testing could be a way of discouraging management from ruining professionally written releases.

The lesson has to be learned by management that PR can only be done 'on the cheap' if it is to be unaccountable. It seems a waste of money to commission PR without knowing what it is expected to achieve, and not caring whether it achieves anything. Yet it is not uncommon for companies to spend an insufficient sum on unspecific PR activity and then complain that it has not done anything. In such a case management is to blame for the waste of money and the ineffectiveness, not PR. That 'sufficient amount' should be sufficient to cover the essential research, and should be enough to cover a PR programme capable of achieving the results which it is hoped the final research will show have been achieved.

The message, of course, is that if you want tangible results it is essential to have tangible objectives. If an architect designs a building he expects the finished structure to represent his plans. Similarly, PR programmes should set out to achieve definite results: at the end of the campaign programme the results should be capable of evaluation. It may not be a pounds and pence, or sales volume, evaluation because PR has more diversified and less commercial objectives. But it may be an evaluation which helps the pounds and pence people to operate profitably. For instance, millions of pounds have been spent on products which have flopped—from the Edsel car to New Smoking Mixture. But they had no PR to create a favourable marketing situation. In both cases only the marketing and its promotional support could be evaluated in cash terms: the PR would have been measured in growth of knowledge and acceptance which would have guided the advisability of marketing the product at all. Again, in both cases, the PR result would have been a measure of the risk rather than the actual profit or loss. In PR we are talking about different things. To take another analogy, for commercial purposes PR can be more like the intelligence work and the artillery bombardment before the attack.

From this it follows that PR is most likely to succeed when management understands what PR can do, and when management knows what it wants PR to do. When the PRO or PR consultant is properly briefed he can plan to operate effectively. Unsuccessful (and intangible) PR programmes result from PR practitioners being obliged to put forward proposals which are not aimed at satisfying management expectations. Worse still, they may be no more than pragmatic, 'playing it by ear' fumblings to support some other activity such as a marketing strategy or an advertising campaign to which, willy-nilly, PR has been attached like a mascot.

PART 4

THE MEDIA OF PUBLIC RELATIONS

22

THE PRESS—NATIONAL, REGIONAL, INTERNATIONAL

The press is the most versatile and resilient of all mass communication media. Sophisticated electronic media have not destroyed the press in industrial countries, and as literacy grows in the developing world so the press develops to satisfy the demand for knowledge, news and entertainment. Radio, television, video-cassettes, video-discs and teletext systems cannot compete with the special merits of newspapers and magazines. What are these attributes? Why does the press predominate?

Special Merits of the Press

1. It can provide information in greater depth than transient broadcasting media.

2. It can be read anywhere, about the home or office, while travelling, sitting out-of-doors, over a meal—at times and in places where electronic media may be inconvenient or unavailable. The press is a portable medium which can be taken almost anywhere. In fact, in developing countries educated members of a family may take newspapers to their villages and read them to illiterate relatives. A readership survey in Kenya has recorded the number of people who 'listen to newspapers'.

3. Newspapers and magazines often have an extended life because they are kept—binders are supplied for some magazines, or back numbers may be looked up in libraries—or because they are passed on to other people. This is proved by the number of enquiries and orders which advertisers receive weeks, months, even years after publication.

4. Items can be cut out and retained, either personally or by libraries which maintain files on many subjects, e.g. the Advertising Association and British Institute of Management libraries. Newspapers—e.g. the *Daily Telegraph* and the *Financial Times*—also keep files of cuttings on numerous subjects which support the information services provided by these newspapers.

The press is therefore very much a living medium, perhaps more so than has been suggested in the past by advocates of electronic media who have tended to deride the press for its lack of participation and intimacy. By comparison with the 'hot' medium of television, Marshall MacLuhan called print media 'cold'.

This is not to say that the electronic media do not have their special merits but here let us consider the advantages and disadvantages of the press as a PR communication medium. What are the demerits?

Special Demerits of the Press

1. Newspapers particularly can have short lives and one has to be wary of the large circulation and readership figures claimed for them. Some copies may never leave—or reach—the home. Other copies may be discarded on a short commuter journey to or from work. Not every section of a paper is

likely to be read by all readers: those who read the sports page may never read the city page, and vice versa. Readerships have to be reduced to likely readerships of certain stories. For example, a reading and noting test showed that the most read feature in the *Financial Times* was not the financial news but the digest of general news on the front page. Similarly, we should not be deluded by the multi-million circulation and readerships claimed for popular newspapers: one such British paper has won a large circulation because it does not have too much to read in it, and its 'readers' are more interested in its pictures, cartoons and contests.

2. Some newspapers and magazines may be biased so that they either do not print certain stories, or, if they do, they distort them. There is seldom truly objective reporting by the press, and it is often true that a good, factual news release from a PR source is more impartial than the average newspaper story. The *Guardian*, for instance, frequently adopts an attitude of mock intellectualism and sneers at PR stories, whereas the *Financial Times* welcomes and uses PR material. In sending PR stories to the press it is wise to understand their peculiar traits. *Campaign*, Britain's advertising trade paper, has a habit of rewriting stories (and even reader's letters) and getting them wrong.

Bias may derive from political, religious, ethnic or simply proprietorial influences as can be seen if one studies how different papers treat the same news story. Many newspapers express political bias but, except for the *Daily Mirror*'s (the Forces newspaper) contribution to Labour's success in 1945, readers are seldom influenced by newspaper politics. If this were so the right-wing *The Sun* would not have a four million circulation while obviously the 'page three girl' compensates for the editorial hysteria on the facing page, even if a grateful Tory premier did knight the editor. Nevertheless, *The Sun* is often good on PR stories, even printing correct ones about ITT.

3. Newspapers, especially, can be unreliable in their reporting, mainly because they are produced very quickly and it is difficult to be editorially accurate. Unfortunately, readers are apt to believe what they read in the papers as if it must be true if it appears in print. This is not always so. One has only to note the number of apologies and disclaimers which have to be published, especially by *The Guardian*. In 1975 *The Guardian* took the unprecedented step of permitting the PRO of ITT to publish a half-page article refuting the reports which *The Guardian* had published during the previous two years! There are times when readers may be entitled to feel that the only reliable material published by the press is that from PR sources, if only because PROs have enjoyed the time and resources to get their facts right.

The stormy saga of Chief M. K. O. Abiola, chairman of ITT Africa and Middle East, as conducted in the Nigerian press is a case in point. It has been going on since 1978 when the controversy was highlighted over the Chief's gifts of calculators to his fellow members of the Constitutional Drafting Committee, and has continued since the civil elections in 1979. The situation has been confused by the fact that Chief Abiola is a wealthy man involved in politics as well as being chairman of an American multinational. Consequently, because he makes lavish gifts it is suspected that the money comes from ITT, which is in turn suspected of being financed by the CIA! In black Africa CIA has to be read for 'reds under the bed' and it is wiser to be seen visiting the British Council rather than the American Centre. The truth is probably that it is foolish to try to buy favour, and as one observer remarked to the writer when he was lecturing in Nigeria in 1980, 'What Abiola needs is a good PRO.'

The following is quoted from *National Concord* (August 26, 1980). Readers may judge for themselves the extent of bias shown by the *Daily Sketch, Nigerian Tribune, Washington Post* and *National Concord* (in which the Chief has financial interests):

Abiola throws challenge to detractors
BRIBE STORY FRIVOLOUS—ITT boss

ITT boss in Africa and Middle East, Chief M. K. O. Abiola, has repudiated the dubious roles attributed to him in publications by the *Daily Sketch*, the *Tribune* and the *Washington Post* over contract awards in Nigeria.

In a rebuttal sent to our Editor yesterday, Chief Abiola said: 'The points made or imputed from a *Washington Post* report against ITT operations in Nigeria and my participation in it, and purportedly reported and analysed by the *Daily Sketch* of Monday, 18th August, 1980, and Wednesday, 20th August, 1980, and the *Tribune* of Wednesday, 20th August, 1980, and Sunday, 24th August, 1980, may be summarised as follows:

1. That ITT, through me, bribed government officials and NPN members to win contracts in Nigeria.

2. That ITT used a Swiss company created for the purpose, to pay bribes through me to those officials.

3. That ITT manipulated invoices to cheat the Nigerian economy.

4. That my role within ITT is dubious and was used to salt away millions of Nigerian money.

5. That when the *Washington Post* report came out, I made myself deliberately unavailable to answer questions or grant interviews to reporters of the *Daily Sketch* and *Tribune*.

I wish to reply, briefly, to each of these allegations as follows:

1. On (1) above, as stated in my statement of 17th August, immediately I heard of the allegation, ITT or myself never took part directly or indirectly in any attempt to bribe any official to secure any contract in Nigeria.

2. On (2) above, ITT, like most multi-national companies have companies in Switzerland, in accordance with the law of that country. It is not illegal, either by Nigerian, Swiss, American or international law to have companies in Switzerland.

The ITT company in Switzerland was established to carry out the objectives of the company, as stated in its memorandum, which objectives do not include the offer of bribes. Our Swiss company was formed long before ITT had any business dealing with Nigeria.

3. On (3) above, the P & T system of tendering, which as stated in various contracts, also form the basis for invoicing, calls for detailed base catalogue prices, as at the date of offer, in such clear itemisation that every component, inclusive of every diode, resistor, capacitor, transistor, size of cable, etc., incorporated in every subsystem is identified, each with its unit price and extended to reflect its quantity.

Government agencies check these figures to ascertain that they are in accordance with the contract before payments are made.

4. On (4) above, my role within ITT is that of a partner with 40% of the shares in Nigeria until I decided to give part of it, free of charge, to my fellow Nigerian staff. It is regrettable that these dubious roles attributed to me, which I totally repudiate, are neither substantiated nor catalogued.

5. I was away to London WT802 at 11.45 pm on Sunday, 17th August, 1980, on Nigerian Airways ticket No.0874201904158 issued on 15th August, 1980. It is clear therefore that the journey was booked two days before the *Washington Post* publications and three days before the *Sketch* publication.

Finally, I challenge both the *Sketch* and the *Tribune* or any other body or bodies to produce any other evidence to the contrary.'

An important company like ITT Africa and Middle East which—with rival companies—is involved in one of Nigeria's most essential developments (a competent national telephone system) has gained an unenviable corporate image as a result of bad publicity during the past three years. Whose fault is it: the indiscreet over-generosity of a man in the limelight or a malicious press? The *Daily Times* (August 28, 1980) and *The Punch* (next day) reported that Chief Abiola had sued the *Daily Sketch* and the *Nigerian Tribune* for 20 million naira (10 million naira each) for the alleged libel, and sought an injunction restraining the two newspapers from publishing any similar libel. On September 6 the *National Concord* carried a front-page story that Chief Abiola had now sued *The Punch* for 5 million naira for libel contained in a front-page story and in a cartoon in a later issue. Or is it simply a case of give a dog a bad name? ITT has been maligned by the press all over the world, usually without justification. Rebuttals like those published in *The Guardian* and the *National Concord* do not undo the harm already done, although on August 25, 1980, *The Sun* was happy to publish and credit another story from ITT Europe's magazine *Profile*.

In Britain, trade unionists were unhappy about the way in which incidents in the 1978–79 winter strikes were overdramatised, and set up the Campaign for Press Freedom (led by trade union leaders) which demanded that the press report both sides of stories about industrial disputes and permit right of reply in exceptional cases of distortion. In addition, the National Union of Journalists submitted a resolution to the 1980 TUC Conference asking the TUC General Council 'to examine ways in which member unions can apply pressure on newspaper and broadcasting employers to ensure a fair hearing for differing opinions'. Mr Bill Keys, general secretary of SOGAT, was reported in *The Guardian* (August 26, 1980) as saying that in extreme cases print workers would be justified in blacking certain copy or refusing to print whole newspapers if managements refused the right of reply.

Inevitably, the resolution was passed. It was, of course, as biased as the press bias it criticised. A leader in *The Times* on September 6 commented on the resolution and remarked: 'In fact most union leaders of any stature are adept in the art of using publicity to advantage, while managers, usually with less experience of industrial conflict, are often relatively inept. It is also true that most industrial correspondents are basically sympathetic to trade news.' In other words, trade unionists are better communicators than management who are notoriously bad at PR during industrial disputes. Trade unionists don't say 'no comment'.

Behind all these controversies lies the illusion of the freedom of the press and the fact that, where they are not state controlled, newspapers are published as businesses to make money. Consequently they will print what is most likely to sell papers. In PR terms, this means that stories are most likely to be printed which editors consider to be of *interest and value to their particular readers*. This will be coloured by the fact that in some cases readers dislike American multinationals or resent industrial disputes. The PRO, in submitting press material, has to reconcile himself to the facts of life about the press and the peculiarities of democracy in a free enterprise society which may not always work in his favour.

History, Location and Distribution

Throughout the world the press varies according to history, location and distribution. History tends to determine location; distribution tends to depend on size of country and population, and the extent of urbanisation, industrialisation and especially transport communications. Press centres tend to be capital cities so that when a number of states or kingdoms have been combined in the past to form one country (as in Germany and Italy) several press centres have survived. If a country is very large, such as the USA or Australia, the principal cities have a localised press.

Britain is unusual in having both a national and a local press. This is because London has been the capital for centuries, the country is small with good road, rail and air communications, and there are many large cities and towns. Overseas visitors are sometimes puzzled to find local weekly newspapers in Britain which have circulations as large as their national dailies. The volume of the British press is phenomenal.

Circulation or Audited Net Sale figures—the average number of copies sold per issue—vary according to the time of year and also according to price rises or industrial disputes. For instance, in recent years the circulation of the *Daily Mirror* and *The Sun* varied between 3½ and 4 million copies daily. Owing to industrial dispute, *The Times* was not published for a year, but upon its return it achieved increased sales, low though these remained by popular press standards.

If we take round figures, the circulations of the London-based British national dailies are roughly as follows (in 1982):

The Sun	3¾ million
Daily Mirror	3½ million
Daily Express	2 million
Daily Mail	2 million
Daily Telegraph	1½ million
Daily Star	1 million
The Guardian	400,000
The Times	300,000
Financial Times	200,000

Readership figures will be higher, taking in 'secondary' readership such as other members of the family or of the office. A popular newspaper may have from two to four readers, whereas the *Financial Times* may be passed round an office and have a dozen readers.

It is important to distinguish between circulation and readership figures, the latter usually being much higher than the figures listed above. **Circulation** figures result from publishers returning audited figures for the number of copies printed, given away and actually sold of each issue to the Audit Bureau of Circulations which periodically certifies the average net sale. **Readership** figures result from interviewing members of the public to discover which publications they have read, and the demographic details (e.g. age, sex, occupation, etc.) of those readers. One is an arithmetic calculation, the other is the result of a national readership survey conducted by an independent research company and published by the Joint Industry Committee for National Readership Surveys (JICNARS).

JICNARS represents the publishers, advertising agencies and advertisers through their trade associations. Thus JICNARS is also independent compared to surveys which are sometimes conducted by individual publishers, or even the old Hulton Readership Survey of the 1950s which attempted to survey the press in general although sponsored by a publisher.

Readership figures are classified according to the social grades A, B, C^1, C^2, D and E, which represent employment as distinct from the former socio-economic groups based on income (which are still used in developing countries where the majority of people are in the poorer groups and employment can be defined less distinctly). In a class-conscious country like Britain the national newspapers can be ranked against the social grades, roughly as follows:

A	*The Times, Financial Times*
B	*Daily Telegraph, Guardian*
C^1	*Daily Express, Daily Mail*
C^2, D, E	*Daily Mirror, The Sun, Daily Star*

Circulations correspond with the *Financial Times* selling only 200 000 copies daily but *The Sun* and the *Daily Mirror* around 3¾ million or more. The *Daily Telegraph* contains the most information, but the young *Daily Star* is said to have won its first million because it did not contain too much reading matter.

In the competition between the intellectual 'heavies' and the popular papers with their youthful pin-ups, an editorial in *The Sun* defined the role of a newspaper in a way which is relevant to the character of desirable PR press material:

We recognise that, since the advent of broadcasting, and television in particular, it is no longer enough merely to INFORM—merely to repeat what was on the box the previous evening.

It is also a newspaper's duty to explain, to educate, to record, to reflect the age it lives in—and to ENTERTAIN.

If it has a message, and *The Sun* believes it has, it is also a newspaper's duty to RECRUIT and MAINTAIN an audience.

Otherwise, there is no point in having a message.

Most popular papers are tabloids. The 'tabloid' (as distinct from the large-page 'broadsheet') newspaper has become adopted by Fleet Street to the extent that it is the format of Britain's five popular newspapers, *The Sun, Daily Mirror, Daily Express, Daily Mail* and *Daily Star* which between them sell more than 12 million copies daily. They are read by more than half the adult population, readership being from three to four times circulation figures.

Kinds of Publication and Circulation Figures

Daily Morning Newspapers

Morning daily newspapers are usually published six times a week—that is, except for Sunday in Christian countries (or Friday or Saturday where other religions exist). According to distribution facilities, the newspaper will be printed many hours earlier (usually overnight) in order to be available at breakfast time or as people go to work. In London, newspapers will be printed in different editions between 10 p.m. and 4 a.m., the final edition being sold in the Greater London area. Where newspapers have to be carried hundreds of miles by road, the first edition may be printed at mid-day on the day previous to sale. This also explains why in large countries like the USA there are no national morning newspapers.

Regional or City Daily Morning Newspapers

Outside Britain, it is common for morning newspapers to circulate within certain population areas, with perhaps a fringe circulation in more distant places. These newspapers may be called 'provincial dailies.' Again, Britain is also unusual in having regional morning newspapers in addition to the London nationals, e.g. the *Western Morning News* (Plymouth), the *Liverpool Daily Post* and the *Yorkshire Post* (Leeds).

The biggest selling British regional mornings have the following approximate circulation (1982): Leeds *Yorkshire Post* (100,000); Darlington *Northern Echo* (100,000); Norwich *Eastern Daily Press* (95,000); *Liverpool Daily Post* (70,000); *Birmingham Post* (42,000); Ipswich *East Anglian Daily Times* (41,000).

In addition to the English regional mornings, there are similar papers published in Wales, Scotland and Northern Ireland which really have their own national press in competition with the London nationals, e.g. the *Western Mail* (Wales), *Glasgow Herald* (Scotland) and the *Belfast Telegraph* (Northern Ireland).

Interesting variations occur in other countries. The popular German *Bild* has a large circulation made up of local editions published in several West German cities. In the USA there are newspaper chains (e.g. Hearst newspapers) which appear under separate city titles but contain some material which is syndicated nationally to all newspapers owned by the group. In Nigeria there are newspapers based on state capitals, but the Lagos *Daily Times* seeks national distribution and achieves a circulation of some 400,000 (comparable to the small UK circulation of *The Times*). But in developing countries like Nigeria the majority of people (80 per cent) are illiterate and outside the market available to a newspaper in industrial and literate countries. A Nigerian paper has the problem of reaching literates scattered throughout a vast country where cities are often hundreds of miles apart (Maduraguri being 1000 miles, Kano 700 miles and Enugu 300 miles from Lagos).

But circulations of newspapers, or numbers of titles, may be restricted by other factors. Newsprint is costly and countries with balance of payments problems (e.g. Ghana and Zambia) may have to limit the number of copies printed. In Nigeria, the competitive and popular *The Punch*—a sort of Nigerian *Sun* complete with page three pin-up—is restricted by lack of machinery, otherwise it would really challenge the *Daily Times*.

The situation is far simpler in Singapore where the *Straits Times* can circulate to a largely literate English-speaking population living on a fairly small island, the paper containing a remarkable number of pages and covering every possible interest. Neighbouring Indonesia, with an area as big as the USA but scattered among thousands of islands, has nationally distributed newspapers. Nevertheless, the total circulation is only 2.2 million against a population of 130 million, and 80 per cent of the circulation is contained in the capital city of Jakarta.

A factor, apart from literacy, which characterises Asian newspapers, especially in the Asian countries, is that in addition to English-language newspapers there are ones published in the languages of the Indian and Chinese communities or in the national Malay and Indonesian languages. English predominates only in Singapore (in spite of a 70 per cent Chinese population), whereas it is the second language in Malaysia, while in Indonesia (where English is widely spoken by the educated and business community) English-language newspapers are read mainly by expatriates and visitors from Britain, America, Canada and Australia.

Wherever newspapers are printed in a variety of languages (e.g. English and Swahili in Kenya, English and Arabic in Arab countries) there are bound to be comparatively small circulations because the total newspaper circulation is dissipated by the different language versions. Thus it is easier for British newspapers to have large circulations because only one language is common, although some immigrant communities (e.g. Indian) have their own language newspapers.

Evening Newspapers

This is a rather ambiguous description because so-called 'evening' newspapers often have early editions appearing in the morning, follow-up sports editions and lunch-time editions until the main city edition appears as people are going home from work. London has its own evening newspaper, the *New Standard*, which has a fringe circulation up to 50 miles around London, but within 40 miles of London and in most of the large cities of England, Wales, Scotland and Northern Ireland there are regional evening newspapers. It is a sign of the times that in 1980 the London *Evening News*, which had once boasted a circulation of $1\frac{1}{2}$ million, was down to 450,000, was losing £9 million a year, and was sold to the *Evening Standard* with a loss of 1700 jobs. There are many more regional evenings than regional mornings but in total about 100 daily newspapers are published outside London, mostly evenings.

The English regional evening newspapers with the largest circulations (1982) are: the Birmingham *Mail* (342,000); Manchester *Evening News* (340,000); Liverpool *Echo* (240,000); Leeds *Evening Post* (180,000); Hull *Daily Mail* (125,000); Stoke-on-Trent *Evening Sentinel* (125,000). These are all old-established papers, but comparative newcomers of the web-offset age have respectable circulations (which nibbled away at the faltering London evenings), e.g. the Southend *Evening Echo* (66,000).

In Scotland the Glasgow *Evening Times* sells 215,000 copies, in Wales the Newport *South Wales Argus* sells 53,000 and the Swansea *South Wales Evening Post* sells 69,000, while in Northern Ireland the Belfast *Telegraph* sells 156,000.

Most British regional dailies are better printed than London nationals because they are printed by web-offset litho. London dailies are printed by old-fashioned letterpress machines, although very slowly photo-typesetting is being introduced. The resistance to new techniques by trade unions resulted in the twelve months' shut-down of *The Times*. Photo-typesetting and web-offset printing require fewer print shop workers.

However, some newspapers have adopted a compromise, replacing Linotype typesetting machines with photo-typesetting but producing plates which can be printed on letterpress machines. This compromise has reduced the number of redundancies, made possible the retraining of employees, and avoided industrial conflict. But in recent decades new regional evening papers have appeared which have been made possible by the economies of web-offset printing—that is, printing from a fast rotary press using reels of paper, and benefiting from the photographic setting and plate-making techniques which have replaced the laborious hot metal techniques typical of letterpress printing.

Sunday Newspapers

The majority of British Sunday newspapers are national, but there are a few regional ones, and there are 'national' Sundays in Scotland and Northern Ireland. The three 'heavies'—the *Sunday Times*, *The Observer*, and the *Sunday Telegraph*—also carry colour magazines which are separate publications, and more popular papers (e.g. *News of the World*) now have colour magazines. Circulations range between about 4 million for the *News of the World* down to 1 million for both *The Observer* and the *Sunday Telegraph*.

A peculiarity of Sunday newspapers is that they carry little news and concentrate on 'magazine' material. In the heavies this 'magazine' material is devoted to politics, business, travel and culture, while in the popular papers it will concentrate on more sensational material. It is interesting that the *News of the World*, the world's biggest circulation Sunday newspaper, lost half a million circulation because it attempted to publish more respectable material. It is perhaps a sad commentary on the mass reader that he or she prefers to read about sex, murder, crime, corruption and disaster and that it is not merely a cynical press which believes that good news is bad news.

English regional Sundays are published in Birmingham, Leicester, Newcastle and Plymouth; Scottish in Glasgow and Dundee; and Northern Irish in Belfast. Of these the top circulations are approximately the Glasgow *Sunday Mail* (760,000) and the Birmingham *Sunday Mercury* (185,000).

Local Weekly Newspapers

In Britain most towns, and even the suburbs of the largest cities, have their own weekly newspapers. In some heavily populated areas there are separate editions with different titles for neighbouring communities. These 'series' (e.g. the *Kentish Times* with editions for places like Beckenham, Bromley, Sidcup and Orpington) will have some pages common to all editions and other pages devoted to local news and perhaps local advertisers. There are also weekly newspapers which are circulated over a wide area, being read by people in towns and villages in two or three counties (e.g. the *West Sussex Gazette*, *Pullman's Gazette*). Thus, local weeklies may range from those confined to single towns, with perhaps modest circulations of a few thousands, to big series with total circulations of a hundred thousand or more.

Freesheets

These weekly newspapers are delivered door-to-door free of charge. Their editorial contents are usually of general consumer interest, such as entertainment, home decorating, gardening, motoring and fashion. Their circulations are large and there is saturation coverage of residential areas, making them increasingly valuable vehicles for PR stories.

Magazines

These can be divided into many categories, and in industrial countries there may be hundreds of titles. In developing countries there may be few magazines of any kind, while some of those on sale will be imported (e.g. the *Reader's Digest*, *Newsweek*) or published abroad and sold locally (e.g. *West Africa*). The 'trade press' may not exist, and overseas readers should make a careful study of the section below on trade, technical and professional magazines. Magazines may be classified as follows:

(*a*) **Consumer magazines.** Covering popular subjects, many of these magazines have large circulations—hundreds of thousands, sometimes more than a million—and women's magazines are the largest group. Sometimes called 'specialist' magazines, they cover every possible interest such as food, sports, hobbies, gardening, politics, religion, travel, house-buying and many other topics. They are called consumer magazines because they are bought by members of the general public and sold by newsagents. A visit to a bookstall at a large railway terminus will give a good idea of the range of subjects covered. Most are printed in colour by either photogravure or offset-litho. All British women's magazines used to be printed by photogravure, but in recent years offset-litho has been adopted by new publications.

In the UK women's magazines top the sales with the weeklies *Woman's Weekly* (1.6 million), *Woman's Own* (1.6 million), *Woman* (1.5 million) and *Woman's Realm* (800,000), and the monthlies *Woman and Home* (700,000), *Cosmopolitan* (480,000), *She* (300,000) and *Ideal Home* (220,000).

(*b*) **Trade, technical and professional magazines,** although quite different, are sometimes wrongly lumped together as the 'trade press'. The trade press is addressed to the trade (distributors such as wholesalers and retailers); technical journals are read by technicians such as electricians, builders, engineers or other craftsmen; professional magazines are published for professionals such as lawyers, doctors, architects, teachers and other qualified people. In industrial countries there are hundreds of such journals. If the subject is very specialised the national circulation may be small and the journals are sold internationally to make them viable, while many of the British and American journals are so authoritative that they are widely read abroad, especially in countries which have no such press of their own.

The size of the circulation may depend on the method of distribution. Do readers **subscribe** to it, which could mean that the circulation is not large? Is it **mailed to members** of an organisation? If so, the circulation will depend on the size of the membership. Or does it have a **controlled circulation**—that is, mailed free of charge to a combination of selected readers and those who have requested copies. Controlled circulation figures can be impressive, meaning good penetration of the subject area.

An interesting example is that until late 1979 there was very poor penetration of the potential PR readership in the UK. The IPR *Communicator* reached only about 2500 members, *Campaign* had mostly an advertising readership and took little interest in PR, and *Hollis PR Weekly* had a small subscription list. But when *PR Bulletin* was issued on a controlled circulation basis it circulated to at least 4000 (eventually rising to 5500) PR practitioners, and for the first time it was possible to reach a substantial number of PR readers. In 1980 *Communicator* ceased independent publication and was incorporated on the back page of *PR Bulletin*.

(*c*) **The alternative press.** This is a curious omnibus classification which has been given to a mixture of publications which do not fit under the standard headings. They include the gay publications and ones for various minority groups and causes. The Royal Commission on the Press published a research paper on the subject called *Periodicals and the Alternative Press*, and defined the alternative press as 'any publication seeking to meet a need not catered for by commercially-published newspapers and magazines'. When including titles under this category the Royal Commission 'took into account important factors such as the expression of attitudes hostile to widely-held beliefs'. Among the titles so included in the Royal Commission survey were *Anti-Apartheid News* and *Gay News*, which would seem to be odd bedfellows, and a choice guaranteed to offend many people in the Third World. It is difficult to understand why the first of those journals could not be listed as a political journal just the same as *Labour Weekly* or *Liberal News*. The alternative press seems to be a most unfortunate classification: 'Miscellaneous' would surely have been adequate.

Circulation Figures

In this chapter we have given round-figure approximations of circulation or net sale (*not* readership) figures. The **Audit Bureau of Circulations** announces certified figures at regular intervals. These figures fluctuate for at least three reasons: (i) increases or decreases in sales; (ii) seasonal fluctuations; (iii) loss of copies due to industrial disputes. Readership figures are published by the Joint Industry Committee for National Readership Surveys. Circulation figures are averages based on audited net sales; readership figures are estimates based on marketing research techniques.

The Varied British Press

There are so many different publications in Britain that it is difficult to classify them all. Like freesheets, there are give-away magazines such as *Girl* which is handed out to office workers in the street; some publications such as *Exchange and Mart* contain nothing but sale and want advertisements; there are women's magazines such as *Family Circle* and *Living* which are sold at the check-out points of supermarkets, and customer house magazines like the North Thames Gas *Modern Living* which are sold in showrooms. Some local authorities, dissatisfied with local press coverage, publish their own local newspapers and magazines. There has been a growth of Arab publications which may be sold to Arabs in Britain or in their home countries or to British readers interested in Anglo-Arab relations and trade. So far we have dealt with newspapers and periodicals (as magazines are also called). There are also annual publications.

Directories, Yearbooks, Annuals

In some of these publications entries are free, in others they are paid for, while in both cases charges are made for more prominent or more displayed entries. Absence from such publications, or inadequate information, can be very bad PR. An essential task of a PRO is to see that his organisation is properly listed wherever possible, otherwise it may be interpreted that the organisation is not worth including. Absence can create some very unfortunate suspicions.

For example, the PRO or press officer of every British organisation should be shown in *Hollis Press and Public Relations Annual* so that any editor can contact him or her when necessary, and PROs may contact one another.

The author has known cases where contracts (or invitations to tender) have been lost simply because a company was not listed in the appropriate directory. Certain yearbooks contain articles giving advice to readers: it may be in a PRO's interest to make sure that such advice is correct, up to date or refers to his company's products or services if this is permissible.

A large part of a PRO's skill lies not so much in having personal contacts with editors and journalists—they may be too numerous for this to be physically possible—but in knowing the publications themselves, how they can fit into PR programmes, and which ones to include in mailing lists for news releases or invitation lists for press events. A PR consultant, with a variety of clients, will require knowledge of hundreds of publications, and this will be extended to thousands if he is engaged in international PR.

Standard mailing lists are rarely satisfactory; new lists need to be compiled for each occasion. Nor is it sufficient to select by title since titles can be misleading; the publications themselves need to be known for their types of reader, content and printing process. It is useless sending a release to a publication read by the wrong sort of reader, which does not print news reports, or has already been printed. Yet it is perfectly easy to avoid these mistakes which, unfortunately, are all to common.

How to Know the Press

1. Study newspapers at first hand. Look at copies in other people's houses or in waiting rooms. Look at them in libraries. Browse through copies in newsagents' shops, or at railway or airport bookstalls. Get to know as many publications as possible. This is easy and can become a valuable habit. The writer has done this all his working life. Remember, publications come and go or change their format and style.

2. Read the profiles on publications in *Benn's Press Directory*. No PRO can afford to be without this annual.

3. Make use of the media lists supplied by PIMS (formerly PRADS) and EMA, and the editorial requirements information contained in the *PR-Planner*. (Addresses will be found in Appendix 3.)

4. Keep up to date with news of new publications and publishing plans as announced in *UK Press Gazette*, published weekly.

5. Subscribe to information sources such as *Advance* (Themetree Ltd., Windsor) which lists forthcoming editorial programmes.

With such knowledge maximum coverage is assured. You will save wasting time and money on useless mailings, and you will avoid annoying editors by sending them stories they cannot use, or which are too late for them to use. It is better to send a story to one journal and get 100 per cent coverage than to mail it to 100 and get 1 per cent coverage. Far too many news releases are sent to far too many publications, simply because the PRO did not know the right ones to mail at the right time.

23

BROADCASTING MEDIA—TELEVISION AND RADIO

Broadcasting media are very different from the press, and television and radio have their special advantages and disadvantages, but they have one thing in common, which is that they are transient unless recorded on video or audio tape. Unlike printed messages, it is difficult to retain broadcast messages. They usually have to be absorbed at the exact time of transmission, and one cannot make later or repeated studies of the message. One has, therefore, to be satisfied with instant impact, and to remember that the message can, of course, be misunderstood or forgotten.

And yet these electronic media can be extremely valuable in PR programmes if they are understood and used properly, especially as audiences may well exceed the readerships of newspapers or magazines. In Britain, a networked television programme may have an audience of up to 20 million viewers, 25 per cent greater than the combined circulation of the national dailies. In fact, the *Dallas* sequence which revealed 'who shot J. R.' attracted 30 million British viewers.

Television

It is difficult to generalise about television because there are different systems in almost every country. In the USA there are many commercial television stations in each city, whereas in Britain there is the national BBC (non-commercial) and the fifteen regional commercial stations known as ITV (although the controlling authority is the Independent Broadcasting Authority). The BBC also has some regional programmes. The programmes of either BBC 1 and 2 or of the regional ITV companies may also be broadcast partly or wholly nationally or even at different times or on different days.

In Singapore there are programmes in English, Indian and Chinese, but in Indonesia they are entirely in the national language. The expressions 'commercial' and 'sponsored' television have different meanings in some countries. By commercial television we mean in Britain that a company such as Thames (London) or Granada (Manchester) will be responsible for the programmes, and will sell advertising time not exceeding six minutes in each hour and usually in two-minute slots. But in Nigeria there will be both brief commercials as in Britain, and whole programmes (mainly sports such as major and often international football or athletics) will be sponsored by an advertiser such as Coca-Cola or Cadburys with interpolated commercials. The hours of viewing, except in the USA, are usually less than in Britain and are often confined to the evening.

While the convention of a balance between entertainment, information and education may be the ideal, the tendency is for television to lean towards popular entertainment, especially if audiences are large and there is competition between stations. Sometimes there is competition between the stations of neighbouring countries. Even the news programmes in Britain verge on entertainment with glamorous newscasters, quips between newscasters, and humorous news stories used as tail-pieces. Supposedly serious interviews have this entertainment appeal if the interviewer is provocative and can provoke argument. After all, television is watched as a form of relaxation, and has largely replaced the cinema and live theatre. London theatres are attended mostly by foreign visitors, most cinemas have closed, been converted into bingo halls, or have survived by being converted into smaller multiple cinemas.

In the Third World there has been a major change similar to the forests of aerials which appeared on Council estates following the introduction of commercial or independent television in Britain some thirty years ago. No longer is television an élitist medium in developing countries because not only has television become popular in urban areas but by means of community viewing in public halls it has been brought within reach of those who cannot afford sets. In some countries television is no longer limited to areas served by electricity because portable sets are available which are run off rechargeable 12-volt car batteries. Moreover, in Indonesia, in spite of its size, programmes are transmitted throughout the country by means of a satellite and 96 local stations.

Characteristics

1. Programmes are watched mostly in the home or other social settings, but may also be seen in schools and workplaces such as offices.

2. While not as captive as a cinema audience, the television audience has to view the programmes in a particular place, and remain seated. The viewer cannot be mobile like a radio listener. However, his assured attention can be unsociable and resentful of interruptions. In fact, television can have a time-consuming drug-like fascination, if only because the viewer watches in anticipation of something better turning up on the screen. It is sometimes criticised for its ability to destroy the reading habit in young people.

3. Perhaps its greatest merit is the blend of sound, movement and colour which provides realism. This applies to people, places and things.

4. But a special characteristic of television is that it is a *visual* medium. Viewers do tend to watch rather than listen to television. This means that people such as a company chairman or other representative of an organisation should be visually interesting. This could be through the way they dress, but more especially how they look physically. Television tends to caricature people, highlighting their oddities. This can be critical and can demolish even famous people if they do not come over well. Very few politicians are successful on the small screen. The PRO should be careful not to rush his chief executive on to television, unless he looks *interesting* and is sufficiently *articulate* to hold his own with an interviewer!

Television familiarisation courses can be attended, prospective interviewees being trained in interview techniques under studio conditions.

5. An important aspect of television has been its ability to introduce new interests to viewers who take them up actively and want to know more about them. This leads to a demand for information in more detailed and permanent form such as new magazines, new newspaper features and new books.

6. Recent innovations have made it possible to record and play back programmes; to show one's own programmes with cassettes of films; and to call

up required information by means of teletext systems, always provided that the viewer has the necessary equipment which at present is still costly.

Opportunities for PR coverage

1. **News.** Most stations in most countries have news bulletins which, like newspapers, require the collection, editing, writing and presentation of news. This may be on a national or regional basis. In Britain, *News At Ten* is a good example of a news bulletin that is supplied nationally by Independent Television News, which is jointly owned by the 15 contracting companies. But each company also presents its regional news bulletin. If a PR story is of interest and value to the large television audience it may be accepted for newscasting.

2. **Discussion programmes.** If the organisation is 'in the news', or if it has an attractive personality who televises well, discussion programmes and 'chat' shows may provide a useful PR vehicle.

3. **Series and serials.** Most of these are produced in advance. For example, series about holidays will be shown in the early months of the year when people are planning their holidays, but the sequences will be filmed or taped during the previous holiday season. To obtain coverage in the series it will be necessary to contact the producer perhaps nine months before the programme appears on the screen. Programmes have to be planned, budgeted, approved, scripted and shot, and all this takes time.

On the other hand, serials like *Coronation Street* or *Crossroads* are rehearsed and shot only a few days before they are shown. If a PRO was concerned with a topic which might suit a character or the storyline without appearing to be overt publicity, the idea might interest the producer and scriptwriters. The Open University has had some coverage of this sort.

4. **Give-away programmes.** On many programmes (e.g. *Sale of the Century*) items will be given to participants, either as prizes or at premium prices. While these awards are not named it may be that they are recognisable and it is good PR to have a product chosen as a prize. Products cannot be given to shows, but if the product is suitable and accepted it will be requisitioned and paid for.

5. **Documentary films.** Non-advertising films of wide audience appeal may be acceptable by television companies, or sequences may be used in special subject programmes. It is also possible for an organisation to make a film on a cooperative basis with a television company. For example, Occidental Oil, in the interests of safety, pioneered a documentary film for television called *Red Alert*, featuring Red Adair, the oil fire-fighter, and Sandy Gaul, the ITN newsreader. Documentary films are often welcomed by television stations in developing countries.

6. **Properties.** For drama productions, sets have to be dressed with authentic articles which suit the scene, and studio property rooms can be supplied with products which can usefully furnish sets. Wall clocks, crockery, furniture and kitchen equipment are typical examples, and if they are of recognisable design they can obtain useful PR coverage. The public can be familiarised with a new product in this way.

7. **Library shots.** Organisations which are likely to feature in drama series and television films can have suitable sequences shot and placed in film librar-ies. Thus it is seldom necessary for special shots to be taken of airliners, trains

or famous landmarks: they can be hired or borrowed from a film library just as music for musical backgrounds (and sound effects) can be hired. Typical examples are the TWA airliners which land and take off in *Hawaii Five-0*. Many airlines make 'library shot' material available. But in the *Rat Catcher* series some time ago, the hero took off from Heathrow in one aircraft and landed at Geneva in another!

8. **Archival film.** Similar to library shots are the archival film services of firms such as Visnews which can provide film (including historical newsreel material) for use in many programmes from news bulletins to documentaries. If an organisation is likely to be 'in the news' it pays to have archival film shot so that it is available when required, although it may be wise regularly to update such material.

The opportunities for getting coverage are clearly limitless if the medium is studied thoroughly, and they can be seen either by watching programmes or going through the pages of the *Radio Times* and *TV Times*. Interviews are among the best opportunities, especially chat shows, of which *Parkinson* is probably the most famous. The Royal National Lifeboat Institute has, over the years, boosted its flag day collections by the coincidental appearance of lifeboat heroes on television programmes, the *Parkinson* interview being a memorable one.

However, there are four problems about television:

1. Facilities—such as a factory background—are often requested and an organisation can go to a lot of trouble without gaining any credit for it. For instance, how many viewers know whose bank was used for the Dover branch bank scenes in the serial *Telford's Change*? It happened to be the Midland.

2. Television can be very time-consuming, both in the negotiations and in the actual shooting. Many hours may be spent on rehearsal and shooting to produce a few minutes of scene time. However, that has to be weighed against the size of audience.

3. If an organisation is asked to provide someone for a programme made up of several interviews, the edited version may be disconcerting when it is found that bits of interviews have been paired with bits from other interviews to produce a controversial juxtapositioning which was not apparent during the original shooting.

4. Television can be a wasteful medium—not only of the PRO's or the organisation's time, but of audiences. While it is true that afternoon shows may be seen by housewives or children, and late shows may be seen by the more serious minded, and different audiences may watch BBC2 compared with ITV, nevertheless the audience is likely to be very large. Peak hour popular programmes may be seen by 10 to 30 million viewers. Is such an audience relevant to the PR message? If it is about a mass consumer product, yes, but if the interest is more specialised, no. This also may govern acceptance of the subject by a producer, but not always. A television commentator may be happy to lampoon a multinational computer company even if few viewers are likely to buy a computer.

Nevertheless, a vast audience may be admirable. A splendid example of this was the launch of the Glass Manufacturers Federation's *Bottle Bank* glass recycling scheme organised by Welbeck PR Ltd in 1971. Reports on ITN and BBC news were estimated to have reached $24\frac{1}{2}$ million people in some 20 million homes. This coverage had to have nation-wide coverage in order to appeal to the public to place bottles in skips with separate compartments for green, brown and clear glass. Bulk loads were then sold by local authorities to a glass manufacturer. In succeeding years the scheme was taken up not only in the UK but abroad, and in 1980 television viewers saw Prince Charles supporting the scheme. By this time there were 50 bottle bank centres in Britain and 10,000 tonnes of waste glass had been recovered—some 35 million containers with 450,000 people making regular deposits.

However, there may be times when it is wise to reject approaches from television producers who are concerned only with exploiting an organisation or a personality for programme purposes. *One is not obliged to accept an invitation to be interviewed!* The negative and even damaging effects of television appearances have to be considered. Cliff Michelmore tells the story of the time he interviewed a famous personality who answered only '*Yes*' or '*No*'. Some of the people interviewed by David Frost have done themselves little credit, to mention only Richard Nixon and Rupert Murdoch. Few people have come over more disastrously than Henry Kissinger on *Parkinson*, and that could also happen to a shy, hesitant or unattractive chief executive!

Additional reference to television as a PR medium will be found in Chapter 34 on broadcasting material and facilities.

Radio

Perhaps the feature that makes radio different from all other mass media, and of special interest to the PR practitioner, is that it can often be an instantaneous medium. Immediate announcements can be made on the radio. This immediacy has been valuable in ending a war (Morocco), calming the effects of a coup (Nigeria), and stopping a race riot (Singapore). In Britain, the state of the share market, traffic conditions and road diversions, the cancelling of trains, the arrival times of British Airways aircraft, sports results, requests for information by the police, and exchange rates for those going abroad are typical examples of instant news and information provided by radio. Local radio (both BBC and ILR)—especially LBC in the London area—have greatly increased this service, and much of it is derived from PR sources or is a form of PR.

The initials ILR stand for 'independent local radio', just as ITV means 'independent television' and is not the name of an organisation. The commercial counterpart of the BBC is the IBA (the Independent Broadcasting Authority). The commercial radio station LBC is, to give it its full name, the London Broadcasting Company.

Characteristics

1. In contrast to the visual nature of television, radio has the intimacy of the human voice, and therefore requires voices which please the ear. The history of radio is one of famous (or infamous) voices, to mention only Franklin Delano Roosevelt, Sir Winston Churchill, J. B. Priestley, Vera Lynn, John Arlott, Peter Sellers, Richard Dimbleby or, more recently, various announcers and disc jockeys such as Dicky Arbiter, Terry Wogan and Kenny Everett.

2. Not unlike the newspaper, radio can be portable thanks to the transistor. Many sets may exist in one household, or a set can be carried from room to

room. Motorcars may be fitted with radios, they are often installed in public places, and the headphone still exists for those who wish to listen without disturbing others, or who are in hospital beds. Radio can be listened to while doing many jobs in factories, on building sites, or even while delivering the milk!

3. The versatility described above also points to a variety of listeners who may tune in at different times of the day. There are the breakfast-time listeners who want to check the time, the commuters, the housewives about the house, the people at work, the businessmen driving their cars, the home-coming motorists, and young people who often listen at night. The radio audience differs from the television audience with its peak hours during the middle evening. Consequently, the PRO can reach particular radio audiences if his material is properly timed for certain programmes.

4. Radio has long been an effective way of reaching people of different ethnic groups and languages in developing countries, including large numbers of people who cannot read, through either personal or public radios. It is easier and more practical to produce a radio programme in several languages, or to broadcast locally in the appropriate language, than to publish vernacular newspapers which people may or may not be able to read.

5. Radio provides companionship, whether it be by means of the human voice or music. But this can also mean that some people like to enjoy a friendly background noise without necessarily paying attention to what is being said. It has been found, for instance, that in landlocked states, where it is possible to listen to a choice of foreign stations broadcast from nearby countries, preference may be given to those which play popular music. In fact, in large countries like Zambia it has been found necessary to strengthen transmissions because people in distant parts of the country were finding it easier or possible only to receive programmes from foreign states.

6. Progressing from the above, it is also true that people listen in to overseas programmes put out by Britain, Germany, Voice of America and so forth, to obtain information and world news. The British World Service in English has programmes such as *New Ideas* which discuss new British products and achievements, and this can be useful to PROs interested in export PR. The BBC External Services broadcast foreign-language programmes too: there is, for example, a large Russian audience for the Russian programme, although it was jammed during the Polish unrest.

7. In Britain, the local radio stations of the BBC and ILR usually cover a smaller area than the regional television stations which makes them ideal for local information such as traffic and public transport announcements.

Opportunities for PR Coverage

1. **News programmes.** As with newspapers, radio stations may welcome news stories. Stations may have their own newsrooms, but just as ITV has its Independent Television News (ITN) which provides a national news service which is networked (e.g. *News At Ten*), so radio has its Independent Radio News (IRN) which all ILR stations can broadcast simultaneously. Similarly, the BBC has its own news service, although different stations will broadcast their own news bulletins: for example, BBC Radio 4 broadcasts a half-hour news programme at 6 p.m., but Radio 1 has a 15 minute *Newsbeat* at 5.30 p.m., while Radio 3 (VHF) has only five minutes of news at 4.55 p.m. Each may present the same news differently, just as newspapers do.

2. **Live studio interviews** are conducted on topical subjects, although sometimes the illusion of a live broadcast is given when the announcer says 'And now we have in the studio Mr So-and-So' when in fact a taped interview is then played back. This, of course, makes it possible to broadcast interviews with people for whom it would be inconvenient to be in the studio for a live broadcast. This is similar to video-taped interviews on television.

3. There is great scope for the **taped interview** which may be produced in the studio for later broadcasting, or may be produced by a professional company such as Universal News Services (UNS) and supplied free of charge on behalf of PR sponsors to radio stations to use as programme material. Supplied tapes should not make direct references to product or company names—they are not to be confused with commercials for which air-time would have to be bought—but the necessary credit is given by the station announcer in introducing and closing the item. The announcer will thus say: 'And now we have in the studio Mr So-and-So who will be telling Mr So-and-So about the new so-and-so.' The tape will be played and listeners will hear the UNS interviewer (e.g. Peter Petts) interviewing a speaker from the sponsoring organisation. A typical interview might be with the author of a new book, the organiser of an exhibition, or an official from a trade organisation.

4. **Phone-ins** are a feature of British local radio, and here are opportunities to present information or points of view to listeners or to contribute to studio discussions. Phone-ins can be prearranged with the producer so that an outside speaker can contribute to a studio discussion. At other times the phone-in can be made by a PRO or spokesman in spontaneous response to a programme, as when the studio commentator invites contributions from listeners.

5. **Tie-ins with series and serials.** It is possible for PR material to be introduced into the scripts for regular radio series and drama serials, provided they are not merely advertisements but are of genuine interest and value to listeners. Characters in programmes such as *The Archers* could refer to topics which suit the storyline of the serial. For example, one of the characters might have a certain medical problem such as diabetes and the script could include sensible advice supplied by a voluntary organisation. Many PR stories have, quite legitimately, been introduced into programmes in this way, and producers may welcome topical or useful ideas from PR sources.

From these suggestions it will be seen that television and radio are entirely different media with quite different PR opportunities. Each needs to be studied carefully to see how PR coverage can be achieved. If the PRO can help producers to produce interesting programmes, their ideas, facilities and co-operation will be welcomed, but attempts to secure free advertising will be rejected. These opportunities will vary from country to country.

In Nigeria, for example, a distinction may be made between what is rightly or wrongly regarded as 'commercial' and 'educational' material and payment may be expected for a commercial topic even in a magazine programme. This would not happen in Britain where the so-called 'commercial' reference would be accepted as news or legitimate programme material. For example, a London course run by the Frank Jefkins School of Public Relations was filmed and given 15 minutes' screen time on BBC2 Television, and the School received a small cheque afterwards. But when a new motorcar was introduced on a Nigerian television magazine programme the advertising agents had to pay for the air-time.

24

DOCUMENTARY FILMS AND VISUAL AIDS

Now we enter into the specific field of created or private PR media, which are distinct from advertising or mass media. Usually, such media are created in order to reach special, private and sometimes small audiences. In public relations we are concerned not only with mass communications, and it is often necessary to reach separate publics or groups of people who cannot be addressed directly through the mass media.

Documentary films and audio-visuals (AVs) are sometimes regarded as separate media, perhaps because documentaries are such a dominant and long-established PR medium, but they are of course a form of audio-visual. This is especially true when we consider that film can be transferred to tape, tape to film, and cassettes are alternatives to reels of film. Stills may also be taken at the same time as filming to provide slides.

As Kodak have emphasised when promoting AVs, we remember only 10 per cent of what we hear, 20 per cent of what we see, but *we remember 60 per cent of what we both see and hear*. This is the strength of television, films, video-cassettes, video-discs and slides with an associated audio tape.

Documentary Films

These are sometimes called 'industrial' or 'sponsored' films, and the expression industrial should *not* be read to mean that such films are limited to industrial subjects. It may seem to be a misleading title, just as 'industrial editor' may seem a misleading title for a house journal editor. However, these terms are part of the accepted jargon of the PR business. Thus, an industrial film means *any kind of PR film* just as an industrial editor may edit *any kind of house journal*. Moreover, sponsored films should not be confused with, say, a film of a sporting event which is shown on television (as in Nigeria) by courtesy of a commercial sponsor who pays for the air-time.

Characteristics of Documentary Films

1. They are not advertising films nor commercials to be shown as paid-for advertisements on the cinema or television screen.

2. They have colour, sound and movement and so can demonstrate the PR message with realism and authenticity.

3. If bias and self-praise is avoided, they can make the PR message credible.

4. In spite of the advances and attractions of new electronic media such as video-cassettes and video-discs, film remains popular because 16 mm sound projectors are universally available throughout the world, whereas playback equipment for video-cassettes and video-discs is costly and not widely available. In fact, it may be found necessary to copy video-tapes onto film for international distribution.

5. It is possible to prepare films for world-wide audiences by one of four methods:

(i)   Dubbing foreign-language sound tracks of voice-over commentaries.

(ii) Separate filming of live commentators speaking different languages.

(iii) Foreign language subtitles.

(iv) Avoiding spoken commentaries altogether, and filming in such a way that by self-explanatory scenes, miming and appropriate musical and sound effect backgrounds, the film is comprehensible wherever it may be shown. Some excellent Dutch and German films have been made in this way (e.g. tourist films about The Hague and Baden-Baden).

6. By their very nature, films have entertainment value so that they are a very pleasant way of communicating a PR message, often being shown on a social occasion and with audience participation.

7. Unlike the transient broadcast media, and the possibly short-lived newspaper, films have a long working life of perhaps five years or even more. Dated sequences can be re-shot. The initial heavy cost of production can therefore be spread over a number of years, and documentary films are actually less expensive than they may at first seem to be. There are some very successful PR films still doing service fifteen years after they were first shot, and some have continued to have PR value for even longer. This long-lasting value of the PR film is sometimes overlooked. A film is rather like a book which can still be read, or a play which can still be produced, years after the original writing.

8. Because a film occupies a substantial period of time its message has sufficient impact to be remembered. This recall effect makes the documentary superior to many other media.

9. Moreover, because of its length and content, the film can often be seen again without causing boredom because, like a piece of music, new aspects may be appreciated on further acquaintance.

10. Films also have an impressive effect on the minds of viewers who are likely to respect the maker for the time, trouble, skill and expense that have gone into a production. This can enhance the corporate image. In a sense, the viewer is flattered by the attention paid to him.

11. More will be said about this later but, as we shall see, the documentary film can be used for many PR purposes: it should not merely be placed in a film library in the hope that people will borrow it. Films are very versatile forms of communication.

12. Joint or cooperative films are possible so that an even larger audience can be addressed, as when one company supplies equipment for a client and both agree to the sharing of the production costs of a film which is of mutual benefit, the cost to each being halved but the audience doubled.

13. Films themselves have publicity value for they can be reviewed and so draw attention to the sponsor. There are well-known industrial film critics who write about them in newspapers (such as the *Financial Times*) and the trade press (e.g. the *PR Bulletin*).

14. Further attention may be drawn to films and their sponsors through the award-making film festivals and contests which are held in many parts of the world. Winning an award is likely to increase demand for the film.

Special Considerations

Before making a documentary film, three special considerations should be taken into account: (*a*) the **purpose** of the film; (*b*) how the film will be **produced**; and (*c*) how it will be **distributed**. At the outset, a definite policy should be decided covering these important decisions for they will ensure the maximum success of the film and justification for its cost. Films should not be isolated exercises but should be an integral part of an objective PR programme. Let us further analyse these vital considerations.

Purpose. A documentary film may serve more than one purpose, or a specific one, but there is no point in making a film unless the reasons for making it are clearly understood. This will also help the producer to make the right sort of film. You must know what you want before you start, not complain when the film is made that it is not what you want.

There are three stages in the production of a film. Based on the sponsor's brief, a **treatment** will be written outlining the proposed content of the film and the way in which the subject will be treated. It is at this early stage that the sponsor must agree or disagree with the producer's proposals. The second stage is the writing of the **shooting script** which contains dialogue, scenes and camera instructions. Third, the film is **shot and edited** and 'rushes' can be seen to decide on the final version.

The following are some possible purposes for making the film and, in some cases, there could be a combination of purposes. It is essential to be clear about the intended audience or audiences for it is no use making a general film which attempts to be all things to all people. A medical film aimed at doctors should be very different from one made for a lay audience.

1. To demonstrate a product to distributors and customers.
2. To demonstrate the use of safety equipment or precautions to employees.
3. To provide induction material for employees, and also perhaps as an introduction for visitors to a plant.
4. To produce a permanent record of an achievement such as a major civil engineering project, or to tell the history of a company's development.
5. To show a company's contribution to society such as the improvement of agriculture, the preservation of the environment, or the conservation of natural resources.
6. To demonstrate a company's contribution to and place in the economy of a country.
7. For presentation purposes at a business conference.
8. To provide evidence of the work of a charity or other voluntary body for the purpose of gaining supporters or raising funds.
9. To educate new and prospective markets for a product, including children.
10. For recruitment purposes, demonstrating job opportunities and explaining the policy of the organisation.
11. To explain a company report and balance sheet to shareholders at an annual general meeting, and also to employees.
12. To explain a government policy or service, either to gain support or to show how benefits may be enjoyed.
13. To explain the work of the police, Armed Forces, fire brigade, ambulance service or some other organisation in order to get the cooperation of the public.

14. To explain a major changeover from a traditional system to, say, decimalisation, metrication or driving on the right-hand side of the road.

Production. The quality, costs and success of a documentary film will depend on decisions made about production. A film does not have to cost a fortune to be a good film. One of the most successful documentaries ever made, Rentokil's *The Intruders*, was made within the confines of a laboratory. On the other hand, a film can be static and dull if there are too many stills shot in a studio. The costs of a film can escalate according to the number and distance of locations and the use of professional actors. The budget is therefore a major consideration. The following are essential production considerations:

1. Will the film be made by the company's own film unit or by an outside production company? Some companies make a lot of films and find it pays to have their own film unit, but the majority of sponsored films are made by independent film makers.
2. The length of the film has an obvious bearing on cost, but it may be determined by the subject or the audience, preferably the latter. A documentary should be long enough to be adequate, but short enough to maintain the interest of the audience. For Western audiences, 20 minutes is a good average length. This is also a useful length for those who want to put on a film show and wish to show more than one film. Too many documentaries extend to 30 or 40 minutes which could inhibit their being shown, or run the risk of creating a restless audience.

Modern films tend to have short, sharply edited sequences which mean either shorter films or the inclusion of more sequences. For unsophisticated audiences, especially those in developing countries where people are probably unfamiliar with Western environments and life-styles, eight to 10 minutes is often sufficient, otherwise concentration and interest will falter.

3. Should the characters be performed by professional actors or company staff, and to what extent should people be seen performing their normal jobs? Is a well-known actor, actress or perhaps television personality needed to give the film authority? For example, a film about motoring could be made more credible if a well-known motoring personality was the storyteller or principal character. But, alternatively, a film about banking might be more authentic if bank officials played their normal roles. Similarly, a film about farming could be more acceptable if the central character was a real farmer, yet one about a tourist attraction might call for the services of a well-known travel writer or television holiday programme personality. An example of an economical use of a well-known actor is the training film on report writing in which Arthur Lowe, particularly famous as the *Dad's Army* captain, plays a variety of roles.

4. The choice and number of locations and the number of visits to locations have to be considered. If the film is about a construction job it will be necessary to film succeeding stages of the work, and filming may be extended over weeks, months and even years. John Laing's famous film about the building of Coventry Cathedral had to be filmed throughout the nine years of building and required visits to the various workshops of different craftsmen. The already mentioned film of Baden-Baden was shot throughout the seasons of the year, although all at one location, the spa itself, and its attractions and activities. But a film about a horse-race associated with a sponsor's trophy

could be filmed entirely on the day of the race. Goodyear's airship film follows the flight of the airship across Europe.

5. The author of the dialogue or commentary should be decided carefully, whether or not it is spoken by a well-known 'voice'. A professionally written script is usually advisable, but it should not be too literary or effusive. A home-made script, even if technically correct, can sometimes be very stilted and made dull by either platitudes or jargon. Humour can be welcome in a script, and that calls for an expert writer. Some travel films have been spoilt by over-enthusiastic commentaries. The blend between words and voice can make all the difference between sincerity and falsity. A film about a firm of printing machine manufacturers was spoilt by the intrusion of the commentator's regional accent and declamatory style.

6. Sound can be recorded on location, which can be costly, or dubbed in afterwards. It all depends on whether it is necessary to record actual sounds and people's voices at the scene, or whether a voice-over commentary can be recorded after shooting.

7. Is special music to be composed, or will library music suffice? Is live sound necessary, or can sound effects be dubbed in?

8. Will the film be live or is animation required, or will a mixture of both be required? Animation (cartoon drawings) is expensive yet some things cannot be filmed or require the use of diagrams with changing sequences. It is perhaps easier to demonstrate by animated drawings something which normally happens out of sight than to attempt expensive filming requiring, say, a deep sea diver. Another example is the action of oil in an engine.

9. If the film is likely to have theatrical showing on British cinemas it will have to obey trade union rules calling for the employment of a full professional film crew.

10. If there are possibilities that the film may be distributed overseas by the Central Office of Information it is sensible to have preliminary discussions with the COI. The film must not have any advertising content. Some makers of documentaries cannot resist inserting 'plugs' or displays of packages bearing the product name. Occasionally this is unavoidable, as when company premises or vehicles are included in shots, but even these sequences can avoid blatant advertising.

Distribution. This, again, is a primary consideration at the onset. To whom and on what occasions will the film be shown? This really delves into the PR opportunities for making the film work hard, and make expenditure on production and prints an investment. It should not be forgotten that costs do not end with the making of the film: prints have to be made, and they have to be distributed and maintained in good condition. It should also be remembered that the despatch, showing and return of films takes time—maybe a week per showing—and that a sufficient number of prints should be available to meet demand. The following methods of distribution should be considered:

1. Invited audiences may be the principal use of the film, and members of the audience should be given a take-away synopsis leaflet. A good example of the use of invited audiences is when an organisation has many branches and local managers can invite customers and prospects to receptions, film shows and talks. Some companies have their own cinemas, or hire private cinemas to which guests may be invited to attend film shows.

2. If the film is of educational value it can be advertised in journals read by teachers, while if it is of specialised interest to, say, engineers, architects, printers or other technicians it can be advertised in their respective technical journals. Organisations such as BP, ICI and Shell advertise catalogues of their films in publications such as *The Times Higher Education Supplement*. Esso, ICI and Unilever jointly offer free loan of a Foundation of Wealth series of educational films and video-tapes for schools. To quote from an advertisement in the *THES:* 'They are designed to appeal to pupils in the middle years of their secondary schooling who are studying the economic and social aspects of modern society.'

3. Films can be placed in libraries such as the Central Film Library or the services of the Guild Sponsored Films division of Guild Sound & Vision Ltd can be used for library and distribution services, the latter also organising film shows for local organisations and public 'road shows' in market squares and other outdoor venues. Guild Sponsored Films of Peterborough reach 70,000 groups each year with presentations throughout the UK. As the UK member of the International Association of Information Film and Video Distributors, the division is also involved in the international distribution of sponsored films in 24 countries.

4. Overseas distribution through British government offices overseas is possible if the film is accepted by the Film Acquisitions Department of the Central Office of Information. The COI catalogues films and supplies them on free loan, and also supplies them to overseas television stations.

5. A film can be shown on an exhibition stand or in a showroom, using a continuous loop with back projection.

6. For press receptions, a company film can form a useful part of the programme.

7. Films are also useful for press facility, customer or distributor works visitors, trade commissions, and other occasions when there are visitors to company premises.

8. Clips from documentaries may be used in television programmes.

9. Films may be used at sales conferences and other staff events.

10. They also make useful induction material for new recruits, or on staff training courses.

11. A company may be able to show its film to delegates at trade, professional and industry conferences.

12. Road shows can be arranged, shows being given in market squares, or a cinema van can be used for giving outdoor film shows at agricultural shows, gymkhanas and other events. In developing countries, the mobile cinema which tours villages is a well-known form of communication, a screen being hoisted on top of a Land Rover and films shown to a crowd assembled in the open.

13. Another method of distribution is to offer a film show and talk to local clubs, organisations and societies, the speaker being a representative from the sponsor's local branch or office. There is tremendous scope for this sort of PR activity which can produce both goodwill and sales leads provided the talk is not too sales promotional.

14. Some films—e.g. tourist films—may be of sufficient general interest to warrant taking a hall or theatre and combining a film show with a stage entertainment, the public paying for admission. Similarly, the public may be

invited free of charge to a film evening at a local theatre, run by an organisation (or even a country seeking immigrants) which has a subject of popular appeal.

15. Or, with the cooperation of organisations with suitable demonstration facilities such as gas and electricity showrooms, motorcar showrooms or department stores, films about appropriate products or services can be shown to invited audiences, especially if the subject can be purchased at the premises.

From the above list it will be seen that supported by a film or films, the PRO can greatly extend his PR activities and coverage. These are among the reasons why he may recommend the inclusion of a film in his PR programme proposals and budget. It makes sense of film-making, and films—when made to work in these ways—can be valuable forms of communication. When some firms say they cannot afford to make a film it may be pertinent to ask can they afford not to make a film when it provides so many opportunities of reaching the right audiences effectively and economically?

While the documentary film is likely to remain the primary visual aid for a long time to come there are many other forms of visual communication which can be used in addition to or in place of films.

Video-tape

'Movies' can also be shot on video-tape. Although the quality may not be as good as 35 mm or even 16 mm film, there are advantages of speed and flexibility. The tape can be played back immediately whereas film has to be processed and prints made. And as television viewers are aware when watching sporting events, it is possible to have replays. Video-tapes are smaller and easier to handle than film, and can be contained in cassettes. With VCR equipment, video-tapes can be played back on a television screen in the home, office, factory or anywhere where the equipment is available, and larger screens are also available. It is possible to transfer film to video-tape and vice versa.

A complication regarding video-cassettes and VCRs is that there are many competing systems, and a video-cassette must be compatible with a particular system. The main domestic systems are:

(i)   V200 (Philips and Grundig recorders).

(ii)   Betamax format (Awai, Sanyo, Sony, etc., recorders).

(iii) VHS (Akai, Ferguson, JVC, Hitachi, National Panasonic, etc., recorders).

This means that if video-cassettes are to be produced for general distribution, versions must be produced for playback on the recorders for each system. At the time of writing, organisations producing video-tapes for internal use are using the Sony Umatic 'industrial' system which cannot be played back on domestic Philips, VHS or Betamax VCRs. However, Umatic tapes can be transferred to other tapes. Several organisations such as Rentokil, Midland Bank and South Eastern Gas produce Sony Umatic video-cassettes for training, documentary, and house journal purposes. Cassettes can be distributed more conveniently than cans of film.

Video-discs

Slower to achieve acceptance is the video-disc, which is not unlike a long-playing gramophone record except that it reproduces pictures as well as sound. Picture and sound quality is superior to that of video-cassettes. A popular use is the production of a visual pop music album which can be played back in the home. The durable fast-rotating (one frame per revolution) 12-inch disc produces an hour or more colour programme. The American RCA Selecta Vision system, made and distributed by CBS, uses a diamond stylus, while the Philips MCA VLP system, in association with MCA of America, uses a laser beam. There is also the JVC Video High Density (VHD) stylus system which is marketed in the UK by Thorn-EMI, and the Thomson-CSF laser system. In the USA, MCA and IBM have combined to market the Discs Vision player, and an example of its use is General Motors' distribution of players and discs to their dealer network to give instructions on the maintenance of their new motorcars. In January 1982, Mothercare introduced video-discs into some of their stores as a promotional tool.

The educational and information possibilities, and the application to PR needs, are a portent of future communications techniques available to the PRO. Costs and availability of replay equipment have to be considered, but it is not so long ago that colour television was unthinkable. Philips' discs of a full-length feature film cost only about £15 compared with about £40 for a video-tape version. Being thin, they are easily stored and distributed.

In 1980, Guild Sound & Film Ltd of Peterborough (already mentioned under film distribution) launched a subsidiary company, Guild Home Video Ltd, to sell or hire video-cassettes and video-discs to domestic viewers. Initially, they are entertainment programmes but there is scope here for educational and instructive cassettes and discs of PR origin provided they are kept scrupulously free of bias and advertising. New releases in VHS and Beta-max formats are added monthly, retailing at around £40 or hiring at about £5.

This sort of domestic distribution provides a new outlet for PR video cassettes not unlike that for schools, whether made through a distributing agency like Guild Sound & Film who distribute documentary films, or supplied direct by a company's AV library or PR department. Taking PR direct into the home is probably the biggest advance in business communication since the advent of commercial television.

Filmstrips

This is an economic form of visual aid, still pictures being put on film. The presenter can give a spoken commentary based on supplied notes, or a cassette can be supplied with commentary and audible cueing. Interesting examples are the Coca-Cola *Man in His Environment* and *You and Your Community* kits, comprising four 15-minute audio-visual filmstrips, commentary cassette and teaching notes. Produced in association with the Educational Foundation for Visual Aid, and supplied at under £15 a kit, they have been used in many schools.

For many years the Electricity Council has made available a series of education filmstrips in their *Understanding Electricity* library of films, filmstrips, information sheets and publications. These filmstrips are intended for schoolchildren aged 9 years upwards and deal with subjects such as circuits and connections, switches and controls, or using refrigeration.

Slides

The simple slide presentation, using a carousel and remote control, is an excellent way of illustrating a talk. Again, 35 mm slide projectors, like 16 mm film projectors, are commonly available. But there have been interesting developments which have made slide presentations competitive with films.

The continuous sound and slide presentation, with fade-in, fade-out or cross-fade, supported by vocal and musical effects on audio-tape, gives a film-like illusion even though the pictures are stills. This can be a very inexpensive visual aid when the cost of making a film or a video-tape is not justified, as in the case of a single presentation at a conference. For regular use the method has the advantage that slides can be replaced. It is necessary to have special twin slide projectors, which may limit the presentations to locations which have the equipment unless it is conveyed there or hired for the occasion.

Another development which has been used in permanent exhibition centres or theatres is the multiple screen presentation, where computerised banks of slide projectors fill the screen with one picture or divide it into perhaps four, eight or sixteen independent pictures. A good example is the *News At Ten* presentation at the IBA Broadcasting Gallery in Knightsbridge, London. There is also *The Singapore Experience* for tourists in Singapore.

Exhibits, Scale and Working Models

Other visual aids of a portable or permanent nature may include screens with displayed photographs or samples; paper or expanded polystyrene sculpture; and scale and working models, all of which can visually communicate information. They may be used for mobile exhibitions, used at press events, or form part of a permanent exhibition on company premises. It may be far simpler to explain an oil rig, a dam, a harbour or a new aircraft by means of a model when it is inconvenient or difficult to show people the real thing.

Visual Aids and Internal Relations

The use of visual aids is becoming—when we are not so much if at all concerned with the mass media—increasingly important in the rapidly growing field of internal communications. (That the British Association of Industrial Editors has opened up its membership to 'internal communicators' as well as house journal editors is evidence of this trend.) Management is having to recognise the need to communicate with employees and electronic media are serving that need.

Touche Ross & Co. of Oxford have published excellent research reports on this theme, such as *You See What I Mean?* which reviews the techniques of audio-visual reporting to employees. As its author Roger Hussey says; 'The most important potential development of a.v. that we foresee appears to be in the role of catalyst—as part of a strategy not merely for communicating but for actually bringing about change in an organisation. . . . Such results as are available indicate that a.v. may be particularly helpful in achieving progress in areas where events seem to be stultified.'

The Touche Ross report emphasises that employees enjoy learning more about their organisation. But this must not become one-way communication like the 'wakey-wakey' domination at the holiday camp. To be really successful employees should be able to participate in upward audio-visual communication with their management, something which has developed in the more traditional printed internal media. Management should be an audience or public too.

Such upward communication could be achieved visually by shooting video-tapes of 'live readers' letters', staff discussion groups, or of actual working conditions. What is a deliveryman's, secretary's, factory worker's or office clerk's day actually like? Management can rarely have any idea since they never spend a whole day in the company of any employee. A lot of management decisions, a lot of dissatisfaction, and much industrial strife could be averted if management were better informed. Modern AV techniques now provide the opportunity to inform management of what goes on outside the boardroom and the managerial office. This can be just as much a mystery to management as balance sheets are to fitters and mechanics. Upward communication can be a major responsibility for the PRO.

South Eastern Gas won the Best Company Video Programme award, presented in Las Vegas by the International Television Association, for their SETV news on video-cassette service. Thousands of SEGAS employees in 38 locations see a 17-minute monthly news programme on television sets. Topics have included preventive medical treatment for staff, an interview with a girl engineer, and a staff trip 120 ft. up the Epsom gas holder. The £250,000 studio at Croydon with its audio and visual mixers, video machines and copiers, cameras, lights and microphones, is directed by Geoffrey Mills, senior public relations officer of SEGAS. The shooting and technical work is carried out by Hugh Letchworth and production assistants Christopher Chapell and Andrew Taylor. Compared with a cost of £1000 a minute of film made by outside producers, the SEGAS operation is very economical. Training material is also produced.

The importance of the technique in management–employee relations was stressed when a pictorial feature, 'Segas taps TV as a source of news power', appeared in the *Croydon Advertiser* (December 5, 1980) from which the following is quoted:

It will never take the place of the printed word in the in-house magazine, says Geoff.
But he intends to continue with the positive policy of being controversial—in the sure expectation that his bosses will not bring out the censor's blue pencil.
His main fear in presenting the 17-minute news programme was that mistrust from both management and workforce would produce no cooperation.
By being scrupulously unbiased, says Geoff, he has convinced them that his programme is vital to get across management policies on one hand and workers grievances on the other.

Thus this enterprising PRO and his organisation are achieving the PR principle of two-way communication as expressed in downward and upward internal communication. An equally enterprising newspaper is to be congratulated on publicising this PR venture for the paper has a large circulation in a major industrial and commercial area.

25

HOUSE JOURNALS

The house journal is one of the oldest forms of PR, the Americans being pioneers of this medium with *The Lowell Offering* (1842), the *I. M. Singer & Co.'s Gazette* (1855) and the Travelers Insurance Companies' *Protector* (1865). This medium therefore supplies evidence that PR is not such a new activity as is sometimes supposed. In Britain, Lever Brothers launched a house journal towards the end of the nineteenth century.

House journals have been given a variety of names such as house organs, employee newspapers and company newspapers. They are **private publications** and are therefore discussed separately from the commercial press. Over the years they have tended to change from pulpits for management to more candid forms of management-employee relations. The John Lewis Partnership, a London retail organisation with an Oxford Street department store and Waitrose supermarkets which has pioneered employee participation, has long been noteworthy for a house journal containing readers' letters which are published anonymously. Many journals have also changed from letterpress printed magazine format to web-offset tabloid newspaper format.

There are also two distinct kinds of house journals; **internals** for staff and **externals** for outside publics. The two are distinct and internals should not be expected to serve the dual purpose of serving, say, employees and customers.

House publications are not confined to the world of commerce and industry even if house journal editors have been given the curious title of 'industrial editors', and their professional association in Britain is called the British Association of Industrial Editors. In fact, private magazines and newspapers are published by almost every kind of organisation whether it be in the public or private sector, commercial or non-commercial.

Types of House Journals

There are basically five types of house journal:

1. **The sales bulletin** which is a regular communication, perhaps weekly, between a sales manager and his salesmen in the field.

2. **The newsletter** which is a digest of news for busy readers.

3. **The magazine** which contains feature articles and pictures and may be published at monthly or quarterly intervals.

4. **The tabloid newspaper** which resembles a popular newspaper and contains mostly news items, short articles and illustrations and may be published weekly, fortnightly, monthly or every two months.

5. **The wall newspaper** is a useful form of staff communication where the staff are contained in one location such as a factory, department store or hospital.

These are general descriptions. In very large organisations all five may exist, addressed to different types of reader. Tabloids are generally addressed to the

154

majority of workers whereas the newsletter may be for executives and the magazine for more serious reading. Externals are likely to use a magazine format since they are more educational and informative, less full of news items, personal stories and gossip.

House journals are popular throughout the world, and in developing countries they help to supplement a meagre commercial press. Indeed, some house journals—especially externals—may be seen on sale at bookstalls where there is a dearth of indigenous magazines. In Indonesia, for instance, Caltex Pacific Indonesia have for 30 years published a daily news bulletin containing company news and a digest of general news.

House Journal Techniques

There are special considerations concerning the publishing, editing, production and distribution of house journals which are best discussed under the following separate headings:

1. **The Readers.** It is important that the sponsor and the editor of a house journal should be absolutely clear about who are to be the readers of the publication. Technicians will want to read about the technicalities of products; factory workers will enjoy reading about themselves and their companions; salesmen will appreciate a journal which informs them about the company and helps them to sell. It is difficult for a journal to be all things to all people, hence the need for separate publications to cater for the different interests of different people. This is not always appreciated, and too many journals attempt to appeal to too wide a readership.

2. **Frequency.** For reasons of cost, it may be decided to publish a journal only so often, but there should not be too large a gap between issues otherwise the sense of regularity and continuity will be lost. Readers should look forward to the next issue, and it should appear on a regular day such as the first of the month. Frequency can also be determined on a cost basis by the number of pages and whether there is black and white or colour printing. There are obvious permutations such as 12 issues of an eight-page tabloid or six issues of a 16-page one. Frequency may also be determined by the need to publish news as soon as possible or the greater timelessness of feature articles. Another cost factor concerning frequency could be the number of copies required to reach all readers.

3. **Title.** Just as the naming of a company or the branding of a product is a form of communication which creates distinctiveness and character, so the title of a house journal establishes the image of the publication. If it is a newspaper it may be a good idea to incorporate a typical newspaper name like 'Times', 'News', 'Express' or 'Mail' into the title, while if it is a magazine a typical name such as 'Review' may be used; or a very distinctive title may be invented such as *The Black Dragon* if perhaps that is part of a trade mark. But one should avoid rather hackneyed titles such as *Link* or over-clever titles such as *Smoker's Smile*. Moreover, a title should be a permanent one, which makes it all the more important to decide on a good name.

4. **Free issue or cover price.** Some people argue that a company journal should be issued free of charge, others say a journal will be valued more highly if there is a cover price. It all depends on how important the journal is to the readers. Do they consider it is worth paying for? This will depend on

how far the journal represents real upward and downward communication between management and employees and how valuable the contents are to readers. Some of the biggest circulation house journals are sold like commercial newspapers, *Coal News* and *Rail News* being good examples.

5. **Distribution.** There is no point in going to a lot of trouble to produce a fine journal, only to let it suffer from ineffective distribution. If an organisation has many branches or locations, and bulk supplies are sent to each address, there should be a systematic distribution to individual readers. If employees are merely expected to pick up copies from a central point they may not bother and copies will be wasted. Similarly, if copies are handed out at the work bench they may be discarded on the floor. Although this may be costly—in terms of wrappers, envelopes and postage, and the mailing list must be kept up to date—the best method is to post copies to home addresses. Employees can then read the journal at their leisure, and it may also interest their families.

6. **Advertisements.** The inclusion of advertisements can help to make a journal look more realistic and may be of value to readers. Three types of advertisement may be included: (*a*) those inserted by the organisation about its own products or services or, perhaps, situations vacant; (*b*) outside commercial advertisements if the circulation makes the journal a good advertising medium; (*c*) readers' sales and wants advertisements. The latter can be a reader service which adds to reader interest.

7. **Contributors.** There should be a planned supply of editorial material, the editor planning future articles which he has agreed with contributors, while correspondents can be appointed who are responsible for collecting news and submitting regular reports. The editor should also organise the taking of photographs of newsworthy events. One of the advantages of web-offset printing is that generous use can be made of illustrations, costly half-tone blocks not being necessary as with letterpress printing. It may also be necessary to commission features from professional writers, while the PROs of other organisations may offer house journals free articles.

8. **Production.** House journals call for a combination of writing, print design and print buying skills. A very amateur-looking journal can result if there is weakness in one of these departments. Some editors are principally journalists, have little or no design or print knowledge, and rely on a printer to convert copy into a journal. The result can be disappointing. At the other extreme, there are sponsors who appreciate these deficiencies and appoint an expert house journal consultancy to produce a professional journal. Well-known specialists are Sam Weller & Associates, IH Publications and Norman Thompson.

On the question of production quality, the mistake is sometimes made of using a paper which is either too highly finished or of too heavy a weight, and this looks incongruous in a web-offset printed tabloid newspaper. Whatever the format, a journal should have a realistic appearance and not be over-lavish or resemble sales literature. Again, care should be taken not to have a journal designed by a studio which is so design-conscious that legibility is sacrificed. House journals should seldom be entrusted to advertising agencies since they are usually unfamiliar with journalism and public relations.

Externals

Most of the above remarks also apply to externals except that the policy, readership and contents must concern readers outside the organisation. Externals should not normally be aimed at a general external readership, like some of the lavish prestige journals of the past. An external should fit into the PR programme as a private medium directed at a defined public for a precise purpose. There are some excellent technical externals, and the circulation list may include the relevant trade, technical and professional journals with the invitation to reproduce features free of charge. For instance, material from ITT Europe's *Profile* has been distributed by Reuters and published in journals as diverse as the *Financial Times* and *The Sun*. These chosen publics could be:

(*a*) **The trade.** Distributors can be educated about a company and its products, with advice on business matters and how to display, demonstrate or sell the products.

(*b*) **Users.** Specifiers, formulators, designers and others can be shown how to use products such as materials, components or ingredients.

(*c*) **Professionals.** Products and services of interest to professionals can be described and explained, ranging from products they may recommend or use to services they may buy.

(*d*) **Patrons.** The in-flight magazine is a good example, as are the journals supplied to hotel guests. Added to these are the tourist journals provided by tourist information organisations which, again, may be found in hotels.

(*e*) **Opinion leaders.** Some journals of a perhaps wider appeal are distributed to those who express opinions about the organisation and need to be kept informed.

Video-cassette and Viewdata House Journals

In the previous chapter, reference was made to the video-cassette house journal which can be shown, whenever convenient, on VCRs located throughout the organisations. The presentation resembles a newsreel.

Other organisations, such as ICL, have introduced the electronic newspaper, using the Prestel Viewdata system. Information is edited, 'pages' are stored in the computer, and viewers at numerous locations can call up 'pages' on a Prestel-equipped television receiver. The editor collects or receives information, and new 'pages' are produced daily.

26

CORPORATE IDENTITY

History

Corporate identity should not be confused with the corporate image, although the latter will include the former. The **corporate image** is the impression one has of a total organisation and it will be derived from its behaviour and reputation. This may be assisted by visible forms of recognition such as a logotype or colour scheme.

Corporate identity has an historical background. Centuries ago a king would lead his army and identify himself by means of an emblem on his shield, such as the cross of St George or the cross of Lorraine. But since this was rather dangerous it became the fashion for all the king's knights to wear the same emblem, which was confusing to the enemy. Emblems became flags. When transportation began to develop, stage coaches were decorated distinctively. Then steamships were given funnel colours. Buses and trams had their colours, as did railways. The colourful buses of London disappeared as the General Omnibus and then London Transport amalgamated them in London red. More recently, numerous provincial motor-coach companies adopted the insignia of the National Bus Company. The oil companies have their road tanker liveries. But the most splendid liveries are those of the world's airlines which make the aprons of Heathrow and Kennedy Airport look like artists' palettes.

Livery is one of the most effective ways of establishing corporate identity. The expression 'corporate identity' was coined by Walter Margulies: with offices in London, New York and Toronto, Lippincott & Margulies have been responsible for some of the best-known corporate identity schemes. They have a checklist of 62 items which can be included in a total identification exercise. In 1980, Rentokil adopted a new look which was based on the lettering for the word 'Rentokil' and the use of Pantone 483 red and white as a colour scheme. The simple one-word logo was applied to all print, packaging and advertising, and vehicles incorporated the red and white livery.

Corporate identity may also include a change of name as when S. Smith & Sons (England) Ltd, became Smiths Industries or when Channel Islands Airways and Air Anglia were fused into the one name Air UK. But it can be confusing when there are too many name changes and identities, such as Rootes becoming Chrysler and then Talbot. Woolworth used aggressive television advertising to change its identity from that of a popular bargain bazaar to one selling more sophisticated merchandise.

Internationally, we have seen problems when countries have become independent and changed their names and it has become difficult for foreigners to keep up with such changes and know exactly where these countries are located. The fact that such names have more realistic local significance than former colonial names does not help foreigners who have constantly to amend their geography. This is a corporate identity problem that every new nation has to cope with in its international relations.

Fig. 9. Reproduced from *Sales & Marketing Management*, April 1981, where it appeared to illustrate an interview with Jeremy Bullmore, Chairman of J. Walter Thompson.

The need for a corporate identity often occurs when either a number of organisations have been united by amalgamation, merger or acquisition, or when the nature of an organisation's activities has changed and the old identity is misleading or inadequate.

Four Basics

Four things are usually basic to a corporate identity scheme: the **name of the organisation**, the **logotype**, the **typography** and the **house colour**.

The **logotype** may be a special way of presenting the name of the company, or a badge or symbol. The initials ITT and the name SEIKO are drawn in a slab serif or Egyptian type, whereas Boots, Cadbury's, Ford, John Collier and Coca-Cola are represented in handwriting. The Midland Bank uses a bold black-face type in upper and lower characters plus the symbol of a lion in a ring of dots. Some symbols last for years, then disappear and return like Player's bearded sailor.

Obscure logotypes should be avoided since they may be distinctive but scarcely meaningful, and this sometimes happens when initials are linked in a 'clever' design which is not readily comprehensible. There are also some designs which tend to be repeated, such as swastika-shaped 'S's' and arrow effects like British Rail's. One of the cleverest symbols is possibly Plessey's oscilloscope effect, while the wise-looking Penguin of Penguin Books is very apt.

Trade Characters

Corporate identity may also be associated with a trade character, some of which seem to live on forever like Johnnie Walker, Bisto's urchins and the Michelin rubber man, and although these are mainly used for advertising purposes they are popular forms of corporate identity.

Slogans

Certain evocative advertising slogans—because they have been retained or even remembered long after disuse—also belong to the devices of corporate identity. Although Guinness have not used the slogan *Guinness Is Good For You* in British advertising for many years, few people realise this, so characteristic is this slogan. In Nigeria the slogan does appear on the neck label on Guinness bottles.

Items Involved in Design Change

The introduction of a corporate identity scheme is often an expensive and extensive business, and the following are some of the items which may be involved in design changes:

    1. The livery of road vehicles, trains, ships, aircraft and other forms of transportation.

    2. All stationery, including letterheadings, invoices, order forms, compliment slips, business cards, tickets, etc.

    3. Name displays on premises such as factories, offices, shops, warehouses, depots, garages, etc.

    4. Sales literature, price lists, catalogues and other publications.

    5. Advertisements in all media.

    6. Labels, packaging and containers.

    7. House journals.

    8. Instruction leaflets and manuals.

    9. Uniforms, overalls, pocket and lapel badges.

    10. Point-of-sale display material.

    11. Credits on documentary films, video-tapes and slide presentations.

    12. Diaries and calendars.

    13. Financial reports.

    14. Cutlery, crockery, serviettes and menus.

    15. Drip mats.

    16. Ash trays.

    17. Ties.

    18. Cuff Links.

    Not every item applies to every organisation but those which are much in the public eye, and organisations which operate very close to their customers, such as airlines, will take up a long list of such items.

    Instructions are usually contained in a corporate identity kit which specifies how the identity shall be applied, setting out the **logotype** design and specifying

typography and shades of **colour.** An advertising agency, for instance, will have to comply with these instructions and will have to avoid deviations from stipulated colours when tints or half-tone screens are applied to solid colours.

Some very ingenious applications are possible, as when door handles, furniture or display windows are specially designed in the shape of a logotype motif of a special recognisable shape such as a star, flower or leaf.

Few companies have made such remarkable efforts to establish and maintain their corporate identity as Coca-Cola, even to the extent of legal battles with rival firms. It is significant that Coca-Cola have scored on a massive international scale by their consistency. The well-known script logo has scarcely changed since 1886 when it was penned by Frank M. Robinson, bookkeeper to the creator of Coca-Cola, Dr John T. Pemberton. True, the freehand copies of the script have been tidied up and the logo containing the trade mark script has changed shape from time to time. The Company has issued a style guide worldwide and ruled that only faithful reproductions may be used. Corporate identity has also been associated with the pack, the bottle with a bulge. This goes back to the company's early days when a bottle to confound imitators was designed which could be recognised even if held in the dark, and even if it were broken.

Generic Terms

It may be flattering to the original companies when everyone refers to vacuum cleaners as 'hoovers' (except to Electrolux) or to thermos flasks, pyrex dishes and sellotape, but there can also be loss of identity and a product may be unfairly associated with inferior or different products. Some of these names have slipped into the language and are even included in dictionaries. For example, the *Oxford Dictionary* says: 'hoover *v.* to clean (a carpet, etc.) with a vacuum cleaner.'

The press dislike capital initial letters and many companies insist on protecting their registered trade names such as Pop rivets, Tannoy, Burberrys, Thermos, Fibreglass and Vaseline to the extent of supporting a quarterly journalists' guide to registered trade names in *UK Press Gazette* about their correct usage. The guide gives a glossary of trade names.

Formica, in one advertisement, insisted that FORMICA 'is used all in capitals when describing one of our products. You see, it is an adjective. Definitely *not* a noun.' This was surely going too far—as bad as underlining copy in a news release to achieve status. It is one thing to insist on an *initial capital*, but too much to instruct editors on their typography. To print Formica as FORMICA would be next door to puffery.

On the other hand, in another advertisement in the *UK Press Gazette* feature it was fair enough for Coca-Cola to argue 'The case for Upper Case' on behalf of Coca-Cola and even Coke, and nice to say 'please use Upper Case 'C''.

The feature, in the 4 January 1982 issue, made a point of listing the following *unregistered* names which are accepted as part of the English language. They are unprotected and do not require a capital letter (except Portland, which is a geographical place name):

aspirin	launderette
cornflakes	lino
derv	mac(k)intosh

dynamite	melamine
escalator	mimeograph
gramophone	petrol
hovercraft	Portland cement
kerosene	polythene
lanolin	shredded wheat

27

PRINTED MATERIAL

Print of various kinds, in addition to house journals, is another private PR medium which serves the informative, instructional and educational role of public relations. It can be excluded from no PR budget; the news release heading, the invitation card and the photo caption blank are necessities. The range of PR print is great, and this chapter is confined to an analysis of 20 examples.

1. **News release headings.** The astonishing thing about British PR is the array of gaudy news release headings which seem to represent an advertising agency's studio nightmare. Too many news release headings devote too much space to colourful displayed lettering which gets in the way of the story. In fact, the best headings—and the ones which editors prefer—are those which place the source details discreetly but clearly *at the foot of the sheet*. This then gives prominence to the headline and opening paragraph so that the editor is immediately made aware of the subject of the story.

2. **Photo caption blanks.** An excellent idea is to print photo caption blanks bearing, preferably at the foot, the name, address, telephone number and perhaps logotype of the sender.

3. **Invitation cards.** These are best printed for each occasion since each invitation card should state the programme, location and timetable of the event.

4. **Film synopsis leaflets.** Give-away leaflets presenting a brief summary and reminder of the content of the film and giving credits to producers, cameramen, scriptwriters, actors and commentators are valuable at showings of documentary films.

5. **Calendars.** While business calendars may be regarded as an advertising medium, they do create goodwill and may also be considered as PR print. They can be informative about an organisation.

6. **Posters and wall charts.** Very popular with trade associations for products such as tea or coffee, PR posters can be very detailed and instructive when the intention is to distribute them to schools. They can also be used to educate the public about safety precautions, or to provide information of public interest. Such posters are usually small bills or placards, the standard sizes being crown (15 × 20 in., 381 × 508 mm), double crown (30 × 20 in., 762 × 508 mm), or quad crown (30 × 40 in., 762 × 1016 mm).

7. **Educational leaflets, folders, booklets.** Here we refer to informative literature which is different from sales literature. Subjects might concern lawn treatment, home decorating, care of clothes, or how to use a gas oven. Such literature helps the customer to gain benefits from the product, and should not plug the product in persuasive copywriting style.

8. **Handy aids.** Under this general heading may be included items which help the customer, such as calculators for quantities of wallpaper or metric conversion tables.

9. **Instruction leaflets and manuals.** Even if the PRO is not directly

responsible for instruction and maintenance manuals he should advise on their production for they can so easily cause ill-will if they are not simple yet comprehensive. It may be that pictures and diagrams can say more than words. When producing for export markets it is more than ever important that translated instructions should be clear and accurate. Some manuals for Japanese products contain some very odd English.

10. **Annual reports and accounts.** Simplicity of presentation has become the hallmark of the modern balance sheet. With so many people interested in company performances—including the staff—the annual report and accounts has become an exercise in good communication.

11. **Postage stamps and first-day covers.** The postage stamp has become a PR medium in many countries of the world, promoting public knowledge of road safety, 'grow more food' campaigns, industrial accident prevention and so forth. Germany has issued many such sets, and the British issued a set to coincide with the first elections to the European Parliament. First-day covers can be used to celebrate PR events (e.g. IPR and IPRA conferences) or, when there is a new stamp issue, charities can issue appeals to prospective donors in first-day covers. Concorde has provided a whole philatelic theme with stamps depicting the aircraft and special covers flown by British Airways and Air France.

12. **Press kits.** Although many press kits suffer from over-kill and are irrelevant, there are times when a useful wallet can be a convenient means of containing a number of loose items at a press event.

13. **Picture postcards.** Apart from advertising the subject, a picture postcard can be very useful and will promote goodwill, examples being those supplied by hotels, airlines and shipping lines.

14. **Questionnaires.** Confidence may be inspired when a hotel guest, airline passenger or customer is invited to complete a questionnaire which requests his praise, criticisms or suggestions.

15. **Pocket and desk diaries.** Lasting a year, diaries extend goodwill over a long period and even more so if annual refills are supplied.

16. **Company histories.** Provided these are not biased and pretentious, they can be important sources of information, especially if the organisation has a good story to tell. The Americans are rather good at this, and Coca-Cola have an excellent full-colour volume. Centenary celebrations provide a good opportunity for such publications. The *Daily Telegraph* has produced a record of news stories as printed since the paper was first launched, making a very interesting historical record.

17. **School project packs.** Many industries and large companies receive requests from students who are undertaking projects, and very sensibly and generously some organisations have responded by producing informative school project packs.

18. **School information material.** Similarly, some organisations regularly supply schools with educational material (e.g. North Thames Gas) in leaflet or pamphlet form.

19. **Induction material.** For any company which is frequently recruiting and training staff, good concise material about the organisation, including charts of management structure, can be a PR responsibility.

20. **Reprints of feature articles.** Ready-made pieces of print with a variety of uses as give-away material in showrooms and on exhibition stands are the reprints of PR feature articles.

28

CORPORATE ADVERTISING

There was a time when corporate, institutional or prestige advertising was an advertising agent's idea of PR. It was even dubbed 'chairman's shaving-mirror advertising'! Corporate advertising has grown up since then, and nowadays it is not so much a way of saying nice things about a company as of using the control and urgency of the advertising columns to communicate a serious corporate message. Writing in *Advertising* (Autumn 1978), Roy Birch of Charles Barker City said: 'Today, however, the situation is changing fast. Partly motivated by a general decline of public confidence in industry and business, American companies have led the way with large-scale campaigns—and have achieved measurable success.' For example, ITT have run corporate commercials on American television.

Corporate advertising is no longer restricted to the business or cultural press; at a time of sugar shortage Tate and Lyle used the popular press to explain its case to housewives. And in recent years ICI, Stirling Winthrop, Glynwed, TI, British Gas, ITT and others have put corporate commercials on British television.

Richard Owen of Interlink Advertising had this to say in *Advertising* (Spring 1980): 'A modern corporate campaign has one over-riding objective—to create a sympathetic public environment for the company. If the economic and social role of the company is fully appreciated, many benefits may follow. It will not be criticised for making fair profits, and is better placed to reject unfair media criticism and to explain controversial aspects of its policy or operations. In short, if society regards a company highly, it is far more likely to leave it free to pursue its commercial and social aim. If, on the other hand, society does not regard a company highly, it may, by accident or design, eventually restrict or control that company's commercial activities.' Thus in the battle for commercial survival, companies apply the PR technique of 'gaining credit for achievement'. Interlink Advertising have handled excellent corporate advertising campaigns for organisations such as Vickers, BP, Tube Investments and the Department of Commerce for Northern Ireland.

At the beginning of this book we showed that PR and advertising were totally different, that PR was not a form of advertising. Now we are dealing with the use of advertising as a form of PR. This may seem like a contradiction but it amounts to this: there are times when we cannot depend on the whim of an editor or a producer to publish or broadcast our message. We have to buy advertisement space or time to deliver our message where, when and how we desire. We must have the ultimate control. To do this we have to become an advertiser.

Modern Use of Corporate Advertising

The modern use of corporate advertising is very different from the old prestige ads which told of achievements and research and often employed famous writers to pen literary copy. Some £12m a year is spent on corporate advertising in Britain alone. Some of the corporate ads of the late 1970s and 1980s have been exciting, aggressive and challenging. They have attacked misconceptions or presented the facts in a controversy.

Or, like Esso, the tiger reappeared to assert the company's 'spotless pedigree', which seemed to ignore the skeleton in the cupboard of Standard Oil's robber baron founder, John D. Rockefeller. More recent Esso corporate advertisements have taken justifiable credit for concern about the energy crisis and the company's efforts in fields of alternative energy supplies, chiefly in the USA.

Corporate advertising can be divided into two classes. First, there is **advocacy** or **issue** advertising which projects a point of view, states a case, challenges attacks made by activists or seeks to correct misconceptions. Second, there is **image** advertising which seeks to establish both corporate identity and a clear understanding of what the organisation does or stands for. Inevitably, there are campaigns which present a case and seek to establish an image.

The use of commercial television, pioneered by the ICI Pathfinders series, has been a novel extension of a mass market medium. At first, viewers were perplexed by non-selling commercials which seemed out of place among the usual hard-selling advertisements. Glynwed showed that the medium could reach shareholders, distributors, customers and employees. ITT, although running only an experimental British version of an American corporate ad on Southern Television, were pleasantly surprised that their employees were impressed by the company's achievements. And Tube Investments used Ronnie Corbett in nine different character roles which was a very lighthearted way of handling corporate advertising. The campaign succeeded in creating awareness of the range of TI products among housewives who were unfamiliar with Tube Investments. The campaign was also brought home to TI's employees through internal media.

For a number of years Tate and Lyle (for example, the Mr Cube ads) have used corporate ads verging on propaganda to combat the threat of nationalisation by Labour Governments, and used the headline *Tate not State* in its 1974 campaign. The copy showed how the company was operating in more than 25 countries and was engaged in other businesses apart from sugar. The Mr Cube character had a sword and shield.

Another company which had to explain its diversity was Vickers. It was famous for aircraft and shipbuilding, but these were nationalised. By means of corporate advertising it told the financial community, prospective investors and top management of its involvement in other enterprises such as North Sea oil. Awareness of Vickers' new activities and its profitability was achieved in six months of corporate advertising.

Really aggressive were the ITT ads during their three-year campaign in 1974, 1975 and 1976. The first of these advertisements devoted half of the full page to a reversed white on black shock headline *Who the devil does ITT think it is?* It looked crude and out-of-place in *The Times, Financial Times, Guardian,* and *The Observer,* but it had resulted from the advertising agency rejecting six milder versions as a result of copy testing.

American multinationals are frequently criticised, and not only by the Left. They straddle continents and present security problems, especially if the parts of, say, a computer are made in different factories in different countries. O▶

course, this is no more contradictory, or a security risk, than the fact that much of Russian industry is based on Western expertise, payment being in the form of cheap products which compete with those in the West. ITT is not the only American multinational to be sensitive about criticism. IBM has met the criticism of the 'buy British' lobby with corporate advertisements carrying headlines such as *How patriotic is it to buy a computer from IBM?* Supporting copy stated:

'Last year alone, our capital investment in Britain amounted to £90 million.
'We've increased our staff from six when we started in 1951, to 15,000 British people working in Britain and for Britain.
'They're working at Hursley, in IBM's biggest research and development laboratory in Europe. At Greenock and Havant, manufacturing machines that help keep British products competitive in an international market and at the same time building our exports.'

This ad copy is very similar to that of the earlier ITT campaigns of 1974–6.

It may be argued that corporate advertising is a form of last ditch PR, and that had there been a consistent PR programme in the past it would not have been necessary to indulge in media advertising. In the case of ITT there was need to challenge persistent misreporting in the press. But the argument may be supported in those tug-of-war corporate advertising situations when a take-over is threatened. In 1962 Courtaulds were nearly taken over by ICI until several thousands of pounds spent on advertising by Courtaulds convinced shareholders that the ICI bid was unwelcome. More recently, in 1979, Spillers—having suffered a financial decline after pulling out of plant baking—had no PR back-up from the past to support it against a bid and in spite of defensive advertising was taken over by Dalgety.

Perhaps the strangest corporate advertisements, if they can be called such, are the two-page spreads taken by the governments of less familiar states. Thousands of words set in small type are crammed into the space, and the advertisements look far too verbose and forbidding to be read. They are little more than bonuses for the advertisement department of the newspaper.

A very successful series of corporate advertisements was linked with a well-organised PR campaign to win respectability for the motorcycle. This was sponsored by the Institute of Motorcycling, and the advertisements appeared in popular newspapers such as *The Sun*.

Generic Advertising

Corporate advertising tends to fall between two stools as the poor (but not inexpensive) relation of both advertising and public relations. A good question is who should be responsible for the production of these campaigns: advertising agencies (which rarely understand PR) or PR consultancies (which rarely understand advertising)? The advertising agency often confuses the idea by asking 'will it sell the product?', while the PR consultant may be too pretentious. It begs the further question: is corporate advertising really necessary?— a theme which repeatedly bothers the advertising and marketing trade press.

Another name for this form of communication when concerned with products and services such as wool, milk, bricks, glass, gas, electricity and insurance is **generic advertising**. In an article headed *Can Generic Ads Pay Off?* (*Campaign*, May 19, 1978), John Emmerson commented:

'The generic campaign, however, faces the difficulty of trying to stimulate demand for a particular type of product, without being able to monitor the success of the advertising in any but the most isolated way, and at the same time fulfil "corporate" objectives in developing a favourable public reaction from sectors which are not prime sales projects.

'The campaign to promote wool seems to be a good example of how such things can be done best.

'Wool, as such, is not a product—the consumer is not being asked to buy the wares of a specific manufacturer, but is being provided with positive image-building associations through "soft" television commercials about the merits of the product category.

' "Look for the Woolmark" is the message. . . . This is the generic activity working effectively.'

Of course, it could be argued that generic advertising is really no more than *cooperative* advertising, which is not strictly speaking corporate advertising. This is rather like saying when is a blonde a brunette, it all depends which wig she's wearing. Something of this confusion is shown in John Emmerson's remarks when first he talks about 'image-building associations' (which is PR) and then refers to 'soft television commercials' (but PR is *not* a soft sell). Generic or cooperative ads are primarily a form of advertising which has PR overtones, whereas corporate advertising is a form of PR which has no advertising overtones. *Their basic intentions are different.*

Production of Corporate Advertising

Corporate advertising must be handled by agents who understand its PR nature and purpose. Some advertising agents, having won such an account, have announced in the trade press that they have been appointed to 'polish the tarnished image' of a client whose reputation is in question. You cannot *polish* images, only seek a deservedly correct image when faults have been put right in the organisation.

An example of a cooperative generic advertising campaign which did not overtly sell a product or service, but performed the essential PR purpose of educating the market, was that of the British insurance companies in July 1977. Its aim was 'to explain some of the principles of insurance, the services provided and the contribution made to the economy'. The sponsors were members of the British Insurance Association, the Life Officers' Association, Associated Scottish Life Offices and the Industrial Life Officers' Association. Whole-page advertisements were placed in most of the London and Scottish national dailies and Sundays. It was part of a long-term effort to develop a better understanding of what insurance is about. There have been other such campaigns. In this particular one on *how insurance works* the ads were very original and interesting, neither blatant nor merely prestigious. The ads were modern-day parables, presented either humorously or factually. One of the most amusing read thus:

THE TREASURE THAT SHRANK

Once upon a time, there was a young pirate. He had already filled his first chest with treasure, for his old age. (He had a crew and several wives to support, so he needed all the treasure he could get.)

One day, he went off secretly and buried the treasure. (Because it was a bit risky keeping it under his bunk.)

'That's a start,' he told his wives and crew, 'Stick by me mates, we'll be alright.'

Then suddenly, cutlass in hand, he died.

And no one knew where the treasure was.

The crew had to join the navy to earn a living.

The wives spent years searching for the treasure. And when they finally found it, it was worth just enough to buy them each a new dress.

What the wives said about that isn't the sort of thing you find in stories like this.

This whimsical copy, designed in handwriting style, occupied seven eighths of the page. Below it was more serious copy explaining the benefits of insurance services.

Beautiful advertisements aimed at counteracting the environment lobby were those for Shell in October 1980. They were two-page spreads in magazines such as the *Observer Colour Magazine*, and full pages in newspapers such as *The Guardian*. In the magazine format the right-hand page was completely occupied by a full-colour picture of a fox in the long grass with Stanlow refinery on the skyline. The picture occupied the greater part of the newspaper advertisement. The copy (quoting Terry Gracie, Shell Environmental Technician, whose portrait was set against the opening words) read as follows:

A SHELL REFINERY ALIVE WITH WILDLIFE
WHAT'S THE STORY?

An oil refinery is not the first place you'd look for herons, or a marsh harrier, or a kingfisher, or a fox. Yet, strange as it may seem, the open spaces in and around Shell's Stanlow Refinery literally abound in wildlife.

Some of it is common. Some is rare.

I have counted 61 species of bird—including seldom seen varieties like the little ringed plover and the sandpiper.

There are scarce plants as well.

The noddingburr marigold and the celery-leafed crowfoot are a couple of the least known varieties.

Stanlow Refinery in Cheshire is the size of a small town. A small, but busy town.

It processes 30,000 tons of oil daily. A tiny percentage of this escapes as spillage but everything that gets away is filtered out of the drainage water by a line of traps which will catch the smallest concentration.

As a check that all is well, we sample the water several times a day.

We also check the atmosphere. An automatic camera takes a timed shot of the skyline every fifteen seconds. If the plant makes smoke, we have an infallible witness.

And there's more. Unhappy with conventional waste disposal, we have also invested £4m in waste *consumption*.

The oil and chemical residues which once had to be dumped (in safe places) are now burned in an advanced furnace to produce the energy equivalent of twenty megawatts.

Water, air and waste pollution control is just where we start'.

This impactive corporate advertising is reminiscent of the campaign conducted by the Central Electricity Generating Board in the 1960s when, among other things, it engaged a game warden to protect wildlife in the vicinity of its power stations at Dungeness, Kent. Appearing at the same time as the Shell ads was an oddly weak corporate advertisement from Mobil. At best, it carried a picture of a sailing ship which may have appealed to devotees of the television series, *The Onedin Line*, but this ad was reminiscent of the prestige corporate ads of the 1950s which one had hoped were relics of bygone decades. The flat old-fashioned, narrative style copy read:

SUPERTANKER, 1901

The dawn of the century marked twilight time for the age of sail—with one notable exception. Kerosene oil for the lamps of China was big business and wind power was still the best way to get it there. The *Brilliant*, built for Mobil in Scotland was the biggest kerosene clipper of them all, carrying four thousand tons on every voyage out.

About the time of World War I, though, newly developed oil-fired steam tankers proved to be better than sailing ships for transporting fuel in bulk to far eastern storage terminals. That meant an end to kerosene clippers.

Today, however, a Mobil *Brilliant* still plies the high seas. The clipper's modern namesake carries more than 100,000 tons of crude oil as part of a Mobil Tanker fleet—both owned and chartered—with a total capacity of almost 10 million tons.

Our fleet goes on evolving. By replacing steam turbines with diesel engines, we are cutting fuel consumption by up to a third. This saving keeps transport costs down and frees valuable oil for use elsewhere.

For these reasons, Mobil's marine engineers are now studying the possibilities of applying alternative energy sources—including coal and even sail—to tankers of the future.

No one is immune to the rising costs of energy—not even an oil company.

This is surely the kind of corporate ad which ITT considered old-hat when it launched its aggressive *Who the devil does ITT think it is?* and put the clock forward for this form of public relations.

Researching Results of Corporate Advertising

The criticism is sometimes made that the value of corporate advertising is difficult to assess, yet research can be applied to it just as it can be applied to general advertising. There have been post-advertising surveys to evaluate the insurance campaigns, and this author has been interviewed at home as a result of a researcher knocking on the door.

Market and Opinion Research International operate a regular monthly omnibus survey 'to measure the effectiveness of corporate advertising'. Known as the **CAS-omnibus**, it can be used for long-term image tracking, pre- and post-advertising tests or 'once-off' image measurements. It can thus be applied to corporate identity as well as corporate advertising studies. Generally, the surveys measure familiarity with and favourability of organisations who subscribe by inserting a number of questions in the omnibus questionnaire. The sample consists of 2000 adults aged 15+ throughout Great Britain in 165 constituency sampling points. Calls are made on homes five doors apart, and only one interview per household is permitted. For a few hundred pounds a very economical assessment can be achieved.

Reverting to Ray Birch's article in *Advertising*, he was able to quote that when one of ICI's series of corporate commercials was put to the test it was shown that 'people who had been exposed to the television campaign were more likely—by a varying but significant margin—to rate ICI highly on a whole range of attributes'. He also recommended that corporate advertising should be tested before it was run. (As already mentioned, the ITT campaign developed out of copy testing.) Roy Birch also quoted the Yankeclovich, Skelly & White study, published in the USA in 1977, which (using a sample of 800) showed that five companies which had used corporate advertising 'were more favourably perceived, both overall and in detail' than another firm which used no corporate advertising. The net difference ranged from 1 to 13 per cent, and of the 16 traits examined the average net difference was 8 per cent.

Corporate Ads Addressed to the Press

A special form of corporate advertising is that placed in journals such as *UK Press Gazette*, occupying perhaps a page or a special four-page centre-spread supplement on art paper. They are usually inserted by organisations which feel they are misunderstood, misreported or maligned by the press, and they have ranged from British Rail to the South African Government.

Few products have had a worse press, rightly or wrongly, than the DC-10 airliner. In the *UK Press Gazette* (September 29, 1980) McDonnell Douglas showed their confidence in the aircraft by printing a whole-page advertisement illustrated by a picture of Pete Conrad standing beside the plane. The copy read:

> 'The more you learn about
> our DC-10, the more you know
> how great it really is.'
> *Pete Conrad*
> *Former Astronaut*
> *Division Vice-President, McDonnell Douglas*

'I've watched airplanes and spacecraft take shape for much of my adult life. I'm certain that nothing made to fly has ever been designed or built to more exacting standards than our DC-10.

'Eighteen million engineering man-hours were invested in this plane's development. That includes 14,000 hours of wind tunnel testing, as well as full-scale "fatigue testing" for the equivalent of 40 years of airline service.

'I'm convinced that the DC-10 is the most thoroughly-tested jetliner ever built. Along with US Government certification, the DC-10 has passed structures tests just as demanding, in their own way, as those required of US Air Force fighter planes.

'The DC-10 fleet demonstrates its dependability flying more than a million miles a day and serving 170 cities in 90 countries around the globe.'

To learn more about the DC-10, write: 'DC-10 Report', McDonnell Douglas, Box 14526, St Louis, MO 63178, USA.

29

SPONSORSHIPS

Sponsorship is a development of patronage. In days gone by a monarch or nobleman would sponsor a composer, a painter or a poet. Today, industry sponsors symphony orchestras, art exhibitions, books and so on, and this has been extended into other areas, especially sport.

There may be different reasons for sponsorship. Some famous businessmen, from John D. Rockefeller to William Morris, were philanthropists, endowing universities, libraries and art galleries. But nowadays there is usually a more commercial purpose associated with marketing, advertising and public relations, sometimes a combination of all three.

Christopher Shale, managing director of Omnisponsorship Ltd, has defined sponsorship for marketing purposes (which may well have a PR content) in the following terms:

Sponsorship is essentially a business deal intended to be to the advantage of both the sponsor and the sponsored. Although sometimes funded from advertising budgets, it should be treated as an entirely separate element of marketing. The sponsored activity may or may not be closely linked to the prime commercial function of the sponsoring organisation. Unlike

    patronage   —fundamentally an altruistic activity,
    subsidy   —aid from national or local government sources, or
    endorsement—payment in return for the agreed use of specific equipment or cloth-
                ing—

sponsorship is the provision of resources for an independent activity in return for benefits which, it is anticipated, will accrue by virtue of that support.

Examples of Sponsorship

Tobacco companies have aroused controversy by associating an allegedly harmful product with healthy leisure activities and sports. Banned from television advertising, they have circumvented this by sponsoring events which are televised, such as golf, tennis and cricket, with the inevitable acknowledgements, while racing cars decorated with the sponsor's name are visible on the television screen.

When Yardley diversified into men's toiletries it used motor sport for a time and sponsored a young man's sport as a medium for establishing this new product image. This idea has been picked up by Fabergé for their Brut 33, the name being painted all over Dave Fuell's rally cross car. Similarly, since 1978, Cornhill Insurance has created awareness of itself in a new market segment by sponsoring test match cricket so that the 'Cornhill Tests' have become a well-known expression. Raleigh have sponsored a cycle racing team with excellent coverage from international events such as the spectacular Six-Day Race in France. In April 1981, Nigeria became the first African nation to take part in a major international cycle race, their six-man team competing in the Sealink International race from Le Touquet to Manchester.

Show-jumping, which is popular with viewers, enjoys two kinds of sponsor-

172

ship. Prizes for events are awarded by sponsors, while the horses and riders may have their sponsors such as Sanyo, Harris Carpets, Everest Double Glazing or the Irish cigarette firm Carroll. This also happens in horse-racing with its Schweppes, Mackeson and Whitbread gold cups, while the Grand National enjoyed different sponsors each year, including The Colt Car Co. and *The Sun* newspaper. Swimming events are supported by Coca-Cola, for some years Gillette infused new life into English county cricket by its sponsorship, and there are the John Player League and Schweppes Championship cricket sponsorships.

Sponsorship does not rest with the event itself and the resulting media coverage. There can be merchandising spin-offs ranging over T-shirts, souvenirs, gramophone records and toys. When Wills Embassy cigarettes sponsor an orchestra the recordings credit the sponsor on the record sleeves.

From this brief summary it will be seen that sponsorship has become a major commercial activity. Not all of it is spectacular. Supplies for expeditions and one-man voyages may not make a lot of news. Specialist consultancies such as West and Nally are responsible for big sponsorships like the Gillette London Marathon. There are people looking for sponsors, and potential sponsors looking for something to sponsor, and consultancies can bring them together.

Kim Pearl and John Clemison, in an article (*Marketing*, October 1, 1980) summed up by saying: 'Perhaps the most convincing reason for any kind of sponsorship was given by LRC, who described the object of its Durex campaign in just four words—"to normalise the name".' LRC's sponsorship of motor and motorboat sport over five years 'achieved most of the objectives we set ourselves', and 'the BBC's refusal to televise rallies in which our car appeared resulted in a mass of press coverage which, while not generated by us, was beneficial to the campaign'. So Ted Wallbutton, LRC marketing controller, was quoted in the *Marketing* article.

Why Sponsor?

Why do firms invest money on sponsorships? Hundreds of firms are involved in financing numerous activities. In some cases there may be a genuine desire to make an activity financially viable. Industry has been responsible for saving cultural institutions from ruin. It is also true that motor-racing has contributed to safer motoring because brakes, tyres and gearboxes have been tested under exceptional conditions and modified accordingly.

But the over-riding characteristic of sponsorship is its *ability to communicate a name*, and to do so repeatedly. It cannot advertise a product in the sense of describing it or persuading people to make purchases. Sponsorship achieves **familiarity** through repetition and impact. This exploits the psychology that we tend to prefer the things we know best.

Among Japanese company and product names Daihatsu is a less familiar latecomer on the British scene but the director of sales, George Griffith, stated in a letter in *Campaign* (October 24,1980): 'Some three weeks after the event we are already certain that orders for our new Masters IV golf cart and sales of Daihatsu vehicles directly attributed to the Bob Hope Classic have paid for our sponsorship. On the basis of this we look forward to participating in the event again next year.' The golf cart was not being advertised or promoted in any way at the time of the Bob Hope Golf championship sponsored by Daihatsu.

There is a second aspect which is the **goodwill** that is derived from being seen to be generous; and also because the sponsor has provided interest, pleasure or something else of value to members of the associated public.

Is Sponsorship Wise?

A prospective sponsor should know why he wishes to indulge in sponsorship, and with whom he wishes to communicate. Approaches are frequently made to prospective sponsors but proposals have to be evaluated carefully. Will the investment achieve tangible objectives, or is the activity of such fringe interest that results may be negligible? Even a big firm like Alcan withdrew from golf because it felt the game was too remote from its marketing objectives. And the *small family car* pun no doubt seemed a brilliant idea to the London Rubber Company except that the BBC did not think it should be presented on the domestic television screen.

Some sponsorships may baffle British audiences. The reason for sponsorship by a foreign firm may be that the television programme will be shown in the home country, as with the Japanese Suntory whisky which is unobtainable in Britain!

Some Forms of Sponsorship

Reference has been made to some of the well-known forms of sponsorship but there are many areas in which sponsorship can be undertaken and they may be analysed under the following headings:

1. **Books.** Sponsored books can be business propositions in themselves, Michelin Guides and Maps, Rothman sports annuals and the *Guinness Book of Records* being well-known examples. The 1981–82 edition of *Rothman's Football Yearbook* was the 12th edition. One of the most famous cookery books is McDougalls *Better Baking*, now in its 30th edition.

Reputable publishers will put their imprint on books by authoritative company authors, costs of production being shared between company and publisher, and distribution also being shared. Thus, the company may supply free copies to clients, and the publisher will sell the book through the book trade. In this way some excellent technical books have been published which have been good PR for the sponsor, and useful additions to the publisher's book list. An example is the Rentokil Library published by Hutchinson.

A variation on this is when a publisher produces books which a sponsor may buy in quantity, bearing his name. The different maps and guides produced by Francis Chichester are typical examples, and there are also weekly visitors' guides which may be sponsored by hotels.

2. **Exhibitions.** The seal of authority and repute can be placed on an exhibition if it is sponsored by an official body, while many trade associations and publishers sponsor exhibitions as a shop window for their organisation. They represent a blend of PR and business initative. Sometimes they are combined with a conference. Some examples are:

Ideal Home Exhibition	*Daily Mail*
International Motor and Commercial Motor Show	Society of Motor Manufacturers and Traders
Accounting Systems and Equipment Show	Business Equipment Trade Association
Arts Accessory Retailer Trade Show	*Arts Accessory Retailer*

OCCA Technical Exhibition	Oil and Colour Chemists' Association
EIA Engineering Exhibition	Engineering Industries Association
MICRO	Royal Microscopic Society
International Machine Tool Exhibition	Machine Tool Traders Association
Royal Show	Royal Agricultural Society of England
International Motor Cycle Exhibition	Institute of Motorcycling
Frozen Food Exhibition	British Frozen Food Federation

3. **Education.** As well as patronising education this kind of sponsorship may be an investment in training and recruitment. Chairs at universities are often possible only by industrial support. In Britain, Chairs of Marketing are comparatively new, and we have yet to see a Chair of Public Relations to be sponsored at a British university. However, many companies do endow bursaries, exhibitions, travelling scholarships and research projects relative to their industries, while others donate appropriate equipment to technical colleges or award trophies and prizes to successful students.

4. **Expeditions and special feats.** Feats of endurance, explorations, mountain-climbs and similar activities are costly to equip and carry out and generally depend upon outside financial support. Food, clothing and equipment are often supplied by generous donors. In most cases, the sponsor receives some benefit. It may be an opportunity to test a product under severe conditions, and this may subsequently be quoted in publicity, or the sponsor may be publicly associated with the venture, as with long-distance yacht races. When the sponsor is a publisher the story may be printed in a newspaper or magazine.

5. **Sport.** The largest proportion of sponsorship money goes into sport, a subject which interests an enormous number of people all over the world so that the media can be relied upon to provide excellent coverage. Among the sports which benefit from sponsorship are: air racing, athletics, balloon racing, basket ball, bicycle racing, cricket, curling, football, golf, handball, horse-racing, motor rallying, power-boat racing, show-jumping, swimming, table tennis, tennis and yacht-racing. The introduction of Braniff air services from Texas to Britain included the biggest prize tennis sponsorship ever held, the Braniff World Doubles Championship at London's Olympia in January 1979. The Daihatsu Challenge is the biggest women's indoor tennis championship.

Associating a sponsorship with an appropriate personality can double the effectiveness. Two cases are worth quoting. Barry Sheen is not only a successful racing motorcyclist but a popular personality—he comes over very well on television. He is sponsored by Yamaha, and press features appear of him and Yamaha quite apart from his participation in races. At the Horse of the Year Show in October 1980 it was announced that Robert Smith, son of Harvey Smith, had received an £80,000 sponsorship from Simoniz. For this he has to provide, equip, enter and transport two grades of horses whose names are prefixed by the product names Liquid Diamond and Vista, for Team Simoniz. *But why a 19-year-old rider like Robert Smith?* Because (*a*) the prime market for car polishes are 18–28-year-old motorists and (*b*) Robert Smith is an immaculate rider with well-turned-out horses who represents the image of the products. He does not have long hair, he dresses smartly, and he belongs to the target group age bracket.

Among the equestrian sponsorships handled by British Equestrian Promotions Ltd are or have been ones on behalf of Elizabeth Ann, Philips

Industries, Everest Double Glazing, Hoechst, Servis, *Daily Mail*, Basildon Bond, Godfrey Davis, Sanyo, Lancia and Kerrygold. The Midland Bank sponsor 183 one-day horse trials leading to the Midland Bank Horse Trials Championship of Great Britain. The coverage may result from a sponsored event and prize, or from a horse bearing a name such as Sanyo Sanmar (ridden by Harvey Smith) or Carroll's Denham (ridden by Eddie Macken). The Sanyo horses also have Sanyo names on a distinctive blue and white saddle-cloth which is very evident on colour television.

A very attractive sponsorship in October 1980 was that of international figure skating at Richmond, London. The St Ivel Ice International attracted competitors from 11 countries and provided about an hour's programme of delightful television on BBC 1 on four successive evenings. Meanwhile, during the same week, BBC2 televised the Kodak Masters Bowls Tournament on eight successive nights (Sunday to Sunday), the Jack High programmes featuring eight of the world's greatest flat green bowlers. Such can be the extent of coverage on national television, at least three sponsorship events being on television over a matter of days—show jumping, ice skating and bowls.

6. **Arts and culture.** The arts have always depended on patronage, and industry is responsible for financing many cultural institutions which would not otherwise survive. The Midland Bank sponsors operatic 'proms', theatres such as the Chichester Festival Theatre have their lists of business sponsors, and many symphony orchestras receive substantial support from firms such as W. D. & H. O. Wills.

Writing in *Campaign* (August 1, 1980), Alastair Sedgwick, managing director of Marketing and the Arts, said: 'The cost of entry into the arts sponsorship club is much less than many imagine. For example, it is currently possible to sponsor over eighty concerts by a long-established London orchestra for little more than £10,000. That's less than the production cost of one 30-second commercial let alone screen time.' It is not usually wise to compare PR and advertising costs because their purpose and achievement are different, but Alastair Sedgwick's comment is valid in stressing the inexpensiveness of some forms of sponsorship which are not merely patronage.

But possibly the largest arts sponsorship was that of the Philharmonia Orchestra's 1980 series of concerts by BAT Industries' Du Maurier cigarettes, which amounted to £600,000. An artful monetarist government hoped that industrial support would justify a cut in arts grants, but the likelihood of this becoming realistic was refuted by a London Business School study.

7. **Causes and charities.** There are occasions when mutual benefit can accrue from an industrial sponsor giving support to a charity or some other voluntary organisation. Sometimes the cost of a film about a charity's work has been met by a benevolent company, or advertising space for appeals has been donated by an advertiser.

8. **Local Events.** Many opportunities exist for companies with local branches to enhance their community or customer relations by contributing prizes to local events such as flower shows or by participating in carnivals. These sponsorships are witnessed by large numbers of people and usually receive publicity in the local media. In very large towns there will be important events such as tennis and golf tournaments, swimming galas, and other events which gain more than local attention and make sponsorship even more worthwhile.

9. **Films.** Firms such as W. D. & H. O. Wills are well-known for their sponsorship of sports, films, and sponsorship films of this nature can be of sufficiently popular interest to secure showings on the public cinema or on television.

10. **Professional awards.** Long established awards are the *Financial Times* Architecture Award and *The Guardian* Young Businessman of the Year Award. *The Times* has its Veuve Clicquot champagne award for the Business Woman of the Year—with a vine named after her and a visit to Rheims for the christening of the vine. There are also show business awards made by the London *Standard* and the *TV Times*.

An increasing number of awards to journalists are made by industry including:

The *Corning Journalist Awards:* entrants submit two articles on food preparation and cooking in the home, or appreciation of good cooking and eating out. Awards for each category: a crystal glass vase from Steuben, presented at a gala dinner at Glaziers' Hall, London.

The *International Building Press Journalism Awards* are a complex of awards sponsored by the RIBA, Institute of Building, Federation of Civil and Engineering Contractors, Willetts Ltd and Blundell Permoglaze and administered by The National Federation of Building Trades Employers.

The *Lilly Medical Journalism Research Award* is a £1000 travel award for journalists under 30 years of age to pursue 'a line of study in the medical/scientific field in a country or countries outside Great Britain', and is administered by the Medical Journalists' Association.

Glaxo Holdings offer three £1000 awards for the best contributions to science journalism. Three Glaxo Fellowships were first made in 1966, and since then Glaxo has made 114 awards in Britain and the EEC worth almost £100,000. The Association of British Science Writers administer the Fellowship awards.

The *Post Office* makes cash awards to the writers and photographers on provincial morning and evening, weekly and bi-weekly newspapers who published the best features—not straight news stories—on British postal services.

A combined regional award scheme organised by the Merseyside and North Wales NUJ Area Council comprises awards made by local firms such as *Ford Motor Company, Unilever* companies on Merseyside, *Littlewoods Organisation, Pilkington Brothers, Bass North West, B + I Line* and *Kershaw Publications*.

ITT Business Systems, under the auspices of the Association of British Science Writers, offer publications and broadcasting awards, each worth £1000 cash plus £500 for travel and equipment, in their Technology Writers' Award.

The *Qualcast Gardening Feature Writing Awards* are made for the best published features on general gardening, lawn care advice, and technical and product advice.

William Grant & Sons Ltd make the Glenfiddich Awards in several categories for wine, whisky and cooking writers and authors. They are made to writers who have contributed to the civilised appreciation of food and drink. The awards are gold medals and Glenfiddich pure malt whisky, while for the principal Writer of the Year award there is a trophy (held for a year), a silver replica of the traditional pot used in the making of malt whisky, and a cash prize.

Van den Berghs & Jurgens Ltd have a £1000 Reporting Award for the journalist or writer who has created a greater public awareness or understanding of some aspect of human nutrition.

The *British Institute of Management* makes its Blue Circle £1000 top award and five category awards of £500 each for industrial writers and broadcasters whose work has made the greatest contribution to the understanding of industrial, management and labour affairs.

Examples of these sponsorships have been given to demonstrate the popularity and versatility of this particularly happy form of sponsorship. These awards to journalists encourage interest in and understanding of the sponsor's subject and show appreciation of journalists' talents. They are sponsorships which enhance media relations.

11. **Public service and civic.** There are also sponsorships in the public interest contributed by local authorities or businesses. A socially responsible sponsorship in the West End of London has been the provision of additional litter bins on the pavement. The scheme was initiated by the British Tourist Authority in cooperation with Westminster City Council. The green bins bear the name of each local sponsor—a shop or bank—and the slogan 'For a Cleaner City'. This simple effort is perhaps more useful and impressive than the expensive illuminations which help to commercialise Christmas, although it would be hard to beat the lighted Christmas tree effects in streets and office block windows in Amsterdam. A city can sponsor attractions which give it character, like the suspended flower baskets in Bath.

Probably the most spectacular goodwill sponsorship is that of Goodyear with its airships in Europe and the USA. On the one hand they further the technical aspect of this form of aviation, but they also provide aerial platforms for television crews filming sports events, or help with traffic control. At night, the airships have flown over cities with public service messages illuminated electronically on their sides. Goodyear have capitalised on this by making a film about *Europa*, the airship from which the Royal Wedding firework display and procession were filmed in July 1981.

Sponsorship is clearly an important local, national and international activity which contains a large element of PR. It signifies that an organisation has arrived and has a sound reputation. No one wants to be associated with a benefactor of ill repute. To be able to sponsor is therefore a sign of acceptance, good PR in itself.

Sometimes it can be surprisingly profitable as Schweppes discovered following their sponsorship of horse-racing in 1977. It began with a contract for publicans in which the prizes were the prize money won by four Schweppes race horses. The four yearlings cost £10,000, plus the cost of training and entry fees. The winning publicans were also guaranteed the first £10,000 of the price their horse fetched at the two-year sales at the end of the UK flat racing season. Each horse's name was prefixed by Schweppes. This was a real gamble since only a few horses win even one race in their first year. But three of the four Schweppes horses were winners. The publicans won more than £35,000! Schweppeshire Lad was the best two-year-old of 1978, winning six out of seven races, and placed second in the seventh. Schweppes enjoyed a self-financing sponsorship, investment in some valuable horses, and the sort of media interest coveted by a consumer product.

30

CONFERENCES AND SEMINARS

Direct communication with publics which have been invited to attend a conference or seminar can be a very successful way of conducting public relations, and it is another example of the use of a private, created medium very different from indiscriminate mass media. It highlights again the inadequacy of mass communication studies which are sometimes misrepresented or misunderstood as complete PR studies. The field of PR extends far beyond mass communications.

The conference or seminar can combine the media of the spoken word, films, video-cassettes, slides, displays and exhibits. Visual aids such as chalkboards, white-boards, flip-over charts and pads, and overhead projectors can also be incorporated.

Conferences and seminars bring organisations face to face with their publics, the latter in fairly small groups. There can be interchange of views—that is, truly mutual communication. Success depends on retaining an informative and educational atmosphere, and there must be no attempt to dress up the affair with banners, posters, sales displays and other sales promotional devices. The sales department or advertising agency can easily ruin a PR event. These PR events should not be regarded as a form of 'soft selling' but as a prelude to selling and a market education service.

Conferences

A conference consists of a large audience and platform speakers and is less intimate than a seminar which may be attended by no more than 25 people, perhaps less, if there is to be participation.

A conference may last for a day or a number of days. It may be held mid-week or over a weekend. It may be residential or non-residential. Delegates may pay an attendance fee, or admission may be free of charge. Accommodation may be paid for by the sponsors or by the delegates who may be either enrolled or invited. There are clearly many variations on how the attendance will be achieved and how the costs are met.

These organisational details need to be thought out very carefully. The events may be so valuable to participants that they will be willing to contribute to the cost while another event may succeed only if people are invited on a non-payment basis. There is no reason why participants should not pay to attend, and there is always the danger that if the sponsor provides too much hospitality the event may provoke suspicion that it is only a publicity stunt. On one occasion a well-known pharmaceutical company paid all the expenses of doctors who were invited to a conference about new drugs, and the company was criticised afterwards for virtually bribing doctors to attend. Sometimes people will place more value and credence on something for which they have to pay, even if it is run for commercial purposes.

The important thing is to have a worthwhile programme with first-class speakers supported by good films, slide presentations or other visual aids. The speakers should be experts (i.e. designers, technicians, scientists) rather than top executives, marketing or sales personnel. It may be a good idea to bring in outside speakers if they are familiar with the subject, either to give an authentic background or because they are users of the product or service. For example, a customer might present a case history.

Special Considerations

1. **The date.** A day and time should be chosen which does not clash with another events of interest to prospective participants. It should be sufficiently far ahead to permit proper planning, and so that invitations may be sent out (or announcements may be published) in sufficient time for people to make arrangements to attend. The planning may need from three to six months, while the event should be announced four to six weeks in advance.

2. **The venue.** A conference should be held at a venue which is (*a*) well-equipped for conferences, (*b*) attractive in itself or in an attractive location and, (*c*) easily accessible by road, rail, sea or air as the case may be.

3. **Recreational activities.** People cannot be expected to sit endlessly in a hall listening to speeches, and it is usually wise to include some recreation or entertainment. According to the type of audience, venue, time of year and so forth, this lighter side could involve a golf tournament, coach tour, boat trip, fashion show, theatre party, or some such social 'break' in the proceedings.

Planning a conference

When planning the timetable for a conference there are certain fixed times which dictate when sessions should be slotted in. These are the times for opening, coffee, lunch, tea and adjournment or closure. Thus, in a day's programme, there will be eight lecture sessions which can be subdivided into shorter lectures or in order to show films or slide presentations. A day's timetable might work out like this:

```
 9.30– 9.45  Delegates assemble
 9.45–10.00  Chairman's introduction
10.00–10.45  Speaker
10.45–11.00  Questions and discussion
11.00–11.30  Coffee
11.30–12.00  Film
12.00–12.30  Speaker
12.30–12.45  Questions and discussion
12.45– 1.00  Cocktails
 1.00– 2.00  Lunch
 2.00– 2.45  Speaker
 2.45– 3.00  Questions and discussion
 3.00– 3.30  Tea
 3.30– 3.45  Speaker with slide presentation
 3.45– 4.30  Questions and Discussion
 4.30        Close
```

Seminars

A seminar is a smaller gathering, and under this heading we can also include evening receptions. Generally, a seminar will be shorter than a conference and will be confined to an evening, half a day and at most a whole day. A large conference venue will not be required, and a medium-sized public room at a hotel or a lecture room at a professional institution will be adequate. Whereas in a conference with a large audience it will be more orderly to confine questions to question time, it is easier and often desirable during a seminar to permit people to participate at any time and for the speaker to encourage discussion rather than deliver a set speech.

Unhappily, the word 'seminar' is widely misused but the general sense of the word is an informal gathering to discuss a topic with a speaker, and a chairman may be unnecessary. In the academic sense a seminar consists of a group of students meeting with their tutor in a tutorial room to discuss a subject as distinct from a larger and more formal gathering in a lecture theatre to listen to a speaker. A lot of so-called seminars turn out to be conferences with an audience of a hundred people!

Evening receptions can be even more informal. A group of clients may be invited to listen to a talk and perhaps attend a film show on company premises or in a hotel room. The hospitality may range from sherry and biscuits to a private bar and light buffet. Bank managers adopt this modest but effective technique, as do motorcar distributors, and it lends itself to organisations with local branches or showrooms. The host and speaker is usually the local manager.

31

EXHIBITIONS

In this chapter we shall consider four aspects of exhibitions: (i) participation in a public or trade exhibition for PR purposes; (ii) PR support for a participant in a public or trade exhibition; (iii) exhibition promoters' PR; and (iv) PR exhibitions. Under public or trade exhibition we shall include trade fairs, but we shall not include the organisation and running of commercial stands in public or trade exhibitions since that is rightly an advertising medium.

Exhibitions take many forms. They may be indoor or outdoor. They can also be mobile using specially designed road vehicles such as trailers, caravans or buses; there are also exhibition trains and ships. They can be either portable or permanent. Once again, there is the PR benefit of face-to-face communication with its opportunities for eliminating communication barriers. The PR transfer process can be very effective through the medium of the exhibition.

Special Characteristics

1. **Exhibitions are very attractive.** They appeal to the curiosity and have entertainment value. They are also gregarious so that there is audience participation. This blend of social and mental stimulation acts as a magnet and heightens the interest. Few media attract such effortless attention even if the actual walking round an exhibition can be an exhausting experience. Some shows like the *Daily Mail* Ideal Home Exhibition and the Motor Show have been held regularly for many years and attract millions of visitors, while Philips' famous Evoluon science exhibition at Eindhoven in the Netherlands brings coachloads of visitors from many parts of Europe. There is a 'day's outing' appeal about most public and trade exhibitions which puts visitors in a receptive mood.

2. **Visibility.** Unlike printed media and even more effective than film or television, an exhibit can be physically seen. It may also be touched, used, sampled or in some other way physically examined. But even if it is too large or inconvenient to include on the stand the subject can be represented by a model—preferably working—or by a film or videotape. Static subjects like banks can be enlivened by interesting displays.

3. **Personal confrontation.** The ability for exhibitors and visitors to meet, talk, explain or complain is a big asset. Visitors can get first-hand information and resolve problems or misunderstandings: exhibitors can get reactions to new products or prototypes. The exhibitor can get close to the customer, something he cannot do when working through wholesalers, agents and retailers.

From these remarks it will be seen that exhibitions have a large PR content even when they are primarily below-the-line advertising media. That is perhaps why there is unfortunate confusion as to whether the exhibition is an advertising or a PR medium. The answer to that poser lies in the *purpose* of the exhibit: is it *to inform and educate* or is it *to persuade and sell?* The majority of stands or booths in public and trade exhibitions, including trade fairs, fall solidly into the advertising or second category. Nevertheless, it is not uncommon for exhibitions of all kinds to be the responsibility of the PRO which is no doubt a tribute to his organising ability.

It should be explained that a public exhibition is open to the public, but admission to a trade show is limited to those who are sent tickets or who are admitted on showing a business card. In the latter case, irrelevant visitors such as schoolchildren are excluded unless educational visits are arranged.

There are certain organisations such as government departments, state enterprises, trade and professional bodies which may exhibit at public or trade shows as part of their PR programme of communicating with their particular publics.

PR Support

The value of a commercial or advertising exhibit can be greatly enhanced if full advantage is taken of the many PR opportunities created by exhibitions. Too often these opportunities are overlooked, or efforts are limited to placing news releases and photographs in the Press Room, which is rather a last-minute effort. Some exhibitors produce lavish press kits, packed with non-news material such as pictures of the chairman, sales literature and house journals. It is usually a waste of time and money to place press kits in Press Rooms: the author was an exhibition Press Officer for many years and he banned them. Visiting journalists do not carry suitcases, and most press kits are wasted. Some examples of PR support for a participant in an exhibition are:

(*a*) Contact the exhibition press officer as soon as the contract for stand space is signed, and ask what help he requires. Usually, he will be sending out advance information, and needs details from exhibitors (at least about the organisation and what it does even if what is to be shown is undecided or secret). Some exhibitors fail to assist like this because they wish to be secretive, but there is no need to give away vital information. The publicity achieved by the exhibition press officer (sometimes overseas) will help to increase the number of visitors to shows, which is to every exhibitor's advantage.

(*b*) It may be that by finding out, at an early date, the identity of the official opener an approach can be made direct to him or her (even if it is a member of the Royal Family or a Government minister) to visit the stand during the official tour. This can be very important. The tour will last only a short time, and since an exhibition may consist of several hundred stands it is impossible for the official opener to stop at each one. Consequently, well in advance, the official opener will have an itinerary drawn up of stands to be visited. It will be necessary to make such an approach, usually through the VIP's secretary or PRO, weeks and maybe months in advance.

(*c*) Newspapers and magazines may be publishing previews of the event. Often, they contact all exhibitors and seek information, and these invitations should not be ignored. Advertisement space does not have to be purchased unless this is thought to be valuable.

(*d*) The exhibition press officer will usually call a press preview or, in the case of a big show, organise a press day. It is wise for exhibitors to have important company personalities available on the stand. The exhibitor may also invite journalists direct, or have a private press reception on the stand.

(*e*) During the run of the exhibition there are often opportunities to secure media coverage as when a large order can be announced, or the stand receives an important visitor. At some exhibitions there will be facilities for distributing such news (e.g. Universal News Services).

(*f*) If a new product with export potential is to be shown it will be useful to advise the Central Office of Information well in advance as they may be interested in issuing overseas news stories, filming the exhibit or taping a radio interview.

(*g*) Newspapers, magazines and freelance journalists (who may be writing for overseas journals) may prepare reports on the show which will appear afterwards, and advantage may be taken of these opportunities to gain post-exhibition publicity.

(*h*) The producers of relevant radio and television programmes may be invited to gain ideas for future programmes.

(*i*) During the run of the exhibition a special press reception can be held on the stand or in a room at the exhibition hall.

From these suggestions it is clear that an enterprising PRO can obtain a great deal of coverage from a purely advertising stand. But he must know about the company's participation in the exhibition as soon as the contract is signed, not asked to supply news releases for the Press Room at the last minute. This also applies to PR consultants servicing clients who exhibit.

Exhibition Promoters' PR

There have been sufficient references in the preceding section to indicate that the PRO employed by the promoters or sponsors of the exhibition has a special type of PR job to do. His efforts are three-sided: he has to inform prospective exhibitors, then prospective visitors before and during the show, and to achieve follow-up coverage. Moreover, much exhibition PR is of a continuous nature, following on from one event to the next, the coverage for one helping its successor.

Large exhibition promoters like Industrial Trade Fairs of Birmingham have a permanent team of PROs who work on a number of shows. The British Overseas Trade Board has a publicity unit which conducts PR for annual All-British exhibitions and British participation in overseas trade fairs. Smaller shows may employ PR consultants, and sponsoring organisations such as trade associations employ their regular PRO to service their events.

The exhibition PRO may be involved in the following tasks:

(*a*) The organisation of PR activities such as a press reception and issue of news releases to announce a forthcoming exhibition.

(*b*) Issue of details to all publications which publish a diary of forthcoming exhibitions.

(*c*) Cooperation with government agencies which circulate information abroad about exhibitions such as the Central Office of Information and the British Overseas Trade Board.

(*d*) Seek advance information from exhibitors.

(*e*) Distribute advance information, including translated versions to the overseas press.

(*f*) Negotiate, write and publish feature articles prior to the show.

(*g*) Cooperate with arrangements for the official opening.

(*h*) Organise a press preview or press day and media coverage of the official opening, and manage it on the day.

(*i*) Advise exhibitors of press preview or press day arrangements.

(*j*) Invite news releases and captioned photographs for the Press Room.

(*k*) Prepare the Press Room, displaying news releases on tables or racks, and displaying photographs and captions on panels, the photographs being numbered and stocks being kept in a filing cabinet. Press kits are not required.

(*l*) Obtain maximum coverage of the official opening in the press and on radio and television as this can produce important publicity at the beginning of the show and so attract visitors.

(*m*) Maintain the Press Room throughout the run of the exhibition, assisting journalists with information, sometimes arranging to send material to their offices, and providing hospitality as required.

(*n*) Invite exhibitors to inform the Press Room of any activities, such as visits by VIPs, which can be put on a notice board in the Press Room.

(*o*) Some exhibitions publish a daily bulletin or house journal which the PRO will edit, have printed, and distribute.

(*p*) Produce an end-of-exhibition report on exhibitors' comments.

(*q*) Monitor and announce attendance figures, especially if it is a large public exhibition when, say, the millionth visitor will be celebrated.

Different exhibitions will have their special needs and possibilities but the above is a typical list of duties. It is a very busy job and in some exhibition centres the Press Room can be small and placed in an obscure part of the building since most of the area is taken up by the exhibits.

PR Exhibitions

Here we refer to the use of the exhibition as yet another private or created PR medium, with or without a large audience. They may be portable or permanent. The various kinds are:

(*a*) **Portable exhibitions.** These may be designed and constructed so that they can be taken apart and transported to a venue. They may be working models, or sets of panels or frames, forming mini-exhibitions which can be assembled at a conference, or in hotel rooms, public libraries, schools, theatre foyers, department stores, shop windows or other suitable situations. A number of building societies find that window displays on all sorts of unassociated topics attract attention to an otherwise uninteresting space, and these can be mini-exhibitions organised by enterprising PROs and toured from branch to branch.

(*b*) **Permanent exhibitions.** These are usually on company premises, but for a number of years Monsanto have enjoyed a permanent exhibition at Brussels Airport in the form of long stretches of Acrilan carpet which millions of passengers have to walk on when they arrive or depart. A permanent exhibition is ideal for an organisation which receives groups of visitors. At its Lambeth headquarters the Pharmaceutical Society has a beautiful exhibition appropriate to its profession, serving as part of the décor of the building. Permanent exhibits can also be mounted at trade centres which governments set up in overseas markets (e.g. the American and Japanese centres in London, the British one in Tokyo), or in particular trade centres such as the Building Centres in London and provincial cities.

(c) **Mobile exhibitions.** Great ingenuity has been applied to the touring exhibition which can take a compact show from place to place by road, rail, sea and even air. The possibilities are endless, ranging from a simple caravan to a train which can stop in a bay at a local station or to a floating exhibition like the Japanese trade ships. There are also custom-built exhibition vehicles and converted double-decker buses, or simple Land Rovers that take combined film shows, demonstrations and song and dance teams to the villages in developing countries. Mobile exhibitions using road vehicles are set up in market squares, car parks, school playgrounds, hotel yards, or at agricultural shows, gymkhanas, sports events and so on.

Sponsorship of Exhibitions

This special aspect of exhibitions—the use of an exhibition as a communication activity of an organisation such as a trade association—is discussed in the exhibitions section of Chapter 29.

32

MEDIA IN DEVELOPING COUNTRIES

There are three ways of looking at PR media in developing countries. First, there is the dearth of Western-style mass media; secondly, there are the limitations of the existing mass media; and thirdly there are the problems, special needs and special techniques of communicating with illiterates and people, often remotely located, of different ethnic groups, languages, dialects, religions and life styles.

Dearth of Western-style Mass Media

Sometimes called elitist media, the number and circulation of newspapers, the number of television sets and number and kind of viewers, and the number of radio sets and listeners will depend on the following factors:

(*a*) *The extent of literacy*, which in turn will depend on the extent of primary education on the one hand and adult literacy education on the other.

(*b*) *The sophistication of the economy and the number of people in the cash economy.* This will influence the size of the market, the justification for advertising, and the ability for media to be commercially viable. There are several ways of looking at this. A country may depend on a particular crop or mineral—sugar, cocoa, copper or rubber—and if there is a slump in the world market the economy will suffer. A net exporter may become a net importer so that restrictions will be placed on imports; or a large number of people may be outside the cash economy either because they are subsistence farmers who sell little or no surplus produce and have no spending power, or because they are young people who earn nothing. Developing countries do not have the ageing population common in the West: 50 per cent of the population are often under 15 years of age.

Limitations of the Existing Mass Media

In addition to the above basic factors there are also reasons why the existing media suffer from limitations—press, radio and television will now be discussed separately.

The Press

Limitations may be of the following kinds, or be caused by the following conditions:

(*a*) Because there may be a number of principal languages (e.g. English, Malay, Chinese, Indian) no newspaper will be able to attain the mass circulation that is possible when there is one language as in Britain. Where there are numerous tribal languages people may not read and write in these languages so that vernacular newspapers are not possible, but even if vernacular newspapers are possible the circulations will be small.

187

(*b*) Low circulations usually mean a small number of pages so that their contents will be limited.

(*c*) Political news may dominate so that there is little space for private sector news and information. This may be because the press is a state mouthpiece. However, in Nigeria the return to civil government, the new political party controversies and the frenzy of new developments make political news so interesting that new publications have emerged, to quote only the *National Concord*. But in more autocratic states a presidential speech may fill two or three daily issues of a newspaper.

(*d*) The high cost of newsprint may restrict the supply of newspapers, as in Ghana and Zambia, even though more copies could be sold.

(*e*) There may be distribution problems due to long distances and poor transportation.

Television

In some parts of the world television has become less of an elitist medium as a result of community viewing in halls, or because sets with 12-volt car batteries have overcome the lack of electricity. Nevertheless, television in the Third World may suffer from the following weaknesses:

(*a*) Only a limited number of people can afford a television set.

(*b*) Only urban areas may be electrified, leaving the rural community without power for television sets. The situation varies from country to country. One can find nomads living in tents on the outskirts of town, and enjoying their television. A vast country like Indonesia has a widespread television service, using a satellite, and lack of electricity is overcome by the use of 12-volt battery sets. Yet in Nigeria the battery set has not been adopted (in spite of the demand for electricity having risen from 3 per cent a year to 70 per cent since the oil bonanza), and prospective viewers look forward to the benefits from the new power station at Sapele.

(*c*) While community viewing has popularised television, programmes are in the evening and since it is usually not the custom for women to go out then audiences are limited to men. Young people are also likely to be excluded.

(*d*) Programme material is usually poor. Video-tape is expensive, studios have limited capacity and equipment, newsreading and acting experience are meagre, outside broadcasts are rare and foreign programmes may be too expensive or restricted by import controls. The poor quality of programmes also deters some people from watching television.

(*e*) The viability of television—which affects the quality of programmes—can be influenced by the lack of advertising revenue if the market economy is limited or depressed.

Radio

There is a common belief that radio is the answer to communications in developing countries because it can so easily penetrate distances, and one does not have to be able to read and write to listen to broadcasts. This has been found to be an oversimplification, and radio suffers its own limitations for the following reasons:

(*a*) In large countries with large rural populations containing a variety of ethnic groups radio may represent a remote and distant centre, unrelated to local interests. Radio can therefore lack credibility, and there can be a great wastage of audience. This may not be realised by the broadcasting authority.

(*b*) Nevertheless, all sorts of people may enjoy radio for its companionship and entertainment. In some countries in large land masses with neighbouring and nearby countries foreign radio programmes may be preferred if they provide the desired programmes such as popular music.

(*c*) It is not always satisfactory to provide multi-language programmes for two reasons:

(i) There may be too many languages.

(ii) If the programmes are broadcast from one station, only a short portion of the day can be devoted to each language with the result that speakers of other languages are deprived of broadcasts. Consequently, radio becomes a very limited medium.

(*d*) Even more seriously, surveys have revealed that although large numbers of people are believed to possess receivers a surprising number of sets are not working. There are two reasons for this:

(i) Developing countries suffer from being sold imported technical products which cannot be serviced or repaired, and they are often too expensive to be replaced.

(ii) Batteries are often expensive, and radios fall into disuse because people cannot afford to buy new batteries.

(*e*) Electricity may not be available so that mains electric receivers cannot be used.

These are problems which do not confront broadcasting in industrial countries. Yet, in spite of all these difficulties radio can penetrate the large populations of developing countries. Box or rediffusion radio is cheap and popular and may be available in public places such as cafés. Rediffusion is common in Singapore homes. Radio can be listened to by illiterates who are beyond the reach of newspapers. Thus, radio audiences are likely to be far greater than newspaper readerships. And radio has been shown to command authority in situations of emergency or national importance touching on the lives of the whole population—for example, in times of war, political upheavals or environmental disasters. In countries of vast distances, radio has also been successful for educational purposes, lessons being broadcast which can be listened to by individuals, listening groups or classes of students.

Other Mass Media

How else can one reach people on a broad scale in multi-ethnic, multi-language, multi-religious societies? One successful technique is through the use of pictures and diagrams which can inform without the need for words. Visual messages can be applied to give-away leaflets (useful in villages) or on posters where sites exist in or near towns. Posters can also be displayed on public transport which travels about the country. The poster method showing, say, parents and two children, has spread the idea of planned parenthood in many parts of the world, especially in Asia. In a similar way, cartoon drawings can be used to explain many things to illiterates. Even so, there are problems and the artist needs to beware of the literal meanings people may place on pictures.

A simple matchstick figure may seem sufficient—but unless the mouth is curved to resemble a smile it may be thought that the character disapproves!

Folk, Traditional and Other Localised Media

For centuries, people have communicated with one another, although in the past only scholars and scribes used written or drawn symbols. Many of these simple forms of communication are still practised. Even in Britain the town crier survives, and in villages in West Africa the *gong man* or court messenger still proclaims the news in the morning and evening, acting as the communication medium between the local ruler and his people. It may be necessary to have PR messages conveyed in this way in order to give them credibility and to reach people who are outside the orbit of Western-style mass media.

But to do this we must first convince the sender of the news—the king, emir, oba or headman. This is where the **innovator theory** comes into play: we have to gain the understanding, sympathy and acceptance of an innovator who will then influence others to adopt his advice. This method is not confined to unsophisticated societies. It has been used the world over: who would ever have flown the Atlantic if Blériot had not first flown the Channel? All new ideas need innovators who take them up so that others may follow. A typical example is the farm machine, the first user inviting neighbours to see a demonstration. In Third World countries the same psychology, the same follow-my-leader system, can apply when the use of modern mass media will fail. The techniques which McCormick used to sell labour-saving machinery to labour-starved prairie farmers is being used today to create a power farming agricultural revolution in Nigeria where urbanisation has drained the little village farms of family labour.

Literacy is not only to do with reading and writing. There can be *visual* and *oral* literacy. So-called 'illiterate' people often possess visual literacy superior to that of Westerners, and have an 'eye-witness' skill which is quite uncanny. Similarly, in West Africa, for example, one finds 'illiterate' street-traders who act as postmen between villages and their friends and relatives in town, carrying elaborate messages word perfect in their heads. These forms of communication should not be overlooked when communicating with people in developing countries.

Yet another important form of vocal communication is **market gossip.** In developing countries with small farms and surplus produce, or local craftsmen with wares to sell, the market provides a meeting place where news is shared. Consequently, market gossip is a medium for spreading information.

Open Air Events

Open air events are more common in warm climates and they appeal to the gregarious instinct of people who have little entertainment. It may be an exhibition or agricultural show, or a mobile demonstration or mobile cinema which tours villages where newspapers are unknown and radio sets may be rare or radio has little impact, while television is unknown. A crowd will gather to watch a film shown on a screen erected on the roof of a Land Rover. These may be called van cinemas, and the terms 'mobile' or 'static' may be used to distinguish between the visiting and the permanent city cinema (covered or drive-in).

But the audience figures and effectiveness of mobile cinema may be subject to doubt. Mobile audience figures have been researched in Kenya, based on an official or policeman estimating crowd numbers. The size of a crowd may not be very helpful if it includes hosts of children! There can be two other problems with mobile cinemas. First, they are infrequent, and even regular monthly tours allow a big memory or impact gap between one showing and another. This applies equally to advertising and information films. Second, the films may be too long to retain concentration, or too sophisticated and contain too many unfamiliar subjects to be comprehensible.

Thus they may defy the **span of consciousness**, the **visual perception time** and be outside the **limits of experience.** To be effective, a film shown to unsophisticated audiences should avoid the 'visual vocabulary block' by *repeating* the message; it should be short enough to hold the attention; and should avoid using scenes or objects which are *foreign* to limited local knowledge and experience.

Very few Western-style documentaries are suitable for such audiences. The sight of a skyscraper to people used to mud huts may arouse howls of derision, disbelief or terror. MGM's lion has been known to empty a cinema in Africa. All this is little different from the fear of American tourists for British double-decker buses which they expect to fall over. It is perhaps hard to believe that Westerners are often more familiar with wild animals than natives of the countries from which these creatures originate. In Nigeria, the author found that a lion at Ibadan University zoo had been donated by Longleat, and when he visited Kano zoo his Nigerian companions were amazed at the huge size of *baby* elephants. Lusaka has a zoo in which Zambians often see for the first time the animals which roam in their great national parks. Such countries rarely have, as in Kenya, giraffes visible from the road and a ban on hoardings because they interfere with the view for the tourists! When Western firms make films for showing to people in developing countries they should remember that the content needs to be credible to people with very different life styles and experiences. And it can be different in the sense that it is more intensely cultural, as in the East, and less materialistic than it is in the West. Different does not mean inferior.

Gregarious people living in simple surroundings often welcome entertainment when it comes to their village. The van may bring films and song and dance teams may accompany it. There may be more local forms of communication such as the **village theatre** which can be used to dramatise a message, something which can be used for bringing new ideas to villagers. You can educate through entertainment.

Very effective when there are linguistic problems is the **puppet show** since messages can be mimed, and this is a medium which has been used for PR purposes in Africa and Asia. In countries where 'public enlightenment' programmes are organised to improve farming, sanitation, hygiene, child welfare and so on, such methods can overcome the fact that millions of people are beyond the reach of so-called mass media. They are not to be dismissed for they buy goods, pay taxes, vote in elections, and have rights to public services.

PART 5

PRACTICAL ASPECTS OF PUBLIC RELATIONS

33

PRESS MATERIAL

In this Part we deal with the 'nuts and bolts' of PR—in other words, how to do it. Strange as it may seem, this is where so many PROs and so much PR fails. This is where PR becomes the great untrained profession. Books philosophise about PR. Courses delve into the sociology of mass communications. But how to do it rarely gets taught. Consequently, a lot of PR practitioners practise press relations very badly, and PR too often has the image it deserves because incompetence abounds. Eighty per cent of the news releases which hit Fleet Street editors' desks every morning are rejected. Ask any editor.

Regrettably, this is true on a world scale. As long ago as 1906 the American PR consultant Ivy Ledbetter Lee established the criteria that PR material should be 'of interest and value' to the reader, but sadly the PR world has often ignored these principles the world over.

In Britain it is common to speak of editors filling their large plastic dustbins with 70–80 per cent of the releases they receive. In the USA the percentage is higher according to *IABC News* (San Francisco, September 1980), which carried the following report:

EDITORS TOSS 9 OF 10 RELEASES
Nine out of ten news releases sent to US daily newspapers from business, industry and organisations never see print, according to a recent study by journalist Professor Bill Baxter at the University of Oklahoma.

Managing editors surveyed at 123 daily newspapers reported using only 9.2 per cent of all news releases received from public relations sources.

Chief reason for rejection was lack of local or regional tie-in. Other reasons for non-use was too much advertising puffery, releases were too long and cumbersome, and, in many cases, they arrived too late to be useful.

'Too many PR people don't know the difference between news and advertising,' said one editor. 'It looks like the copy was written to impress bosses and not necessarily for print.'

'PR people should target their material more selectively and try to write more for individual papers,' said another respondent.

In a similar survey conducted in 1978 among editors in Oklahoma, Baxter found that editors in that state used only 8 per cent of news releases they received from corporations, businesses, organisations and government agencies. Most editors agreed they would rather see improvement in release programmes than curtailment.

Professor Baxter's findings provide ample justification for the pre-testing of releases, as the American PR consultant James B. Strenski suggested in the *IPRA Review* (see quotation in Chapter 16).

The love–hate relationship between journalists and PR practitioners is not only jealousy because colleagues have found greener fields. Most journalists—unless they are senior ones with worldly experience—are unsuitable as PR recruits. Their standard of education is often too low, their experience too limited, and their outlook too cynical and bigoted. Something of this is expressed in journalistic semantics: the use of 'PR' for PRO; 'handout' for news release; 'propaganda' for business news; 'hidden persuader' for PRO.

This is not to deny that some very accomplished PR practitioners were originally journalists, partly because there was a reservoir of unemployed journalists and partly because employers either wanted press officers rather than PROs or mistakenly believed that only a journalist could be a PRO.

Nowadays, while still second or third career people, PR practitioners are recruited from many more fields than journalism, and the trend is towards people coming in with suitable academic training. Eventually, recruits must be those who are vocationally trained and qualified in public relations, as in most other professions such as accountancy, architecture, pharmacy, teaching or the law.

We travelled far in the late 1970s to discover that a great deal of PR had little to do with the mass media, that it also dealt with one-to-one or small group communications, and with non-marketing, financial, internal and international aspects of communication.

Nevertheless, in industrial countries—in spite of all the new and fashionable electronic media—the press remains a huge, diversified and dominant medium. It is still of greater value to the PR practitioner than either radio or television. In Britain alone there are some 6000 publications (according to *Benn's Press Directory*) if one includes newspapers, periodicals, house journals and directories. The press grows continuously in the developing world, matching the growth of education and literacy. So, no matter how more sophisticated the media become and how more far-ranging the activities of the PRO become, the press will, for a long time to come, deserve to be served more proficiently than has been its experience so far.

It is not, therefore, contradictory to say that press relations is only a part of modern PR while at the same time emphasising that in an industrial country the press is a substantial and dominant communication medium.

There is a wilful, obstinate belief by too many people in the PR world that nothing has to be learned about writing news releases. This is intensified by the fact that managing directors, marketing and advertising managers, advertising agents and other press relations amateurs think that not only can *they* write (or re-write) news releases, but that they have the right to be published.

Another mistaken belief occasionally held is that the press is the Fourth Estate, a quaint idea that belongs to the constitution of the United States, not ours. The British press is published by courtesy of mostly Commonwealth press barons plus the advertisers, and sometimes at a financial loss because trade unions are reluctant to accept modern technology which would put many newspaper print workers on the dole. The struggle has in recent years resulted in the year-long stoppage of *The Times*, the demise of the London *Evening News*, and general industrial unrest in the printing and publishing industries.

What is News?

William Randolph Hearst, one-time American newspaper tycoon, once defined news as being *what someone, somewhere doesn't want you to print—all the rest is advertising*. The press of the world seems to have adopted that advice wholeheartedly in its attitude to PR material.

Journalists take a coy attitude to naming names. When the news is bad it is 'good news' and names will be named, but when the news is good this is regarded as advertising. Journalists make little distinction between business or other PR news and advertising. This, of course, is not helped by news release writers who do not understand the difference either!

Just to show how universal is this attitude, here is an example taken from the internationally distributed *South African Digest* (November 30, 1979). It was the caption to a PR picture of a pretty girl with a Smurf doll in the palm of her hand. It read:

> The Smurfs—cartoon characters that have proved extremely popular throughout the world—are now in South Africa. They have been introduced through the national network of service stations of a major oil company. Here a member of the 50-strong Smurf family takes a bow.

One has to be grateful that the editor did not censor the word Smurf!

On one occasion the author attempted to discuss this problem with the editor of the *Daily Mirror* in which a picture story had appeared without naming the company involved. The editor replied with a long sarcastic letter asking why they should not have named the makers of every item in the picture down to the boots worn by the man who was carrying out some special work on Buckingham Palace. Well, they did mention Buckingham Palace. Being a left-wing newspaper it was surprising that the *Daily Mirror* did not describe the Palace as being 'the home of a well-known monarch'.

So, news depends a lot on the bias of the editor or of the particular publication, yet if the news release writer is to be successful he needs to supply original information of interest and value to the readers of the journals to which he sends it. News does not necessarily have to be 'new' if it has not previously been made known, but it must not be stale news in the sense that it is obviously dated.

One also has to be careful about stating that something happened 'recently' for how recent is recent? This depends on how often a publication is published. A monthly magazine may print a story about an event which happened after the previous issue was published, but a daily will not print a story about something which happened the day before yesterday, unless it came from a remote destination from which news travels slowly. A weekly local newspaper printed on Thursday and sold on Friday is usually unable to report Thursday night's events, and will not hold such news for the following week's issue. Even so, if the item is sufficiently important, special efforts may be made as when Prince Charles opened a new police station in Croydon on a Thursday. Pictures did appear in the next day's issue of the weekly *Croydon Advertiser*, but this was a very rare exception which called for some very tight production scheduling.

Credibility

A quality which distinguishes PR news material as being publishable in the eyes of editors is its credibility. We may have said some harsh things about journalists, but the right perspective is necessary. They are not white knights bringing their great reading public the unvarnished truth. They are making a living or a profit by giving people what they want to read. In Britain, what most people want to read will be found in *The Sun* and the *News of the*

World, in Germany in *Bild*, in Nigeria in *The Punch*, and it was ever thus since the crowds cheered in the Coliseum and probably long before. The majority of people do not want to read newspapers like *The Times*. The news release writer needs to understand that on the whole few people want to read what he writes unless. . . .

Exactly. How does one compete with the murder and violence, the sex and corruption, and the other norms which make up the average person's reading taste? How do commercial firms succeed in getting into the dramatic columns of *The Sun* and the *Daily Mirror*? Or in any other publication? We have already said that releases must be of *interest* and *value* to the reader, but they must also be *credible*. Unless people are likely to believe in the story it will not get published.

Nowadays, people are sceptical about advertising, and they will be sceptical of any story which smacks of either advertising or one-sidedness. If an editor suspects that a story is a cover-up or an attempt to put the best side on things, he may well expose this effort to hoodwink the media and the public. Unfortunately, there are many releases which are blatant attempts to pretend things are what they are not. Whatever the biases of the various media or journalists, a news release must be *impartial* and *factual* if it is to be credible.

To be acceptable *a news release has to be like a piece of plain wood which others can cut, shape, polish, paint or use as they wish*. The cutting, shaping, polishing, painting or special use must not be pre-empted by the sender. Bare facts, without comment or self-praise, have credibility. Many rejected releases are simply *unbelievable*.

Local government PROs have a running battle with the media. The media believe that town hall news is little more than propaganda, while the elected representatives and local government officers believe that they are either mis-represented or inadequately covered by the media. In some cases, local authorities publish their own civic newspapers in order to get a fair and adequate press. Nevertheless, Peter Manning, Press Officer of Cornwall County Council, had this to say in an article in *UK Press Gazette* (December 17, 1979): '. . . credibility to a communicator is like topsoil to a farmer who can get a high price for selling it but can only sell it once.'

Originality

It does help if a story has originality. This may be difficult with a mundane subject like soup, but consider what happened when Esther Rantzen, while inviting members of the public to try her bat soup for her *That's Life* television programme was arrested for obstruction. *The Sun* (October 17, 1980) head-lined the story thus:

> BAT'S LIFE!
> ESTHER IS
> RUN IN
> *Arrest stops soup test*

An example of a PR story which achieved remarkable coverage in the press and on radio and television, and which was released by a marketing manager with little PR know-how or experience but a lot of commonsense, succeeded because it was of interest and value and had credibility and originality. It was about camel-milking, not in the Sahara but in Reading, Berkshire. The delightful simple release read:

The Milking Equipment Division of Gascoignes based at Reading are to export a camel-milking parlour for the Royal Camel Herd of King Khalid of Saudi Arabia.

The parlour has been developed over a period of months in conjunction with the agricultural export company, OAD (Agriculture) Ltd, of Hermitage, Newbury, Berks. Managing Director of OAD, Mr Taylor, is also a Director of the West Country Wildlife Park at Cricket St Thomas and his experience with camels proved useful with the development work.

The parlour was tested for size in Reading last week when three camels were loaned by Chipperfields of Longleat to have a trial run.

The development of the camel as an efficient converter of poor quality food and water into meat and milk has aroused a lot of interest from many of the countries where camels are indigenous. Up until now little research has actually been done on the camel.

OAD are now trying to locate an experienced camel milker to go to Saudi Arabia to train the operators of the equipment.

Further details from F. Flatman, Export Manager, or Robin Smith, Marketing Planning Manager.

This was supplemented by half-a-dozen telephone calls to the media. The story was included in *News At Ten* on independent television, there was an interview on the BBC Radio I *Newsbeat* programme, Southern BBC showed film on their news bulletin, reports appeared in the *Daily Telegraph, Daily Mail*, and *Daily Express*, stories and pictures appeared in the local press, the Central Office of Information distributed the story to its Middle East press contacts, and the BBC World Service broadcast it.

As marketing planning manager R. Smith commented afterwards: 'To sum the subject up in one sentence, I would say "Always be aware of, and on the look-out, for a PR story".' This effort was faultless from company, media, reader, viewer and listener standpoints. But it is the kind of opportunity and action missed by so many industrial exporters who cannot be bothered with PR. An important point here is that this story was handled by neither a company PRO nor a PR consultant but by a PR-minded marketing man who had his criteria right. In the words of Max Bygraves, it was a case of 'I wanna tell you a story'.

Language and Vocabulary

It does not matter what sort of story it is—whether it is destined for *The Sun* or the *Financial Times, Heating and Ventilating Review* or *The Lancet*—short words, short sentences and short paragraphs are preferable. If there are unavoidable long technical words, fair enough.

Short words mean that more can be said in the space. Short words will not be broken in narrow columns. Short sentences, provided the effect is not too abrupt, and short paragraphs with their indentations, help to speed the flow of reading and the ease of understanding. Tortuous language and two-page paragraphs may have suited the leisured matrons who read Henry James, but Ernest Hemingway changed all that.

Some examples of short words which are preferable to long ones are the following:

live	*for*	reside	try	*for*	endeavour
death		mortality	climb		ascend
food		sustenance	poor		impecunious
job		employment	tiny		infinitesimal

This is not to say that to avoid the monotony of repeated use a different and perhaps longer word should not be used, but the news release does have a space problem. Longer words are better for articles and books which benefit from a rich vocabulary, a more literary style, and more reading time. Short words, sentences and paragraphs not only help the story to fit space that is scarce, but result in less subediting, less rewriting and less opportunity for editorial staff to get things wrong. It is very hard to alter a sentence which is so tight and precise that there is no better way of writing it.

Dr Rudolf Flesch, in his admirable work *The Art of Readable Writing* (Harper Bros, New York, 1949), set the following criteria: 'Use short words— 150 syllables per 100 words; short sentences—no more than 19 words per sentence. Human interest should be at the rate of 6 per cent names, personal pronouns or words referring to people or having masculine or feminine gender.'

Clichés should be avoided and to add 'at all costs' or 'like the plague' would be use of a cliché. News releases seem to have their own clichés, of which 'unique' is the worst since few things are unique, and 'exhaustive research', 'ultra-modern', 'this point in time', 'facilitates', and 'breakthrough' are common examples. Probably the most hackneyed expression used by all kinds of communicators is 'a wide range', for which there are many substitutes such as 'a wide variety', 'a large range', 'a large variety' or 'a wide choice'.

Apt words should be selected. Repetition of words should be controlled. The news release writer should use his *Roget's Thesaurus* or *The Synonym Finder* to increase and sharpen his vocabulary.

Americans are given to long words, and to words which are peculiarly American. One suspects the German influence on American English! American scholars have tried to stop American newspapers using words such as 'parenting', 'medication' and 'orientation'. To these might be added 'escalation' and 'harassment'. Then there are those double emphatic bits of nonsense such as 'completely destroyed', 'true facts', 'most unique', 'really unique', 'utterly false', and 'totally untrue'.

We also need to beware of generalisations, which may be acceptable in more emotive and less explicit advertisement copy. We should explain why a product is 'economical in use', 'handy', 'easy to make', 'compact', 'lightweight', 'money-saving', 'generous' or 'convenient'. The facts, the details, must be stated in such a way that the attributes are implied.

Similarly, vague expressions such as the longest, tallest, shortest, biggest, smallest, or cheapest should be implied by facts, not used as puffs or left open to challenge. One also has to be very careful about stating that anything is 'first'—are you sure about this claim? Editors dislike receiving contradictions and having to print disclaimers. They may add the derogatory words 'claimed to be . . .'.

Writing the Release

Journalists tend to follow the news story rule of the Five W's: who, what, when, where and why. That is, *who* is the story about, *what* happened, *when* did it happen, *where* did it happen, *why* did it happen, and sometimes adding a sixth, *what* were the consequences?

A news release differs from this slightly if only that it is seldom a personal story. For *who* it is best to substitute the **subject**. But the subject may not be the *who*, and the **organisation** or the **product** will replace the individual. Moreover, the subject is more likely to be what the organisation has done or the product so that *what* displaces the journalist's *who*. We shall return to this again because the subject of the story is so important.

Some excellent advice on news release writing was given by the Council for Small Industries in Rural Areas to local businessmen. To quote:

If space is short, editors will run the blue pencil through the lower paragraphs. They are busy men. The first paragraph must hold and attract.

If you have to wade through three paragraphs before getting to the point, then the chances are that they will have given up before then.

Also write good basic English. Avoid jargon and journalese. Write for the readership and don't try to sell the product or firm.

You are not writing advertising copy and there can be no quicker way of finding the wastepaper basket than to write a thinly-disguised puff.

Also be topical. There must be a basic reason for telling the story and you have to find that peg on which to hang the story.

Robert D. Irvine put it another way in *Journal of Organizational Communication* (Vol. 8, No. 2, 1979) when he wrote: 'Follow the "inverted pyramid" style of writing, i.e. have the important ideas and significant quotes at the beginning followed by progressively more detailed, less crucial information. The lead sentence should capture the one or two ideas that inspired the release.'

Importance of the Opening Paragraph

The above quotations all emphasise the importance of the **subject** and the **opening paragraph**, the two features which can make or mar the success of a news release. This is not understood by those who write the majority of rejected releases.

Nothing has given PR a worse name than the bad news release, not all the gin and junkets for which PR is supposedly infamous.

Nothing is done so badly by so many PR practitioners. *Ask any editor anywhere in the world.*

Yet it is perfectly easy to write a publishable news release. It is also perfectly easy not to write, or not to issue, an unpublishable one.

Remarkable though this may be, some PROs do not expect their work to be published. They expect someone in an editorial office to rewrite it for them. Why should they?

To prove the point, the author has published hundreds of news releases, mostly exactly as he wrote them. Sometimes, of course, they have been adapted to meet the particular style of a publication but in essence the message was identical.

Some releases are not addressed to the reader, but to the editor. They begin with flowery expressions such as 'We are pleased to announce', while others are written like letters with salutations. Pronouns should be avoided: the editor is not going to use 'we' or 'you'.

The easiest way to learn how to write a news release is to read newspaper reports and study how they are written. Most editors are convinced that the majority of PROs never read newspapers, otherwise they would never submit such rubbish. If newspapers are studied it will be found that we are back to where we began—with the **subject** and the **opening paragraph**.

It will be found that in every story in every paper two things characterise press reports. First, **the subject is stated in the first few words.** Second, **the gist of the story is given in the opening paragraph.** There are no teasers, no clever introductions. The whole story is 'blown' or given away right at the beginning. The rest of the report substantiates the story. It is as simple as that. In fact, if one read the opening paragraph of each report one would have a complete digest of the newspaper's news.

Yet it is rare to find the subject of a news release in the first three paragraphs, perhaps not even on the first page.

To return to the advice given by the Council for Small Industries in Rural Areas and Robert D. Irvine, four things are likely to result from writing a release professionally:

1. An editor can see at a glance what the story is about for, as the news editor of the *Financial Times* once told the author, an editor has 'one second flat' to judge each release in his daily pile.

2. If there is little space, *at least* the opening paragraph may get printed. If it is a good summary you are home and dry.

3. If a longer story is printed it will be capable of being cut *from the bottom* up as can occur when a story is printed at length in an early edition—when news may be scarce—and then cut in each succeeding edition until perhaps only the first paragraph remains in the final edition. This can happen in evening newspapers, the first edition appearing early in the day, and the final edition appearing when people are going home from work.

4. If the story is written as the editor would have written it there is no point in him changing it. Editors are busy people. On some publications (e.g. trade magazines) they have no assistants to rewrite stories and may well print the ones that provide them with the least work. Why should they burrow through three pages of terrible prose to find the thirty or forty words they have space to print? A news release has to compete with hundreds of other releases, but the professionally written releases, *the rarity*, really have no competitors.

The Subject

A major fault with too many releases is that they start with the name of the organisation, which is seldom the subject. Unfortunately, to the sender, his organisation is all-important. Some stories begin with a long-winded presentation of the name, e.g. 'The Universal Engineering Company Limited, a member of the International Engineering Group, . . .'. Who cares—apart from the managing director and the company secretary? Of those twelve words only *Universal Engineering* are publishable in an opening sentence. Most journalists will make these the *last* two words of the sentence. Thus, an acceptable sentence might be: 'A new electronically controlled crane for the construction industry is now available from Universal Engineering of Luton.'

What is the subject? It could be different for different classes and categories of journal. It pays to write special versions of stories, not send the same story to every editor, and this will call for careful decisions about the appropriate subject for the opening paragraph. To take the example of the crane, subjects could range from its electronic interest to the fact that it was British, from its local manufacture to its use on an important construction job.

From many of these remarks it will be apparent by now that while it is not difficult to write a good release, the skilled writer will, in the words of Lord Geddes, 'squeeze the orange until the pips squeak'. Maximising press coverage means marketing a story so that the fullest possible coverage is won. We shall return to this when discussing mailing lists.

Seven-Point News Release Model

The discussion so far leads logically to the adoption of the Seven-Point Model which the author has used to provide (*a*) a checklist when researching story material, (*b*) a plot for the release, and (*c*) a means of checking that nothing vital has been omitted.

The SOLAADS Seven-Point Model

1. **Subject**—what is the story about?
2. **Organisation**—what is the name of the organisation?
3. **Location**—what is the location of the organisation?
4. **Advantages**—what is new, special, beneficial about the product or service?
5. **Applications**—how or by whom can the product or service be used or enjoyed?
6. **Details**—what are the specifications or details of colours, prices, sizes and so on.
7. **Source**—if this is different from location, e.g. an airline will fly from an airport but the office may be in the city centre.

This is not a plan for seven paragraphs. The subject, organisation and location will fall into the first paragraph together with highlights of the story. Thus we have an opening paragraph which summarises the entire story and can stand alone if necessary. The story is substantiated by paragraphs which concentrate on certain types of information. Finally, it is a good idea to close with words such as: 'The Rondo lawnmower is made and marketed by the XYZ Company Ltd, Richmond Road, Ilkley, Yorkshire.'

Different Kinds of Release

So far we have concentrated on the *publishable* release since the most typical release is the one we want to get printed. There are, however, other types of release, not all of which are intended for immediate publication. The six kinds of news release are:

1. The **publishable,** as already described.
2. The **background** story which is not intended for immediate publication, but is issued as background information so that journalists are kept well informed and have the facts on file when they are writing about the subject. This kind of release can be especially useful for a long-term project such as a civil engineering job or the development of a new source of energy. Organisations which are constantly in the news such as state enterprises, oil

companies, airlines and new technology developers will issue regular background stories.

Some firms consider it helpful to distinguish between news for immediate publications and background material by having separate release headings printed with the distinctive words NEWS FROM ... and INFORMATION FROM ... followed by the company name and perhaps its logo.

3. The **technical story with summary**. Ideally, a release should be confined to one sheet of paper, but some subjects warrant longer and very technical accounts. In such cases it is helpful to the editor if the main story is preceded by a brief summary.

4. The **summary of a report, speech or document.** The object here is to bring out the important or new features of something lengthy which is being sent to the media. Journalists may not have time to read the whole speech, document or volume, and even if they did they may not know how to make comparisons or evaluations. The accompanying release can pull out the newsworthy and most relevant stories. This may guide the journalist to read for himself what is most interesting; it may provoke questions; it may attract the journalist's interest when otherwise he would have ignored the material; and some busy journalists may take your word for it and print the summary.

In the case of an advance copy of a speech, the opening paragraph technique already discussed is applicable. The summary might begin: 'The smoking of cannabis in public cinemas is opposed by the Conservative Party, Lord Wrigglebury told the Mapleton Conservative Party on Monday, January 10.'

Once again we are home and dry with an opening paragraph which is a self-sufficient message. But the statement may well occur on page 10 of the speech, whereas the summary can put it in the first paragraph of a report.

5. The **extended picture caption.** When the picture is the real news item, a longer-than-usual explanatory caption can replace the news release. There are three ways of doing this. The caption may be attached to the back of the print with Sellotape; a double perforated caption can be attached to the print, so that one copy can be used for editorial purposes and the other left to identify the picture; or the caption can be repeated on release paper, and this can accompany the captioned photograph.

6. The **brief announcement.** There is sometimes a mistaken idea that the submission of a press story is an opportunity to tell the editor as much as possible. Some releases read like confessions. On some occasions—if the sender has studied the media—they should not exceed one sentence or possibly a paragraph. This brevity will make them publishable and unalterable. One example is the change of address: some publications run a change of address column in which the essential facts are stated and no more.

Another example is the 'new appointment' story. Most publications say no more than that Mr X had left one company to join another, the job he is taking up, and maybe his age, or it may be a promotion within the same organisation. Usually, many such items are published in the feature. There may or may not be a portrait or portraits. Only a very few newspapers, e.g. *The Times* and the *Financial Times*, regularly print appointment stories; trade, technical and professional journals print very brief accounts, e.g. the cryptic items in *Campaign*, although somewhat longer stories may appear in some journals. Only the local newspaper will perhaps print a short biography if the person is sufficiently important or interesting. Yet, day after day, editors of countless newspapers receive three-page life stories, complete with large salon portraits, about hundreds of people who have been appointed or promoted. The following are typical unillustrated items from the *Financial Times*:

Professor Samuel Sey, chairman of Barclays Bank of Ghana, has been appointed a director of BARCLAYS BANK INTERNATIONAL

Mr Gordon D. S. Jones has been appointed to the Board of GALLAGHER HINTON AND VEREKER.

The trade magazine *Freight News* is slightly more generous and prints items (some with portraits) such as:

William Menzies-Wilson becomes chairman of Ocean Transport & Trading this month, following the retirement of Sir Lindsay Alexander.
Mr Menzies-Wilson was appointed deputy chairman at the beginning of the year and has been an executive director of the company since he joined the group in 1973.

Coming into our own field, *PR Bulletin* will report that:

Kate Whittaker, previously responsible for Centronics Data Computer (UK) Ltd, has been appointed associate director of MEPR.

These examples are given because this is a favourite area of PR activity. Hours of research and interviewing can be spent to produce an approved biography, and money can be spent on special photography when in fact no more than a sentence or paragraph, and probably no picture, is required. Moreover, the expectations of the person involved can be built up out of all proportion to the coverage which is easily accessible at the start. A couple of lines here and there is all that can be expected.

Presentation of Releases

A news release is a manuscript which provides copy for printing. A lot of releases ignore this requirement, simply because the PR practitioner has failed to instruct his secretary accordingly. A secretary is trained to type letters with block paragraphs, courteously to give the managing director a capital 'M' and 'D', and to insert full points between initials such as 'I.P.R.'. None of these things apply to a news release. Again, in advertisement copy the company name may be written in all-caps, e.g. FORD, and numbers may be written 5, 7 or 9, but again this would be wrong in a news release. From these remarks it is easy to appreciate that if a release is typed wrongly the editor has to correct all these faults before he can send the story to the printer. It is another way in which the release is unprofessional and helps to irritate the editor. The following are essential considerations:

1. **The news release heading.** Flamboyant, multicoloured headings are not necessary. The heading should merely distinguish it from a business letter-heading, identify the sender (e.g. by means of a logo) and give the source details (preferably at the foot of the sheet). *The maximum amount of space should be given to the story*. One colour is sufficient, and this may be the corporate identity house colour. Do not contain the text area in a border or print anything in the left and right margins.
2. **Typing style.** Use a standard typeface—not all-caps or a fancy, imitation handwriting or italic face. Do not use an extra large face because this can

spread a story over an extra page or pages. To comply with editorial and typesetting requirements all copy for print must be in double-spaced typing, with good margins on either side, and only one side of the paper may be used. The editor has to insert amendments and typographical instructions between the lines and in the margins. No one is ever going to look at the back of the sheet.

3. **The headline.** The headline should simply declare what the story is about, e.g. New Soup From Heinz. Do not try to be clever and invent, say, *S'nice Soupier Snail Soup*. Editors write their own headlines to suit the space, to fit the page design, to be different, or in line with the house style.

4. **Paragraphing.** Normal publishing style is as in this book, with paragraphs indented. Most publishers do not, however, indent the first paragraph, a tradition dating back to hand-written Bibles when the first letter (or drop capital) was drawn decoratively and very large.

5. **Subheadings or cross-heads.** Do not insert them in a release (unless they help to clarify a long piece) because the editor will use subheadings or crossheads as he wishes. This may be a typographical device to give a black and grey artistic contrast to the page.

6. **Capital letters.** As pointed out with reference to generic names at the end of Chapter 26, the press use a minimum of capital letters. Not even the *Financial Times* gives managing directors and chairmen or other official or job titles capital letters. Normally, no word should be written completely in capital letters, even if the *Financial Times* chooses to print company names in caps in new appointment stories. (It also prints the person's name in black face.) Only certain top people are given initial caps, e.g. President, Queen, Pope, Prime Minister, Defence Secretary, Chief Whip, whereas job titles are not. One should also be careful about nouns which seem to be important. Some technical writers tend to capitalise nouns indiscriminately. Capital initial letters should therefore be restricted to proper nouns such as the names of individuals and organisations, registered names and geographical place names.

7. **Full points or full stops.** The press do not use full points in abbreviations and print BL, EEC, KLM, IPR, IBM, USA and so on, but retain full points in *i.e.* and *e.g.* A full point does not follow *Mr*, *Mrs*, *Rev*, *mph* and so forth.

8. **Quotation marks.** These should be restricted to quoted speech, not used for product names, ship's names, titles or anything else. The editor will have his own style—quotation marks, italics, black face, caps and so on—which the news release writer cannot anticipate and he must therefore adopt a neutral style.

9. **Underlining.** Nothing should be underlined as this is an instruction to set in *italics*, an instruction which only the editor can give.

10. **Signs.** Do not use the % sign in a sentence. Spell out 'per cent' or 'percent'. Do not use the ampersand (&) in sentences, nor the abbreviation 'etc.'.

11. **Figures.** Except in dates, times, prices, street numbers, weights and measures and similar special uses of numbers, spell out from one to nine, then use figures until they become unwieldy thousands or millions, when it is clearly better to say ten thousand, or 10 million. Thus, one writes: 'Two men spent five hours from 8 am to 1 pm considering whether 10m tonnes of rice could reach the millions of refugees by August 30.'

12. **Dates.** Most secretaries date letters the opposite way round to editorial style. In the press the month is given first, and 'th', 'rd', 'st' and 'nd' are not used. The correct style is December 1, *not* 1st December.

13. **Continuations.** If there are succeeding sheets, make this clear at the foot of the first page and top of the second page and so on if there are more than two pages. Write 'more' in the bottom right-hand corner of page one, and repeat the title at the top of the next page. Succeeding pages should be numbered.

14. **Concluding the release.** There is no point in writing 'ends' at the close of the story as this is obvious if the story is followed by the name of the writer, his telephone number and the date.

15. **Embargoes.** Embargoes are not popular with editors, and should never be used unless there is a very obvious and justified reason which the editor can appreciate. Time differentials between countries, Stock Exchange rules, or the fact that a speech will not be delivered for some time are self-evident justifications. Ideally, an embargo should be a privilege, the editor being given advance information. Press embargoes are widely misunderstood: they should not be used to satisfy the convenience of the PR practitioner. If a story is not embargoed, there is no point in stating 'for immediate release'.

House Style Exceptions

Newspapers and magazines do have their own characteristics, and may not therefore adopt identical styles. Some magazines have an unjustified or 'free' right-hand edge; some business magazines do not indent paragraphs; *The Guardian* sometimes indents opening paragraphs, the *Sunday Telegraph* uses full points between initials (e.g. B.A.O.R.); various newspapers open stories in different ways—with drop capitals, black face type, or all caps for the first word or two. These are 'house styles' over which the news writer has no control, and he should not attempt to copy these individual styles. It is best, therefore, to adopt a printing and publishing style which is acceptable to the majority of editors. They can then introduce their own special styles.

Mailing Lists

The finest news release is useless if it is sent to the wrong media, or if it is sent to the right media at the wrong time. This is another area of criticism: too many PR practitioners are either careless or ignorant about media. It is necessary to know your media—what they print, who their readers are, how they are printed, how often they are published, when they are printed and their latest date for copy. This means for each story a new mailing list has to be compiled, otherwise editors will be annoyed because they have been sent stories which are irrelevant or ill-timed. Here is a letter (*UK Press Gazette*, September 29, 1980) from a well-known and long-suffering London editor:

PR INDOLENCE

Some time ago, when I was editor of *Reveille*, you published a letter of mine in which I attacked lazy and/or incompetent PR people who didn't keep their mailing lists up to date.

I complained then about letters addressed to *Reveille* editors who had either left, retired or died.

Reveille itself has now been dead for just over a year. Yet I still receive communications from PR people.

Since *Reveille*'s demise was accorded its fair share of obituaries in the media, is it not understandable that certain PR firms and personnel are castigated for their indolence and inefficiency? CYRIL KERSH, assistant editor (features), *Sunday Mirror*.

The press was analysed in Chapter 22, and with this knowledge it should be possible to decide which newspapers or magazines are likely to print the story. Good press relations depend on supplying editors with what they want when they want it.

The PR practitioner can become professional at mailing list compilation if he uses the many resources available to him. *Benn's Press Directory* and *PR Planner* provide much of what he needs to know, while news release mailing organisations such as PIMS and EMA provide information and services which are updated regularly.

One of the biggest faults with mailings is that too many releases are sent to too many publications. The rate of success should be considered. If one release is sent to one editor because only one editor is likely to print it, and he does, that is a success rate of 100 per cent. But if 100 releases are mailed and the story appears only once, that is a success rate of 1 per cent and a failure rate of 99 per cent! The point is that standard mailing lists, to which new titles are constantly added and defunct ones are never removed, are unprofessional. Each story requires its own carefully selected list. The skilled practitioner will be so familiar with media that he can practically dictate lists.

In compiling mailing lists it is necessary to restrict titles to those publications which:

(*a*) **Are likely to print the story.** If publications are studied it will be found that some newspapers or magazines regularly, irregularly or never carry your type of story. Therefore it is a waste of time and money sending releases where they are unwanted and unwelcome—yet it is not unusual for releases to be sent to 'all nationals' or 'all women's magazines' or all 'local weeklies'. Editors expect PROs to know what kinds of stories they print. The *PR Planner* is a useful guide to editorial requirements.

(*b*) **Have time to print the story.** It is pointless sending a release to a publication which has been made up or printed already. Mailings have to be timed correctly, and sometimes staggered. What is the lead time between editing and printing? In the case of a daily it could be hours, but a weekly will need the story four to seven days in advance and a monthly two to three weeks, but if it is printed by photogravure it could be two to three months.

These two factors are vital, and with such understanding of editorial and publishing requirements it will be sensible to *eliminate* from the list those titles which are useless if immediate publication is desired. Some stories may be timeless, but few publications will carry forward a dated story.

News Agencies

Several kinds of news agencies exist. The Press Association supplies the UK press with home news, and newspapers subscribe to this service. News releases sent to the PA should not exceed 100 words. Reuters supply and distribute international news. Universal News Services supply PR news stories for their subscribers. These are 'wire' services. There are also news agencies which specialise in the reporting of news and the supplying of features to the press.

Exclusive Signed Feature Articles

An article is not a long news release, but an entirely different literary form with its own special characteristics, uses and values. Here, we are concerned with the article written **exclusively** for one publication. It cannot be reproduced elsewhere without permission. One can, of course, rewrite the article, presenting the same basic information differently and with fresh examples to suit other journals but each article will be an exclusive. When the same article is supplied to more than one publication this is called a **syndicated** article (syndication will be discussed separately).

Whereas a news release is given broadcast distribution, could be printed at any time, may not be printed at all, and could be cut or rewritten, the article will be written for a particular issue of one journal and, if well produced, is unlikely to be seriously edited.

An article occupies a substantial area of space and is usually indexed. It can have permanent value in at least three ways: magazines especially are often retained in binders or libraries; articles are often kept as part of the literature on the subject; reprints can be made for future use as direct mail shots, enclosures with correspondence, or as give-away material in showrooms or on exhibition stands. An article can have a long working life.

It can be authoritative, especially if the author is an authority on the subject, and it can be very informative and well-illustrated. Colour pictures may be possible when they are seldom likely to be printed with news releases.

But an article will be more expensive than a news release because time has to be spent on obtaining permission to write about the subject if others are involved, negotiating publication with editors, researching the material, writing the article, and checking the draft with those who have supplied information. This cost—it may be three days' work in all—has to be set against the cost-effectiveness of its long-term influence, and not against the achievement of only one press cutting.

Two First Considerations

1. First of all there must be an idea, theme or subject, not just a bare description of something. It could be how someone used a bank loan to make a fortune, how a new invention overcame a problem, why a new holiday resort is different from any other, how a dangerous task was made safe or how a new bridge has changed traffic patterns. It is this idea which is going to convince an editor that the article should be written and published.

2. Second, it must be possible to have access to the information which usually means getting permission from owners, contractors, customers or whoever may be involved. Several organisations and individuals may have to be approached. It must not be assumed that everyone will agree with the article being written, and only those with full responsibility for giving approval must be approached. It is both courteous and helpful to make initial approaches through the PROs of the various organisations who can then assist the writer.

Negotiating with Editors

Once the idea and the permissions are settled, the next step is to negotiate with the editor of the selected publication. The article should not be written speculatively and sent to an editor because (*a*) we do not know whether he will print it and (*b*) we do not know what he wants.

Moreover, there is also the question of who will write the article, for PR articles can be written by the following people:

(a) **The editor or a staff writer.** Large publications may not accept articles from outsiders, and will prefer to be provided with the idea and with facilities for visits and interviews. The initiator of the idea will then make the necessary arrangements, probably accompanying the staff writer and perhaps arranging for photography. This has advantages and disadvantages. The article will have the independent authority of the by-lined staff writer, but control may be lost over *what* is written and *how* the article is written. It could look better and less biased if the publisher has produced the article itself, but the piece could be inaccurate or biased by the writer's point of view.

(b) **A contributor.** The article could be written by a contributor as when a professional writer supplies a regular feature to a journal. A lot of gardening writers do this. The PRO may be able to provide an idea and facilities to such a contributor.

(c) **The PRO.** In this case the article could be written by the in-house PRO or by a PR consultant; or a freelance writer could be engaged; or a personality within the organisation could be the author. A fourth possibility is that the PRO, PR consultant or a freelance writer could 'ghost write' the article for a VIP such as the managing director. This is rather like the biographies of famous people being written for them by professional 'ghost writers'.

There are therefore many ways in which PR articles can be produced.

How to Propose a PR Article

There is a false notion that in order to get a PR article published it is necessary to take an editor out to lunch. This is not so if you have a practical proposition. The PRO has the advantage that the editor has neither the idea nor the access until the proposal is put to him. Assuming that the PRO is responsible for producing the article the proposition can be presented on the telephone or in a letter. The author has published hundreds of articles in this way. He has not been known to the editor, and he has not known the editor, nor has he ever met the editor, a situation which can happen if, over a period of years, one is dealing with scores of subjects. The proposition should present the idea, state that permission has been obtained to cover the subject and conduct the necessary research, and say that if the editor likes the idea will he please state:

(a) The number of words required.
(b) Any special treatment required.
(c) If illustrations are required, what kind and what number.
(d) The date of the issue in which the article will appear.
(e) The copy date or deadline.

If the article is accepted the PRO is commissioned to write it, and he must supply on the agreed date. There will be no fee for the article, and in any case it would be unethical for the PRO to be paid twice, once by his employer or client and again by the publisher. It is wise to promise the editor that commercial references will be kept to a minimum, but he will probably safeguard himself by agreeing to publish 'subject to sight of the copy'. It is up to the writer to supply a publishable article.

How to Write Feature Articles

Bad articles result from having too little to write about. A well researched, readable article results from having to select from a wealth of information. The following model is a useful plot and discipline.

Seven-point Model for Feature Articles

1. Opening paragraph.
2. The problem or previous situation.
3. The search for a solution or improvement.
4. The solution or improvement.
5. The results achieved.
6. Closing paragraph.
7. Check draft with sources of information.

This model is useful for writing a case-study article which enhances the current situation or experience by contrasting it with an inferior situation or experience in the past. For example, a journey once took days or weeks by ship, but now takes only a matter of hours by plane. Or production was inefficient and costly by hand or old-fashioned machinery but is now faultless and economic by robotics. This before and after treatment gives a dramatic quality to an article. Points 2, 3, 4 and 5 become the ones requiring research. Then the article needs an opening paragraph to capture the reader's interest and attention, and a final paragraph to bring about a satisfying close to the account.

The topping and tailing of the article can be done after the heart of the article has been composed, and ideas for these paragraphs may spring from the central material. One should not 'write one's way in', and—unlike the release—with an article the opening paragraph should *not* 'give the game away', but should lead the reader into the body of the article by means of an irresistible statement, question or perhaps an intriguing quotation.

The draft should then be submitted to *all* those who gave information or have the authority to approve its publication. This can be both a courtesy and an insurance. One owes it to all concerned, including the editor, that the facts are correct. It may be wise to draw attention to statements, figures and spellings which should be checked. And since a publication date is involved, there must be a deadline for the return of the approved or amended draft. If there is any risk of delay—readers of the draft will be busy people and they could be absent on business or holidays—it is a sensible precaution to state quite emphatically that the draft will be assumed to be correct unless returned by a certain date. This date should be early enough for the writer to supply the editor with a clean and correct final version. Even then, it pays to telephone if the draft has not been returned.

Example of an Exclusive Signed Feature Article

The following is an example of a feature article. This was written by Tony Vanterpool of Barbados as an exercise during a Public Relations Management Summer School held in London by the author.

BANKING IS THEIR BUSINESS

by TONY VANTERPOOL

For all his adult life 60-year-old Joe Jenkins earned his keep as a small farmer and fed his family off the land. It was a two-acre lot on which his little wooden house was located.

Then suddenly one morning it happened!

Joe got out of bed, offered up a brief prayer to his God, brushed his teeth, took a bath and sat down to a breakfast of boiled eggs and codfish, when, out of the blue, he heard a knocking on his front door.

He opened the door only to be confronted by a postman pushing a brown envelope in his direction. He immediately spotted the official marking 'Trinidad and Tobago Government' and, assuming that the letter was from the Commissioner of Inland Revenue requesting him to pay up tax arrears, he shouted to his wife: 'The tax man has caught up with us.'

Instead, when he opened it he discovered to his surprise a cheque made out on his behalf for the sum of $10,000, and an attached note explaining that the enclosed sum was 'royalties' from oil drilled on and around Joe's property.

Joe was speechless for a few seconds. Then he asked his wife: 'Where are we going to put all this money . . . not in that box under the bed!'

'No,' she exclaimed, 'We are going to take it to the National Commercial Bank of Trinidad and Tobago.'

It was in order to cater for people like Joe Jenkins that the NCB was incorporated on June 15, 1970. During that period the country started to experience an oil boom. There was unrest because the major banks were all foreign-owned, resulting in profits from local savings and investments going to shareholders abroad, some of whom had never heard of Trinidad and Tobago.

The head office of NCB is located at Independence Square, Port of Spain and the Chairman/Managing Director, Philip G. Rochford, heads a staff of 550 operating 10 branches across the country.

The objectives of the bank were aimed at expanding the field of banking as widely as possible to reach out to the indigenous population such as Joe Jenkins, and also to introduce as many banking services as possible. Initially, the complete shareholding was in the hands of Government.

However, in March 1978 NCB was converted into a public company and while the Government retained 63 per cent of the shareholding, 30 per cent of the shares were bought up by 1800 local people while the remaining 7 per cent were taken up by the National Insurance Board.

The National Commercial Bank of Trinidad and Tobago Limited came into being as a result of a takeover by the Government of Trinidad and Tobago of the business assets and liabilities of the branch of a foreign bank which operated in that country.

The assets of the bank exceed $400 million and it has a paid up capital of $28 million.

The bank's Board of Directors is representative of some of the major national interests including law, management, labour relations and accounting, bringing many years of business experience to the organisation.

A subsidiary Trust Company, which is owned by the bank, provides a full range of trustee services as well as mortgage financing and acceptance of long-term deposits.

The success of the NCB augers well for the future.

Not an organisation to rest on its laurels, NCB is planning during the current financial year to establish a Mercantile Division and also to establish another six branches.

Its aim is to provide a banking service even in the most remote areas of Trinidad and Tobago.

The result: no more banking problems for people like Joe Jenkins.

Syndicated Articles

Feature articles need not be exclusive, but can be syndicated—that is, supplied to and published in more than one publication—provided care is taken to see that they do not appear in rival journals. It is best not to send out the articles like news releases. Unsolicited articles may be rejected. The procedure is to send a synopsis to a selection of publications which do not have rival readerships (e.g. evening newspapers published at least 50 miles apart), and to supply the article, and any requested illustrations, upon acceptance. When articles are being published internationally one could approach one editor per country. (Overseas distribution of articles is undertaken by EIBIS International Ltd.)

However, rationalisation of the UK regional daily press does mean that nowadays a syndicated article is not likely to appear in newspapers with competing circulations, although this does not apply to national newspapers and magazines. Even so, publication is more likely to result from *offering* an article than from sending it out speculatively.

Syndicated articles are popular in the travel industry. A particularly interesting example of how to publish such articles occurred in *UK Gazette* on November 17, 1980, when a whole-page advertisement announced eight articles on behalf of Global. The 800-word articles were written by well-known travel journalists and covered subjects such as *How to 'read' a holiday brochure, Coach touring holidays, Cost-conscious Canada, Single-parent holidays,* and *Eastern Europe for beginners*. Black and white photographs were also offered. There was an order form which had to be returned to the PR consultants, Stuart Hulse Associates.

Studying the Media

Chapter 22 provided an analysis of and an insight into the number and variety of publications which may welcome PR material, but however observant and vigilant the PRO may be he cannot always be aware of future editorial programmes. A publication designed to help him is *Advance*, published six times a year by Themetree Ltd, Longwood House, Datchet Road, Old Woking, Berkshire, SL4 2RQ. *Advance* reports on features and supplements planned for UK newspapers and periodicals. It gives the topics to be featured, together with the names, addresses and telephone numbers of editorial contacts, plus copy dates. Topics are grouped under some thirty headings. It is supplied on annual subscription.

Sources of Information

The PR practitioner should possess a library of up-to-date reference books and the following are some of the more essential ones:

Advertiser's Annual, Kelly's Directories Ltd, Windsor Court, East Grinstead House, East Grinstead, West Sussex, RH19 1XB.

Benn's Press Directory, Benn Publications Ltd, Directories Division, Union House, Eridge Road, Tunbridge Wells, Kent, TN4 8HF. Two volumes: UK and Overseas.

Hollis Press and Public Relations Annual, Contact House, Lower Hampton Road, Sunbury-on-Thames, Middlesex, TW16 5HG.

PR-Planner-UK and *PR-Planner-Europe*, Media House, 8–16 Cromer Street, London, WC1H 8BR.

Willings Press Guide, Thomas Skinner Publications, 41–43 Perrymount Road, Haywards Heath, West Sussex, RH16 3BS.

Writers' & Artists' Yearbook, Adam & Charles Black, 35 Bedford Row, London WC1R 4JH.

IPR Register of Members, Institute of Public Relations, 1 Great James Street, London, WC1N 3DA.

Roget's Thesaurus, Longman, Longman House, Burnt Mill, Harlow, Essex, CM20 2JE. (Also Penguin edition.)

The Synonym Finder, Rodale Press, Griffin Lane, Aylesbury, Bucks, HP19 3AS.

Press release distribution services

PIMS Ltd (formerly *PRADS*), Greencoat House, Francis Street, London, SW1P 1DH.

EIBIS International Ltd, 3 Johnson's Court, Fleet Street, London, EC4A 3EA.

EMA, Bill Gibbs-PNA Group, 13/19 Curtain Road, London, EC2A 3LT.

News Agencies

Press Association, 85 Fleet Street, London, EC4P 3DP.

Universal News Services, Communication House, Gough Square, London, EC4P 3DP.

Press cutting services

These are listed in *Advertiser's Annual*, *Benn's Press Directory*, *Hollis Press & Public Relations Annual* and *Willings Press Guide*.

International and Overseas publications

In many countries there are public relations institutes and associations which publish membership lists. There are also the following:

IPRA Members Register, International Public Relations Secretariat, 40 Wellington Street, London, WC2E 8BN.

Directory of Business and Organizational Communicators, International Association of Business Communicators, 870 Market Street, Suite 928, San Francisco, CA 94102, USA.

Asian Press & Media Directory, Syme Media Enterprises Ltd, 1303 World Trade Centre, Causeway Bay, Hong Kong.

34

BROADCASTING MATERIAL AND FACILITIES

There is a lot more to broadcasting than sending news releases to the station news room or to Independent Television News, Independent Radio News or the BBC news services. In fact, merely to put the broadcasting services on the mailing list is likely to be ineffectual if only because the story will probably arrive too late to be usable. Airtime on both radio and television is divided into numerous programmes, not unlike the pages and features of newspapers and magazines except that (apart from the London radio station LBC) news is a small part of the total broadcast material.

Although the theory of broadcasting is that it should combine information, education and entertainment, the tendency is for the entertainment to predominate, even to some extent in the information and educational programmes. This is because, as with popular newspapers such as the *Daily Mirror* and *The Sun*, radio and television cater for the mass public which prefers to be entertained rather than informed or educated. That is a statement of fact, not cynicism. Since the advent of colour television, newscasters have dressed colourfully, and the news is presented entertainingly with amusing tail-piece stories and quips by the newscasters.

With British television audiences numbering 15 to 30 million, most PR material for television has to be 'of interest and value' to a very large number of viewers. Much of company news which might suit certain sections of the press, special interest columns or features even in the popular press (e.g. City Page) will be irrelevant. So this is a medium which has to be looked at very carefully. It can be a valuable PR medium if programmes, presenters, producers, script-writers and research assistants are diligently selected, and if approaches are timed correctly. For example, a businessman might appear on *Question Time*, a topic might have a place in *Crossroads* or *Coronation Street*, an export order success story could suit a regional news bulletin, or a holiday subject might be welcomed by one of the holiday programmes on either BBC or ITV. The story has to be marketed! A word of warning: while radio may be only a matter of a studio or outside interview (live or taped), television can be very time-consuming, with many hours taken up for a few moments of screen time.

Before getting involved in television one should consider whether one has the time to spare compared with the value of the coverage. Television can be a temptation and a disappointment. It is a visual medium which invites critical viewing if the subject or personality is not attractive on a small screen in private homes. Some well-known personalities have suffered adverse publicity because they have come over badly on television. The viewing public does tend to look at, rather than listen to, television, but with radio it is the attractiveness of the voice which matters. As an example of this, it does not help PR very much when a contestant for the Miss World beauty contest announces that she is a PRO, whereas when Keith Hopkins, the PR consultant, was interviewed on LBC he sounded sincere, experienced and credible.

It pays to study the programmes printed in the *Radio Times* and *TV Times* (or similar programme magazines in other countries) to see which programmes are being broadcast, and to note the names of presenters, editors and producers. There is no cast-iron rule about this, but for different programmes one may have to deal with the producer, the editor, the presenter or the researcher. If in doubt, it is best to contact the producer in the first instance, setting out the proposition in a letter or a telephone conversation with postal confirmation.

Five Points to Remember about Television

Five things should be remembered about television:

1. Some programmes are live or are produced only a few days earlier. For example, Esther Rantzen's *That's Life* is a combination of pre-taped material and studio performance.

2. Other programmes, such as holiday series, have to be filmed months in advance. You may be able to get your topic into next week's show, or next season's. The author had coverage in a regular weekly programme, but discussions began in January and 15 minutes of a day's filming appeared a week after shooting in March.

3. Sometimes material may be shot for a magazine programme, and one may be kept on tenterhooks wondering in which week's programme it will be used. Even then one may be told 'it's going on tonight' only to find it is held over to a future programme.

4. Television can be not only time-consuming but exasperating. The editing method of breaking up interviews and inserting bits in conjunction with bits from other interviews can be disconcerting. Juxtapositioning can give an entirely different meaning from what was discussed in the separate interviews! This can be unfair because those concerned are unaware of the other interviews from which they are isolated until the programme actually appears.

5. However, if there is a valid reason for seeking television coverage, and if the story is 'of interest and value' to the mass television audience, the PR practitioner needs to understand the technical demands of the medium. While it is simple and quick to tape-record a radio interview, television requires planning time, the use of equipment, proper lighting, sometimes many people, and probably a budget allocation to undertake the job.

This implies, therefore, that the 'idea' has to be 'sold' in practical terms, facilities must be provided, and a lot of cooperation will be required in providing scenes or venues, or people for interview. For instance, it is unlike inviting a group of journalists to a press reception or on a press visit. One has to devote all one's time to one television crew, and do so on a day convenient and for however long it may take to set up, script, rehearse and shoot the story.

The author did nothing else but cooperate for two weeks in the making of a 23-minute television programme, after having negotiated for a year to get the idea accepted. In this case, one of the requests made by the producer was for a farm where part of the action could be shot. That section of the programme occupied a day and lunch had to be provided for a 12-man television crew in the heart of the country!

The PR practitioner has to be aware of the pitfalls and peculiarities of television production which may prove to be merely a device to amuse rather than inform audiences. Inspired controversy based on innocent interviews is a form of entertainment. The wise practitioner may, therefore, find it a matter of responsibility towards his clients or employers to advise them against participation in a television programme. This may require considerable tact since some people may be anxious to 'get on the box', if only to impress their friends. Vanity can prove costly.

Opportunities for PR Coverage (see also Chapter 23)

1. **News bulletins.** There are two kinds of news bulletins: national ones which report major national and international news, and regional ones (e.g. TVS News which follows the ITN networked news on Television South).

2. **Magazine programmes.** Being regular, they are open to suggestions for material that is both topical and of interest to the particular audience, e.g. women, farmers, motorists, businessmen.

3. **Chat shows, discussion panels, interviews.** Opportunities exist for participation by interesting personalities, especially if they or their subjects are topical.

Here is an example of a live television interview with Peter Bateman, Public Relations Director of Rentokil, who discussed a new product which was being retailed by his company. Peter Bateman's job was not stated, nor was his company or the product (Trapsit) named. This is usually the case with a radio or television interview, although sometimes names will be stated in the announcer's introduction. The whole script cannot be reproduced here but the following excerpts show what can be achieved. It was an unscripted women's afternoon programme made in the Bristol studio of Harlech TV, but also shown by former Southern TV and Anglia TV.

ANNOUNCER: Now I don't know whether the Bishop has got bats in the belfry, but I know that some of us, including me, have got mice in the kitchen. So we decided to ask along somebody who knows all about vermin. His name is Peter Bateman, and he's talking to Amanda.

After some minutes discussion about the problems of vermin in the home, and the inadequacy of the family cat as a mouser, this exchange took place:

AMANDA: What about traps then?

MR BATEMAN: Yes, the good old-fashioned trap has been refined. I think it was Emerson who said: 'Build a better mouse trap and the world will make a beaten path to your door', and we have on the table, if you can see it, the latest refinement of this. This is a new all-British steel mouse trap which is very sensitive. The mouse simply has to lean on this, because of its wedge shape. That will go off, you see, very quickly before the mouse has had a chance to drag the bait away.

Thus, Peter Bateman was able to describe a new Rentokil product which viewers could quite easily ask for in their hardware shop. He then went on to describe other products that were available, although not exclusively from Rentokil.

MR BATEMAN: A lot of people don't like the idea of removing messy bodies from traps, and the new mouse killers on the market now are designed to be specifically safe in the home. The ones you can buy over the counter are quite safe provided they're used as per instructions. There are ones that send the mice to sleep and kill them kindly in that way. There's one that gives them an overdose of vitamins, so all the mice die in good health. The modern mouse killers are really much safer than the old ones.

The interview continued with questions from Amanda and answers from her guest until the interview closed with:

AMANDA: But mice have got to go!
MR BATEMAN: But the 'wee cowering timorous beastie' is nothing of the kind and can be a menace.
AMANDA: Peter—thank you.

Two things are essential for such live interviews: the interviewer must be articulate and know his or her subject and be capable of responding instantaneously, authoritatively and sincerely to any question.

4. **Serials.** It may be possible to introduce a public interest subject into a fictional programme if it can be made relevant to the characters or storyline.

5. **Current affairs programmes.** A programme such as *Panorama*, *TV Eye*, *Weekend World* or *World in Action* may require cooperation in covering a subject, or may be interested in a proposed topic.

6. **Series.** These may be produced in advance, and may appear regularly at certain times of the year. We have already mentioned the holiday series shown during the early part of the year when people are planning their holidays. But there are other series, such as those on gardening, which are made at shorter notice.

7. **Archival material.** This consists of ready-made film or video-tape which can be inserted into programmes to give background effects or information—for example, scenes at a seaport or airport.

8. **Library shots.** Action films are often shot in studios, and outside scenes are borrowed or hired from libraries. Famous landmarks and geographical scenes are typical examples. Many airlines make available shots of their aircraft taking off, in flight or landing.

9. **Properties.** Many products have to be used in television films and series. They can be supplied to property rooms, and so used on sets, or they may be supplied for use on location. It is noticeable that Ford cars are often used in both American and British detective series, and credited in the subtitles.

10. **Prizes** for give-away and contest shows. These are purchased by the programme makers and unlikely to be identified (to avoid advertising) but if a product is suitable as a prize and benefits from easy recognition, it could be useful PR to propose it to the producer.

11. **Stills.** Colour slides can be useful for news stories, being televised to coincide with the reading of an associated story.

12. **Documentary films.** Some may be of sufficient interest to be shown in their entirety. (The COI distributes documentary films to overseas television companies and stations where they may be appreciated because of low budgets and shortage of material.) Clips may be taken from industrial films for use in programmes, usually with acknowledgement.

From the above suggestions it will be seen that the scope for television coverage is more versatile and specific than the reference in the CAM Media syllabus for 1981–82 to 'editorial publicity opportunities'.

Differences Between Radio and Television

Before listing the opportunities for radio coverage it is necessary to analyse how radio differs from television:

(*a*) Radio is not confined to indoor audiences. Thanks to the portable transistor receiver, car radios, rediffusion and loudspeakers in public places, radio is available to more people, in more places at more times than television.

(*b*) Even though television is no longer limited to those who can afford to buy receivers or to the availability of electricity—thanks to battery sets and community viewing in many parts of the Third World, plus rental systems— the hours of transmission and the time people have free for viewing is limited. Television also requires the attention of immobile viewers. None of these restrictions applies to radio.

(*c*) While the breadth and freedom of listening has its advantages it has to be admitted that viewers are more attentive. Radio can be a form of companionship, a background sound. One can listen continuously to any kind of enjoyable music—whatever one's tasks—whereas few people would wish continuously to watch music programmes on television. Radio does broadcast a lot of music.

(*d*) Radio is more instantaneous than television. While it is possible to interrupt a television programme with a newsflash, instant news can be typical of radio. A radio programme can be produced at short notice, simply by going on the air. Television programmes usually require advance preparation. A play cannot be read on television—parts have to be learned as on the stage.

(*e*) In Britain, television regions are quite large, embracing perhaps three or four counties, whereas local radio covers smaller areas more intimately.

With these differences in mind, and remembering that radio does not have television's realism and entertainment value of vision, colour and movement, let us now consider how to use radio as a PR medium.

Opportunities for PR Coverage on Radio

1. **News bulletins.** There are national, regional and local radio stations so that news of area significance will interest different radio stations. For example, information about traffic conditions or public transport, which is of interest to people only within one area, can be and is broadcast on local radio.

2. **Taped interviews.** Interviews can be produced by one of two ways. The station may commission an interview, either at the studio or with a reporter outside the studio, or the taped interview can be produced by a PR source and supplied to radio stations. The latter is done more often than listeners realise, which shows that the PR material was broadcast on its merits. The illusion of a genuine studio interview is created by the announcer saying 'We now have in the studio Mr X who is going to talk to Miss X about . . .', and then the tape is played. Afterwards, the announcer will say 'That was Mr X talking to Miss X about . . .'. No commercial reference will occur in the interview, but the identity of the company or product is usually mentioned in the announcer's introduction and close. Sometimes the identity will be obvious if the interview is about, say, a public event, a new entertainment or a new book. Or it could be a trade organisation or professional body giving advice

with the message more important than the source, e.g. advice in late October and early November about how to handle fireworks safely.

3. **Studio interviews, discussions, talks.** Being an audio medium, programmes based on talk and the human voice are characteristic of radio. Interesting voices, conversationalists, commentators or subjects suitable for a talk or discussion are all ideal for radio.

4. **Phone-ins.** Borrowed from the USA, the phone-in produces listener participation and offers opportunities to phone in a PR message if it is an appropriate and genuine contribution to the programme.

5. **Serials and series.** There are possibilities for including PR messages in radio serials, as has happened a number of times on *The Archers*, provided they are of interest and value to large numbers of listeners. In spite of television and local radio, *The Archers* has three million listeners. Voluntary organisations have made good use of radio serials in order to advise the public on matters of health and safety.

Attacks on Television Programmes

Newspapers and magazines as different as the *Sunday People*, *Private Eye*, *The Guardian*, *New Society*, and the *New International* have exposed a great many scandals and strange doings. Some call it the freedom of the press, others call it gutter journalism. It can be either enlightening or mischievous, and either way it helps to build circulations and make money.

But there is a world of difference between muck-raking in publications which are read by selective groups of readers, and an attack on a television programme which is seen by millions of people, often in family groups in the home. There is practically no audience selectivity except between one channel and another. In Britain there are habitual BBC or ITV viewers. We do not have the selectivity that exists in the USA where there are numerous television stations in many cities. An attack or exposure broadcast on television is therefore a more serious matter than one in the press which thousands of people may never read. An exposure on television is discussed afterwards by viewers with people who may or may not have seen the programme, and the topic is often taken up by the press and radio the next day. The message spreads like shock waves.

The victim rightly or wrongly is crucified. An apology or retraction is usually too late. Newspapers may be anxious to avoid libel actions and will publish handsome apologies. Television seems to thrive on threats of libel. Esther Rantzen's attacks on inefficient organisations have produced a response in keeping with the programme, and apologetic victims have retaliated with verses and songs. However, a victim may go to law, but it is a long process and by the time the case has been won it no longer matters. For example, the BBC paid substantial damages and costs in settlement of a High Court libel action brought by a laundry group against Esther Rantzen's *That's Life* show; the BBC also unreservedly withdrew its allegations that the laundry had failed to pay proper compensation for clothes which had been lost or damaged; but it took five years for that victim of a television attack legally to recover its good reputation.

Teletext and Viewdata

Information magazines, whereby viewers can call up pages of information or countless topics, are rapidly becoming a new outlet for the PR practitioner. In the UK there are three systems. Teletext information is free of charge and is transmitted by the BBC (Ceefax) and ITV (Oracle). To receive Teletext 'pages' the viewer needs a receiver fitted with a special decoder, and a handset (like a small calculator) with which to select the required magazine section. While these services offer hundreds of pages of information on the weather, Stock Exchange prices, traffic conditions, sports results, entertainments, shopping prices, farm prices and so on, this is limited compared with the encyclopaedic information available from Prestel. Moreover, with the Post Office Viewdata system (Prestel), information (commercial and PR) is supplied to the computer by numerous sources. The viewer is also able to 'talk back' and ask for specific information.

However, the cost of a Prestel set is at present double that of a Teletext set, the set has to be connected with the telephone, the local telephone call charge has to be paid to use the service, and some pages have to be paid for.

At the time of writing Prestel is in its infancy with fewer than 10,000 sets in use and a limited number of pages being available. A set costs about £1000, there is a charge of £12 plus 50p per quarter for linking the set with the telephone, general pages are free but detailed information costs from 1p to 5p per page plus the time of the telephone call. The viewer does not have to use the telephone but calls up information and feeds in requests or orders for goods by means of the keypad which has numbers 1 to 9.

In the UK the Prestel system is costly for the domestic user, whereas in France, over a period of years, free receivers are being provided instead of telephone books.

Firms such as Mills and Allen specialise in producing pages for clients. Organisations such as the National Building Agency (Contel) feed in pages about their industry. Thus, the information can have a PR service aspect not unlike the 'on-line' information which airlines operate for reservations. The great advantage of the system is its instantaneous nature since information can be constantly revised, unlike a static advertisement, timetable or tariff. Nor does one have to wait for information to be presented at regular times as with news bulletins, sports reports and financial reports. Prestel especially will change life styles. Before going shopping it will be possible to check prices, order mail order goods, and make reservations for meals, hotels, travel or holidays from the home or office. From the PR point of view it promises to be a means of both providing information accurately and quickly and having access to publics efficiently and economically.

Unitel Nation-wide News Service

A flourishing regional press, and the growth of free sheets, plus the development of local radio, encouraged Universal News Services to introduce Unitel on the Prestel system. UNS provides its clients with a nation-wide distribution of news of local interest.

The Unitel service enables PROs to reach local media instantly instead of having to mail news releases. Editors in news rooms around the country can receive news directly relevant to their circulation areas. A single call to UNS will ensure that news is immediately and cost-effectively made available via Unitel, using Prestel television facilities with off-line printers. Most regional editors do not have wire services but now they can receive instant news from London, using Prestel equipment supplied by UNS.

The system operates like this. On the screen the day's headlines are broken down into 17 regions, radio services and features. The editor calls up the list of stories applicable to his region. Then he can select and display stories which are screened complete with contact. By using the screen image printer he can immediately print out the actual story on the screen (see Fig. 10). This costs him nothing. The editor has free access to every story in the Unitel news file.

```
UNITEL                    2551005a        0p
SPONSORED WALKERS TO RAISE FUNDS FOR
EX-LANDLORDS 26/5 Three Pages

A sponsored walk on the scale of the
recent London Marathon is being
organised by Whitbread, the brewers, to
raise funds for one of the country's
leading licensed trade charities.
Several thousand people are expected to
put their walking boots on to aid the
Licensed Victuallers' National Homes
when the "Whitbread walk" is held on
Sunday June 7.

From its headquarters at Denham, Bucks,
the LVNH provides retirement flats and
bungalows for 1,000 former pub land-
lords at 19 estates throughout the
country.

Key 0 Unitel Index Key # To Continue.
```

Fig. 10. Unitel news releases.

UNITEL   2551005b   0p
SPONSORED Continued

Dozens of different walks will be held.
Three hundred people will walk the 270
miles of the Penine Way in ten-mile
stages. A party from a Marlow, Bucks
brewery will walk the 25 miles to
Denham.

In Scotland hundreds of walkers will
step out the 400 miles from John
O'Groats to Gretna Green in relays. A
clifftop walk along the Glamorgan coast
-line is being planned in Wales. A pet
labrador will join the party walking
from Hatfield, Herts, to Denham.

Key 0 Unitel Index Key # To Continue

UNITEL   2551005c   0p
SPONSORED Continued

A Luton landlord will lead a group of
walkers from his pub to Denham. In
London 25 employees from Long John
Whisky will walk along the tow-path of
the Grand Union Canal to Denham.Walkers
arriving at Denham will be met by Mr
Michael Whitbread, the 1981 president
of the LVNH, during the Sunday afternoon.

Contact: George Davies of Whitbread,
01-506 4455.

Key 0 Unitel Index Key 1 For Page One

Fig. 10. (cont'd)

35

ORGANISING PR FUNCTIONS AND EVENTS

Public relations has a bad name for wining and dining, gin and tonics, 'good sloshes', junkets and jollies. This has to be balanced against the normal custom of welcoming a guest with a cup of tea or coffee, a beer or a glass of sherry, a cola nut or a date according to the custom of the country. In some countries a shopkeeper would not begin to discuss business until he had served his customer with a cup of mint tea. Elsewhere, it may be Turkish coffee or saki, maybe palm wine. There is a difference between hospitality which is bribery and that which is courteous. If there are few journals and journalists, a press party may be welcomed and expected, but if—as in Britain—journalists may have to choose between any six press receptions occurring simultaneously, they want the stories, not the drinks. But they may be grateful for something to eat or, on a cold morning, some hot soup on arrival.

In this chapter we shall consider five kinds of PR functions and events: (i) the press conference; (ii) the press reception; (iii) the facility visit; (iv) the open day; and (v) the press lunch.

The Press Conference

This may be a regular event or one called at short notice. Its purpose is to give information to the media and to receive and answer questions. It will be a comparatively simple and informal occasion and hospitality will be minimal, such as a 'thank you' drink at the close. It may be held in the boardroom or conference room, or at a hotel, and if called at short notice there will be no printed invitation cards. The term 'press conference' should not be confused with the more elaborate 'press reception', although some people mistakenly use them as interchangeable terms.

Regular press conferences may be held by heads of government and ministers to keep the media informed on an on-going basis. Sometimes a minister will advise the media 'off the record' or from a 'non-attributable source'. Based on such official 'leaks', journalists will refer the story to 'a usually reliable source'. But most press conferences are held at short notice because something unexpected has happened and a press statement is necessary, or a newsworthy person will be interviewed, for example, on arrival at an airport.

The Press Reception

This is more planned and socialised than a press conference. The planning may begin some months in advance, and it will be as thoroughly organised as a wedding reception complete with venue, invitations, catering and speeches. It will be more than a mere cocktail party. It calls for a timetable and programme of activities which may include an audio-visual presentation and a product demonstration, a bar and a buffet. It must have an adequate purpose—that is, a good story—to win a good attendance.

The Facility Visit

This may be a press trip to a site, a factory, new premises; it could be a flight on a new aircraft or a voyage on a new vessel; it might be an official opening; it could be a visit to a country, an exhibition or a new holiday attraction. One way or another it usually means taking a person or a group of people by some form of transport to the location of the visit. If people are travelling from a variety of places they may have to make their own way. At least a day is usually involved, but overnight stops may be necessary. A great deal of organisation is required. Again, because of the sacrifice of time, the visit has to be worthwhile from a story point of view.

Journalists will not respond if they have to travel 500 miles to see a jam factory that is no different from the one in their home town. They will be delighted to go behind-the-scenes of something unusual or unfamiliar. Such visits should not depend on complicated arrangements which could be wrecked by the weather or industrial action. A new motorcar was once launched many miles from London, but the press failed to arrive because of an air traffic controllers' strike. An example of an actual facility visit is given at the end of this chapter.

The Open Day

This is an opportunity for the press to make a visit and see what goes on, though there is probably nothing new to be seen. Such a visit could be to a factory, college, hospital, mine, town hall, airport, charity home—preferably somewhere to which the press do not normally have general access. There may or may not be a direct story. More, it is a goodwill effort to familiarise the media with the place and what happens there. This may provide background knowledge that may help when news stories are being handled. Planning is still necessary, and management and employees should be aware of the visit.

A fiasco once occurred at a factory with an unfortunate industrial relations record resulting in hostile local press stories. The works manager had told the gatekeeper to refuse entry to the press. An open day was organised by the firm's PR consultants who were unaware of the works manager's instructions. The press never got in.

The Press Lunch

This can be a pleasant way for journalists to meet the personalities of an organisation, get to know them informally, and so discuss topics of mutual interest. It can be helpful in creating understanding between management and journalists. There may or may not be formal speeches, nor may there be an immediate story. Individual journalists or groups of journalists may be given lunch.

A good example occurred when, for no apparent reason, the entire trade press was hostile to a certain well-known company. This situation was reversed after each editor was invited to lunch with the PR consultant and two members of the company's top management. The problem had arisen because an assistant editor of one of the journals had become a member of the consultancy staff but had left their employ after a difference of opinion with the client. Delicate situations can be resolved in a relaxed atmosphere.

Planning Considerations

1. **The purpose.** Is the event justified—is it worth the cost to the organisation and the time of the guests? Or would a news release be sufficient? This is a very important decision. As a consultant the author found that clients enjoyed press receptions, and sometimes had to be dissuaded from holding them.

2. **The date and time of day.** The chairman may think it convenient to hold a press reception at 6 p.m. on a Friday evening, journalists may prefer one at 11 a.m. on a Tuesday morning, and the chairman's wishes will be irrelevant. The event must be held when it suits the press, otherwise there will be a disappointing turn-out, little coverage, and a heavy bill for a wasted effort.

There are two rules for the choice of date and time, and neither of them is easy to obey satisfactorily:

(i) Try to avoid *clashing* with some major event or another press function. To some extent one can check that it is not Wimbledon Week, the Chelsea Flower Show or the Derby. The *Daily Telegraph* information bureau can be helpful. One can also ring press friends and ask if they have heard of anything else on the same day. Many events and press events are listed in the monthly *Diary* which costs about £20 a year from 17 Walton Street, London SW3. However, a problem is that the PR practitioner may plan his reception three months in advance and someone less well organised will choose the same date only three weeks in advance.

Time of day is important, and for most receptions in London it is best if the proceedings begin in mid-morning and close with a buffet lunch—that is, from about 11.30 a.m. to 1.30 p.m.

(ii) Try to choose a day which satisfies copy date needs. Day of the week is important because the end of the week is poor for daily newspapers, and too late for some magazines. The week in the month is important for monthly magazines may go to press before the middle of the month.

So, as a general rule, early in the day, early in the week and early in the month will suit the physical requirements of most publishers. However, if magazines (e.g. many of the big-circulation women's magazines) are printed by photogravure, they will need the story three months in advance. That is why receptions for Christmas gifts are held in July/August, ones for central heating in April/May, and those for summer holidays (January editions) are held in September/October. To publish stories coinciding with the March Ideal Home Exhibition, the press reception needs to be held in November.

3. **Venue.** Again, the convenience of the guests is a first consideration, rather than the glamour of the place. In a city centre, like London, the venue should be easily reached on foot or by taxi. Remember that journalists may have more than one reception to attend. In provincial cities it may be more import-ant that there are good car-parking facilities if guests are coming in from surrounding towns. The venue should have good conference facilities ranging from catering to AVs.

4. **Programme.** A timed programme should be drawn up when the event is being planned. If it is a facility visit, the timetable must include everything from the assembly of the party at a railway station, coach pick-up point or airport to their return. There may not be a great deal of actual visit time if a factory stops work for lunch at 12 noon and closes for the day at 4 p.m. How is the party collected early enough to reach the venue in time to make a tour

or see demonstrations before and/or after lunch? This may determine the form of transportation, perhaps require the provision of breakfast. It may be necessary to go over the route and tour and time the various stages—on foot, by car and so on—allowing, for example, for the time it takes to get a certain number of people on and off coaches and from point to point during the day.

The maximum number of people to be accepted may be determined by the size of a coach, aircraft, demonstration theatre, luncheon room or by the number of people who can be taken round. With most visits there is usually some such factor which controls the size of the party.

5. **Guest list and invitations.** People are naturally flattered if their names are known and they are invited by name. This may mean taking the trouble to telephone round and check names (unless one is a subscriber to PIMS or EMA and has a regularly updated list of names). If the guest list is large enough, a printed invitation is better than a letter. The invitation should state exactly what the event is about, not vaguely invite people to a reception or visit. A timetable can be printed on the back of the card. To ensure prompt acceptances or refusals there should be some means of reply, not merely an RSVP note at the foot of the card. This can be a tear-off reply coupon or a separate reply card, which should bear not only the PRO's postal address but a printed square for the stamp so that it becomes a postcard, otherwise recipients will put it in an envelope.

6. **Rehearsals.** Events need to occur without hitches—'like clockwork'—and while a timetable provides the basis for a well-organised event, and it pays to time each stage, it is also important to rehearse wherever possible. Speeches, demonstrations, film and slide presentations should be rehearsed.

7. **Press material.** Guests should be supplied with only the minimum of material necessary for their information so that they can print a story. A news release, copy of a speech, a photograph and, on a visit, an itinerary should be sufficient. The mistake should not be made of overloading guests with elaborate press packs filled with irrelevant items. Remember, the guests may be standing, eating, drinking, smoking or walking round the site or premises. They will not enjoy having to carry a weighty press kit. The guest should be informed, not impressed. If there is a lot of useful information it may be better to supply it on the point of leaving, or on the return journey. Many an unwelcome press kit has been dumped under a seat!

Example of a Press Facility Visit

John Laing Press Day at Berkshire Brewery

The common claim that journalists attend press events 'only for the beer' was tested when Richard Humphries, press officer to builders John Laing, organised a press day at Courage's new Berkshire Brewery at Reading. A number of other big firms had been involved in the building project, and it was expected that many specialist journals would be interested.

The brief was to organise a press day purely for the construction, architectural and specialist trade press at the brewery, which was nearing completion. Courage had already taken possession but planned to arrange their own press days for the brewery, national and local press.

Construction of the brewery was managed by a member company of the John Laing Group, Laing Management Contracting Ltd. Like other companies within the Group, they contribute an annual sum towards the cost of maintaining the group public relations department. The direct costs for the press day were photography, press kit folders printed in the LMC house colours of brown and gold, and coach hire. The catering costs were shared by Courage's in-house caterers and the Laing site team.

It was planned to receive 45 journalists on the day. They would be divided into three groups of 15 for the guided tour of the brewery. Tuesday, September 23, was the given date, although this was awkward for trade weeklies which went to press that day and were least likely to have staff to spare.

Because the project was so vast (a total of £90m, £35m being construction costs) it was decided to invite the principal subcontractors to supply news releases for the press pack. Some of the subcontracts were multi-million pound jobs. Again, a management contract differs from a building contract. Although Laing are builders—they built Coventry Cathedral—they were engaged by Courage on a fee basis to manage the construction, using their expertise to control the project but not doing any of the building work themselves. It was therefore important that those who had contributed to the actual construction should be able to participate in the press day.

There was the risk that the event could be regarded by the press as a 'jolly', and journalists might come along 'for the beer' rather than for the story. From past experience, Richard Humphries knew that a normal turnout would be about 20 journalists, but a brewery could be a different matter. About 70 invitations were posted, and about 30 acceptances were received. Refusals were because of press days—understandable since some trade journals have small staffs—but they asked for information to be posted to them.

Arrangements were made to cater for about 30 journalists plus about 20 Laing and Courage representatives.

On the afternoon preceding the event apologies began to come in: 'pressure of work', 'staff on holiday', 'illness', 'prior engagement overlooked', 'too many press "do's" on that day'. They were certainly not coming for the beer. In the end, 18 came, some doubling for sister journals. The Laing management was disappointed, but journalists who did come told the managing director it was 'a very good turnout for the trade press', and that very often there were fewer on press trips to which all sections of the media had been invited.

It proved to be a successful day. Each journalist had the opportunity of talking in detail on a one-to-one basis with a senior-ranking specialist, and all left with good stories. The Courage PR department gave them presentation packs containing two engraved goblets and two bottles of Bulldog ale.

The itinerary gives an insight into the planning that was required (including the timing of the coach journey), and the cooperation that was required and given by important personnel both inside and outside the Laing organisation.

BERKSHIRE BREWERY PRESS DAY
Tuesday, September 23, 1980

Programme

09.15	Coach departs from 14 Regent Street London SW1.
10.30	Arrive at Berkshire Brewery, Reading, and proceed to restaurant.
10.30–10.45	Welcome by Terry Fleming, Managing Director of Laing Management Contracting Limited, who will introduce James Hampton, Production Director, Courage Central Limited, and Gerald Coveney, Group Chief Architect, Courage Central Limited.
10.50–11.10	Background description of project by G. N. Coveney, Courage Central Limited.

Programme

11.10–11.30	Audio-Visual display by T. W. Fleming, describing the construction project.
11.30	Division into three groups for conducted tour of the complex:

Group 1: Construction press. Led by T. W. Fleming (Laing), C. C. Birch (Laing).

Group 2: Architectural and consultant press. Led by G. N. Coveney (Courage), K. N. Fisher (Laing), N. H. Viney (Laing).

Group 3: Specialist press. Led by J. Hampton (Courage), D. Green (Laing), M. Stubbins (Laing).

12.45–13.15	Return to Hospitality Suite for pre-lunch refreshments.
13.15–14.30	Lunch.
14.30–15.15	Questions panel: T. W. Fleming, K. N. Fisher, J. Hampton, G. N. Coveney.
15.15	Summing up and thanks by T. W. Fleming.
15.20	Board coach.
16.30 (approx.)	Arrive at 14 Regent Street.

The event justified a press pack and this contained the above timetable, a site plan and three photographs, a list of the names and addresses of the 106 main subcontractors and suppliers, five pages of background information on the project, a full-colour company brochure, and news releases from Degremont Laing Ltd, Costain Group Ltd, Boulton & Paul (Steel Construction) Ltd, Crown House Engineering Ltd, Drake & Scull Engineering Ltd, Frankipile Ltd, Kitson's Insulation Contractors Ltd (Pilkington), H. H. Robertson (UK) Ltd, and Tarmac Ltd. Courage also supplied independent releases.

Some independent observations by the author are as follows:

1. The date of a press event should be chosen for its convenience to the guests, not the hosts, otherwise maximum press coverage—the object of the exercise—is unlikely. Management should accept advice from the PRO.

2. No matter how attractive the event, the PRO should be pessimistically realistic about the likely response.

3. When other people are invited to take advantage of such an event they should do so as professionally as the organisers. The press kit contained news releases from eight other firms, most of them big ones. Only five of these stories were written professionally; four were in single-spaced typing; three were produced on business letterheadings and badly photocopied; one was a single paragraph of 230 words! This carelessness over press material only emphasises the comments made at the beginning of this chapter.

There was immediate coverage of the visit in *Architects' Journal, Building, Building Design, Construction News*, and *New Civil Engineer*, and a dozen other magazines prepared later features.

36

PR PHOTOGRAPHY

Editors frequently complain about the poor quality of PR pictures. The reason why PR pictures are sometimes bad is that the PR practitioner does not understand three things:

1. How to tell a story with pictures.
2. The sort of pictures editors want.
3. How to work with a photographer.

Without this knowledge and ability it is inevitable that the PR practitioner will fail to make the best use of photography, and will disappoint editors. It does help if the PR photographer can use a camera himself, and with modern cameras such as the Canon and the Olympus it is not difficult to take good pictures. **The secret is to know how to compose a picture.** With this knowledge one can create with a camera just as one does on a typewriter—and *instruct* a photographer. Let us now consider the three points set out above.

Telling a Story Pictorially

A PR picture should convey a message, not be a mere record. But it should not be a blatant advertising message, and product or company names—if shown at all—should be discreet.

Human interest may improve a picture, provided it is relevant and helps to explain the subject. For example, a holiday picture is more realistic if people are shown enjoying themselves, but a typical family might be better than a model in a bikini. A brick looks better if a bricklayer is laying it, a sewing machine is better demonstrated by a dressmaker using it. But a power mower looks ridiculous if it is being driven by a blonde in a bikini and high-heeled shoes. People in pictures should be *concentrating* on what they are doing, not decorating the picture or grinning at the camera. If the size of the subject is difficult to judge the message is made clearer if, say, a tiny object is held in the palm of a hand, or a human being is seen standing beside something very large. A lot of PR pictures could be made interesting and publishable if people were used properly. They do not have to be professional models.

Action is another device for giving pictures interest and realism. An aircraft in the air looks more interesting than one on the ground, while a static object such as a building looks better if someone is walking up the steps, or passing through the entrance. Action can thus be real or induced.

Three-dimensional effects give a picture depth. It is more interesting to see three sides of a matchbox than just the side. This applies to many subjects. Do not face the subject head-on: stand to one side and take it at an angle, whether it be a portrait, a piece of machinery, a ship or a loaf of bread.

It is more dramatic to *allow a little to tell the whole* story. A section of a building can look more impressive than if one stands back to get the whole building in the picture. The cricketer at the wicket, with the wicket-keeper crouched behind him, makes a better picture than a bird's-eye view of the match in progress. Close ups and telescopic lenses help here.

Show the subject in use. If it is a lorry, give it a load, show the crane working, have the fork-lift truck lifting things. Have the bus driving along a well-known street, the weighing machine weighing a parcel, and the pop-singer clutching a mike.

What Editors Want

Editors want pictures that enhance the page and flatter their ability to please their readers. Most of the PR pictures they receive do neither.

They also want pictures which reproduce well according to the printing process and paper they use. For a newspaper printed by letterpress on an absorbent paper, 'soot and whitewash' pictures and big subjects are wanted. They have to be sufficiently black and white and simple to contend with the loss of definition caused by a coarse screen halftone and spreading ink. They should not have large pale areas which will show the print on the reverse side. They should not have small detail which will become indistinct. For example, the face only is better than a head and shoulders portrait or full-figure picture.

However, if the journal is printed by photo-offset litho, advantage can be taken of the finer screen and better paper used. Now the picture can have a larger range of tonal values—shades of grey—and it can be more detailed, perhaps distant or landscape, because by this process the picture will reproduce more nearly like the original.

Does the editor want black-and-white or colour pictures? It is a mistake to suppose that since we usually take colour pictures as amateur photographers, a good picture must be in colour. Hardly any PR pictures should be in colour, unless this has been agreed with the editor. The majority of pictures in newspapers are in black and white. An exception is television: if photographs are sent to support a news story they must be in colour.

Editors want sharp, well-focused glossy (*not glazed*) prints. They should not be snapshot size, but they do not have to be large prints if the subject matter fills the picture and cutting or cropping is unnecessary. A half-plate print without borders has the advantage that it is unlikely to be damaged in the post. Even card-backed envelopes are liable to be bent if the postman puts a string or elastic band round the bundle of letters for a particular address. Words such as 'Do Not Bend' are often ignored. Large prints really need personal delivery.

Working with the Photographer

It follows that working with the photographer means knowing what kind of pictures are required. The photographer is not an expert who knows best and must be left to do as he pleases, although this attitude is all too common among those who, in the end, supply editors with pictures they refuse to publish.

The photographer cannot produce pictures which convey the PR message, suit the printing process and encourage publication *unless* the PR practitioner knows what he wants and instructs the photographer properly. The photographer is not a mind-reader. If a building is to be designed the architect has to know whether it is to be a bungalow, a house or a block of flats and then he will want to know what kind of bungalow, house or block of flats. Similarly, it is useless sending a photographer to take pictures unless he is thoroughly briefed. In fact, the PR practitioner should accompany the photographer, help to set up pictures, and even look in the viewfinder to see if the right picture has been composed. When a good relationship has been developed with a photographer he will probably invite the PR practitioner to look in the viewfinder.

Photo Captions

One of the strangest faults with PR pictures is that they are often sent out without captions. The caption on the back of a picture should not be confused with the caption which the editor prints under the picture. The two can be very different.

Photo captions are essential on any picture when it is sent out and to whoever it is sent. It does not have to be an editor. It could be someone requesting a picture. Unless there is a caption the recipient does not know:

(*a*) What the picture is about.
(*b*) Who sent it.
(*c*) Who owns the copyright.

Thus, **the caption should say what the picture cannot say for itself.** If it is a picture of a ship it is no use merely putting the name of the ship on the caption. Who owns the ship? What is its tonnage? Where is it going?

What is the **source** of the picture—what is the sender's name, address and telephone number?

Whose is the **copyright?** Is there a reproduction fee or is it free of copyright? The PR practitioner should never submit pictures for which his client or employer does not own the copyright. When receiving a picture from PR sources editors will assume that it is the copyright of the sender and can be reproduced free of charge.

When a photographer is commissioned to take a picture the copyright of the negative belongs to the photographer, and the copyright of the prints belongs to the commissioner. If the pictures are ordered by a PR consultant the copyright is his, unless it is assigned to the client. If the photographer is employed as a staff photographer, the copyright of pictures taken during his working hours belongs to his employer. The copyright of photographs supplied by photographers or photo agencies belongs to them, and they are entitled to reproduction fees. These fees are usually higher for advertising than for editorial purposes.

The PR practitioner may receive pictures from newspapers or private individuals and he must remember that *they* own the copyright. He can, of course, negotiate to purchase the copyright. Some photographers offer to take pictures of personalities, but they will expect to receive reproduction fees from editors if the pictures are published. Some editors may not wish to do so and will not print such pictures, even though they may be distributed by PR practitioners. If a PR practitioner invites photo agencies to cover a story they will do so on the expectation of selling news pictures to editors.

Captions should not be *written* on the back of the print, but should be duplicated on a piece of paper firmly attached to the print, Sellotaped rather than stuck. A strip of tape top and bottom will fix the caption securely. Do not use a small single piece of tape so that the caption dangles and is likely to get ripped off. **Flapped captions** are best reserved for pictures in photo libraries.

Photographers should be told not to put their **rubber stamps** on the backs of prints, but a PR rubber stamp may be used as well as the caption.

The caption should provide the information from which the editor may create his own caption. He will not remove the caption and send it to the printer for setting. The caption will remain with the picture to explain the picture and identify the source.

Even when captions are fixed to pictures it is extraordinary how often the senders forget to include their name, address and telephone number. The most efficient captions are those which have **printed headings.**

Fixing captions takes time, which is why they are often omitted: the reason may be that too many pictures are sent out! This may be related to the indiscriminate sending out of news releases on excessively large mailing lists. One fault leads to another.

Ways of Avoiding Wasteful Distribution of Pictures

(*a*) Pictures should be sent only to those publications likely to print them.

(*b*) Editors can be telephoned and asked if they would like a picture—for example, before sending an appointment story to the *Financial Times* which prints numerous appointment stories, the majority without pictures—but if a PR appointment story is sent to *Campaign*, *PR Bulletin* or *UK Press Gazette* a picture will probably be printed.

(*c*) Pictures can be reproduced on the news release, and editors invited to request prints.

(*d*) If there is a set of pictures, a sheet of miniatures can be supplied with the story so that editors may choose which picture or pictures they want sent to them.

(*e*) At the foot of a release one can state that pictures are available.

If these methods are adopted a great deal of money can be saved and fewer pictures will be wasted. Editors are normally inundated with pictures they cannot use.

From these remarks it will be seen that it is not difficult to produce publishable pictures, nor to get them published. It costs no more to produce a good picture than a poor one. The careful distribution of pictures is a budgeting consideration.

37

WORKING WITH THE PRINTER

Printing is a craft on its own, and one that is rapidly changing with the introduction of computerised technology. A modern print shop resembles a hospital compared with those where hot metal was in use. While the PR practitioner does not need to have expert knowledge about printing, it can increase his efficiency if he has a working knowledge of printing processes and techniques, and can work intelligently with printers.

He will find it extremely helpful to possess a brilliant little book called *Printing Reproduction POCKET PAL*, published by the Advertising Agency Production Association, c/o Institute of Practitioners in Advertising, 44 Belgrave Square, London SW1. No better, simpler, more compact and inexpensive guide to printing has ever been published.

There are three aspects to working with the printer:

1. **An understanding of the different processes** so that he can use the best process for the job, and supply suitable material for printing by that process.

2. **An understanding of production time schedules** so that a print job can be delivered by the desired date.

3. **An understanding of proofreading** and correction.

This chapter will concentrate on these three aspects. There is great rivalry between printing processes and each is continually competing with the others through the introduction of new machines. Many years ago most magazines were printed by letterpress, then photogravure took over for large-circulation magazines such as the women's press and the Sunday newspaper colour magazines, but in recent years many such magazines have been printed by web-offset-litho. Similarly, while silk-screen printing was confined to short runs of rather crude posters, the process has become sophisticated with photographic reproduction, long runs and specialities such as printing vandal-proof posters on vinyl.

Printing Processes

The four main printing processes are **letterpress, lithography, photogravure** and **silk screen.**

Letterpress (Relief)

Printing is achieved by having all printing surfaces raised or in relief so that when ink is applied and the inked surface is impressed on paper the image is transferred to the paper. This is similar to the typewriter or date stamp. Letterpress machines may be flat-bed with the printing material lying flat on the bed of the machine, sheets of paper being fed in and pressed down on the printing surface by an impression cylinder. Faster printing is achieved by moulding a copy of the metal printing material to produce a curved plate or stereo which is wrapped round a cylinder. This becomes rotary printing, the method used for letterpress newspaper printing.

The 'printing material' referred to above consists of metal type, line blocks to reproduce line drawings and halftone blocks to reproduce artwork such as photographs. This metal printing material together with spacing material which is not 'type high' and so cannot accept ink, is assembled in the forme and locked up in a frame called a 'chase'.

However, one of the developments by which new technologies have been introduced into newspaper and other printing is that the photo-typesetting, paste-up artwork, and finer half-tone screens used for offset-litho—methods which do not require metal type and blocks—can be applied to letterpress printing. The pasted-up page or pages can be photographed and a plate, not unlike a litho plate, can be made for wrapping round the cylinder of a letterpress machine. The effect is to print a newspaper with a quality of reproduction difficult to distinguish from litho printing.

Letterpress printing has many advantages by which it retains its popularity. There are machines of all sizes and varieties so that the process can be used for work as small as a business card or as fine as a four-colour art book. It can also be used to print on a great variety of papers from cheap newsprint to chrome art. With heat set presses, which have driers, four colour work can be produced as a continuous process.

Lithography (Planographic)

Lithography—which is often referred to in familiar terms as 'offset' and 'web offset'—differs from letterpress in that the printing surface is not raised but is flat on the surface of the plate (see Fig. 11). Years ago printing was made from a limestone surface known as 'the stone'. (This is not to be confused with 'the stone' in letterpress printing which is the steel-topped table on which printing metal is assembled in the forme for locking up in the chase before being placed on the bed of the machine, or moulded to form a stereo.)

The principle of lithography is that water and grease will not mix, which is why the porous limestone was used originally. In those days a litho artist would draw, say, a large poster in reverse in each colour on a slab of limestone. The drawn image would be greasy so that when ink was applied it stayed on the greasy printing image when water was next applied, washing away the unwanted ink from the non-printing areas. Although the process is today photographic, using metal or plastic plates, the same principle applies.

Offset means that the inked plate prints onto a rubber blanket which offsets onto the paper. On the rotary press there are three cylinders—the plate cylinder, the blanket cylinder and the impression cylinder—the paper passing between the blanket and impression cylinders to receive the image.

Web-offset means that a web or reel of continuous paper is used instead of single sheets of paper.

The advantages of offset-lithography are many. Machines are more compact than letterpress machines; inks have a lot of pigment and gloss so that rich colours are reproduced; the paper is not indented by metal printing surfaces (as with letterpress); the text is clearly produced because with photo-typesetting each character is of identical quality and there are no irregular or damaged letters; a good range of papers is now available whereas at one time hard surface cartridge paper was typical of the process; and fine halftone

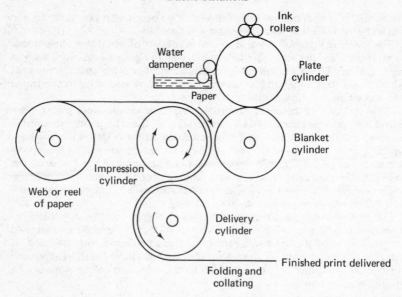

Fig. 11. Diagrammatic representation of the web-offset lithography process. The paper feeds from the web or reel. The plate prints on to the blanket which offsets the image on to the paper as it is fed through by the impression cylinder. The delivery cylinder feeds the printed paper through to the folding, collating and delivery sections of the machine.

screens (about 100 to 120 screen) are used when letterpress might require much coarser screens (e.g. 65 screen for newsprint). The difference can be seen by comparing a letterpress-printed London newspaper with a web-offset printed regional one which may also have colour pictures. In Nigeria in September 1980, the *Daily Times* switched from letterpress to web-offset, with a colour picture on the front page. Fleet Street was still lagging behind such enterprise! By October 1980, *The Times* of London, with all its new technology unacceptable to the unions, was looking for a new owner.

Lithography is used for the printing of inexpensive but beautiful picture books, and also for catalogues and sales literature such as holiday, horticulture, motorcar and fashion brochures.

Photogravure (Intaglio)

There are two chief kinds of photogravure: the kind which economically produces large quantities of popular full-colour print on 'cheap' supercalendered paper, e.g. women's weekly magazines and Sunday newspaper colour supplements (which are sometimes mistakenly called 'glossies' because the paper is shinier than newsprint), and the second kind for the superb printing of reproductions of paintings plus the excellent printing of postage stamps.

Most gravure printing is by means of a recessed plate or 'sleeve' since it is cylindrical, the printing area being *below* the surface and consisting of minute cells etched to the depth required to contain the amount of ink required to print the graduation of tone. The surface of the sleeve is a square grid known as the 'resist'. Ink is applied and then scraped off the resist by a doctor blade, the paper passes through the machine and the ink is sucked out of the cells. Being a volatile ink, the pigment stays on the paper and the solvent evaporates. A piece of photogravure print can be distinguished by the smell of the ink. The effect of the grid is to lay a fine square screen over the entire print area, and not just over halftone picture as with the dot screens used in letterpress and lithography.

The quality of photogravure magazine printing (sometimes called roto-gravure or colourgravure) tends to be poor, definition being lost by the velvety effect of reproduction, while the text is given a ragged effect by the resist.

However, as with the other processes, there have been revolutionary developments in photogravure. German print engineers have introduced the Klischograph hard dot cylinder which is not only a vast improvement upon the traditional photogravure sleeve with its comparatively crude reproduction but surpasses the fine definition of offset-lithography. Hard dot gravure still uses the cell system but instead of the cell being of varying depth it is of varying surface area. This is not unlike the halftone dot being of varying size, except that in Klischograph photogravure it is square, of varying size, and recessed.

Silk Screen (Stencil)

Probably the oldest printing process of all since the Chinese, centuries ago, stencil-printed through a mesh made of human hair, this is a remarkably versatile process. The principle is the stencil, a printing area being cut out to permit the passing of ink to the paper below. It is so simple that a home-made silk screen press can be made. In factories the process is used to print clock faces and instrument panels, and it can be used to print on curved surfaces such as soft-drink or beer bottles.

Its versatility lies in its ability to print on all sorts of materials such as paper, cloth, glass, plastic, foil, wood and so on. Readers will be familiar with ties, T-shirts, balloons, carrier bags, drip mats and other articles which have been printed in this fashion. It can be used for printing the price of goods posters seen on supermarket shop windows or pictorial posters seen on hoardings. But unlike the metal cut-out stencil used for marking crates, the silk-screen press has a mesh through which the ink is pressed. Presses can range from simple ones, hand operated with a squeegee roller, to electronically operated ones with photographic stencils capable of producing half-tone effects.

From these brief remarks it will be seen that printing is a fascinating subject, and a better understanding will be obtained by visiting printing works. However, most printers specialise in certain classes of work such as news-papers, books, commercial print, packaging, labels, picture postcards, calendars and so on, so that no one printing works will provide a complete picture of the craft.

For the same reason, when obtaining quotations for print it is necessary to pick the right printer for the job. Printers' estimates can vary astonishingly for the same job. This will be because they have different machines—faster or slower ones or ones printing from larger or smaller sheets and capable of printing larger or smaller quantities per hour. The price may also depend on how the job is set and made up. Human and machine time all have a bearing on price. It pays to talk to printers and ask them how the job will be produced, and to understand what they are talking about.

Production Time Schedules

The customer may want delivery by a certain date. The printer will say he can deliver by an agreed date provided a time schedule is followed. This is a discipline which must be obeyed, otherwise delays will result in rushed work, the need for overtime working and an increased price. A machine can set or print or bind only one job at a time, and production has to be planned to cope with the different stages of different jobs for different customers. A print schedule may look something like this:

Copy to printer	April 1
Proofs from printer	April 14
Corrected proofs to printer	April 21
Revised proofs from printer	April 28
Corrected revised proofs to printer	May 5
Delivery by printer	May 19

Obviously, there can be many variations on this example. It all depends on the job. 'Copy' means the layout, wording and pictures. If there is a lot of text, galley proofs may be supplied first (that is, long proofs without spacing and not made up into pages), then page proofs will follow. If there is colour printing, machine proofs will be checked at the printers. If it is a lithographic job, photostat proofs will be supplied before the paste-up is photographed. There are various kinds of photo-typesetting and proofs come in different forms. To avoid costly work, it is wise to heed the printer's instructions on making corrections, and to understand at which stage further corrections should not be made.

If one is used to dealing with a printer who sets metal type it can be a very different experience dealing with a printer who is using computerised photo-typesetting and has all the copy stored on a magnetic tape or on a floppy disc and not in movable metal type. With photo-set work it is so simple to make corrections that a proof may be submitted which is full of errors. It can be a frustrating experience to engage in the task of finding more errors than would have existed on a mechanically set proof, which had been read and corrected before submission. Printing has gone through a revolution from craftsmen printers who were artists in metal, to keyboard operators and paste-up artists whose attitude to print is as different as that of horse-carriage drivers and motorists to transport.

Correcting Proofs

Two things should be remembered about correcting proofs:

1. It is too late at this stage to start rewriting copy. However, if serious amendments are vital, they should be made in such a way that the length of the column or page is not exceeded, otherwise subsequent columns and pages will have to be altered to take in the overflow of extra material. When deleting and replacing copy, the new copy should consist of the same number of characters, which includes punctuation marks and spaces between words.

2. The corrections should be made clearly so that the printer can understand what is required. They should not be scribbled all over the proof, but confined to the margins and the proper correction signs used. Proof correction signs have been changed in recent years to conform with international needs, rather like traffic signs. The long-used *stet* (meaning 'let it stand' when something has been deleted in error) is now replaced by a tick in a circle. The current correction signs follow at the end of this chapter.

The following advice is helpful when correcting proofs:

(*a*) Author's corrections (i.e. changes introduced by the author or customer) should be made in black or blue. They may be chargeable!

(*b*) Corrections of printer's errors should be in red. (If the printer has read the proof he will make his own corrections in green.)

(*c*) Mentally divide the work with a vertical line down the middle, placing corrections on the left-hand half in the left-hand margin and those on the right-hand half in the right-hand margin.

(*d*) Read syllable by syllable slowly.

(*e*) Check the spellings of all names, especially those with alternative spellings such as Allan, Alan, Alain, and Allen, Francis and Frances, Sidney and Sydney, or Davis and Davies.

(*f*) Check figures, especially when there are noughts.

(*g*) Look up dates. It is easy to transfer dates from one year to another, or even look at the wrong year's calendar in a diary.

(*h*) Check prices. Have they changed? Is the currency correct?

(*i*) Check measurements—are there metric changes or requirements which have been overlooked?

(*j*) Watch out for transpositions of dates, such as 1918 for 1981.

(*k*) Check captions below illustrations. It is easy for a paste-up artist to paste captions wrongly, especially names of people. Such errors are very common in lithography.

(*l*) With litho proofs especially, look out for blank spaces where copy has run short. Can you fill it, perhaps by introducing a subheading? If in hot metal the printer can lose the space by leading out the lines of type.

(*m*) Watch out for words like 'of' and 'or' which are commonly mistyped in original copy, or misread by typesetters. Or 'i's' and 'e's' which can result in 'blind' instead of 'blend'. One of the most difficult things about proofreading is spotting an error which could make sense because it makes a normal word, as in the last example.

(*n*) Watch out for the typesetter's habit errors, or even the original typist's! There are some people who simply cannot spell certain words, e.g. 'seperate' for 'separate', 'liason' for liaison', 'personel' for 'personnel' and—although this has slipped into usage—'all right' is better than 'alright'. There are also times when a peculiar, or even an American, spelling is correct for the job, e.g. 'disk' and not 'disc' in connection with computers or 'Travelers' with one 'l' for the American insurance company. Certain place names have special spellings: Jakarta is nowadays not spelt Djakarta, and the country is Malaysia and not Malaya. One must not become confused between the different countries of the People's Republic of China (mainland China) and the Republic of China (Taiwan, formerly Formosa), the Democratic People's Republic of

Korea (North Korea) and the Republic of Korea (South Korea). Both tend to use the name China or Korea as if the other did not exist. One also has to be careful about the People's Democratic Republic of Yemen (South Yemen, formerly Aden) and the Arab Republic of Yemen (North Yemen). The Dutch prefer their country to be called The Netherlands rather than Holland which is a province.

(*o*) Finally, never be afraid to invite other people to check proofs, especially strangers to the copy who may well find errors which are overlooked by readers who are so familiar with the copy that they tend to read into it what they expect to find there.

New Symbols for Correcting Proofs *

The symbols for correcting proofs used here are taken from a British Standard BS 5261: *Part 2 1976 Copy preparation and proof correction—Specification for typographic requirements, marks for copy preparation and proof correction, proofing procedure.* It was prepared by the British Standards Institution following discussions on an international standard for proof correction symbols to replace the former British Standard which used several English words or initial letters unacceptable internationally.

Extracts from the new Standard are given below and all authors, printers, and publishers are recommended to adopt the new correction symbols.

Instruction	Textual Mark	Marginal Mark
Correction is concluded	None	/
Leave unchanged	– – – – – – under character to remain	Ⓙ
Push down risen spacing material	Encircle blemish	⊥
Insert in text the matter indicated in the margin	⋏	New matter followed by ⋏
Insert additional matter identified by a letter in a diamond	⋏	⋏ Followed by for example Ⓐ

* Reproduced by permission of the British Printing Industries Federation, from *Authors' alterations cost money and cause delay.* . . .

Instruction	Textual Mark	Marginal Mark
Delete	/ through character(s) or ├────────┤ through word(s) to be deleted	⌒
Delete and close up	⌒ through character or ⊃──────⊂ through character e.g. charaᶜacter charaᵃacter	⌒
Substitute character or substitute part of one or more word(s)	/ through character or ├────────┤ through word(s)	New character or new word(s)
Wrong fount. Replace by character(s) of correct fount	Encircle character(s) to be changed	⊗
Change damaged character(s)	Encircle character(s) to be changed	✕
Set in or change to italic	——— under character(s) to be set or changed	⊔
Set in or change to capital letters	≡≡≡ under character(s) to be set or changed	≡
Set in or change to small capital letters	≡≡≡ under character(s) to be set or changed	═
Set in or change to capital letters for initial letters and small capital letters for the rest of the words	≡ under initial letters and ≡≡≡ under rest of word(s)	≡

Instruction	Textual Mark	Marginal Mark
Set in or change to bold type	~~~~~ under character(s) to be set or changed	~~
Change capital letters to lower case letters	Encircle character(s) to be changed	≢
Change italic to upright type	Encircle character(s) to be changed	⊔
Invert type	Encircle character to be inverted	↻
Substitute or insert full stop or decimal point	/ through character or ⋀ where required	⊙
Substitute or insert semi-colon	/ through character or ⋀ where required	;
Substitute or insert comma	/ through character or ⋀ where required	,
Start new paragraph	⌐_	⌐_
Run on (no new paragraph)	∽	∽
Centre	[enclosing matter to be centred]	[ ]

Instruction	Textual Mark	Marginal Mark
Indent		
Cancel indent		
Move matter specified distance to the right	enclosing matter to be moved to the right	
Take over character(s), word(s) or line to next line, column or page		
Take back character(s), word(s) or line to previous line, column or page		
Raise matter	over matter to be raised / under matter to be raised	
Lower matter	over matter to be lowered / under matter to be lowered	
Correct horizontal alignment	Single line above and below misaligned matter e.g. $mi_{sa}l^{ig}n_ed$	
Close up. Delete space between characters or words	linking characters	

Instruction	Textual Mark	Marginal Mark
Insert space between characters	between characters affected	Y
Insert space between words	between words affected Y	Y
Reduce space between characters	between characters affected	⌒
Reduce space between words	between words affected ⌒	⌒
Make space appear equal between characters or words	between characters or words affected	X

38

THE FUTURE OF PUBLIC RELATIONS

Because public relations is concerned with converting negative attitudes into positive ones, and has the educational task of spreading knowledge in order to create understanding, it has an exceptionally valuable role to play in our rapidly changing world.

Of course, the world is always changing. It is always easy to be dazzled by the prospect of what may happen next. But nowadays we have means of communicating so quickly and so thoroughly that there is a danger that the bombardment of information could become incomprehensible. The escape from that lies in selectivity—selecting information and selecting those we wish to inform. Viewdata is one such means. Mass media may disappear. Video-cassettes and video-discs may provide more direct communication with individuals when and where they are willing to be informed. Mass media tend to relieve the boredom of people doing dull jobs and leading dull lives, the penalty of the passing industrial age. What will happen when it is realised that the problem in an age of greater leisure is unempayment, not unemployment?

Prophecies are sometimes foolish, and this is not the place to indulge late-twentieth-century fantasies along the lines of Jules Verne and H. G. Wells. Let us look at three topics of urgent concern to the PR practitioner during the next few years. These are: (1) new fields for PR activity (2) media changes and (3) the training of PR practitioners.

New Fields for PR Activity

This, again, can be divided into three main sections: (*a*) employee-management relations; (*b*) educating people about changing life styles; (*c*) corporate responsibility.

Employee–Management Relations

While this is not something new, PR techniques can give it a new look and help to bring about more practical and liberal communications.

Circumstances may help. The powerlessness of trade unions when confronted by mass unemployment and the failure of poor management in times of crisis situations may be helped by greater cooperation on the one hand and greater candour on the other. Each will need to know more about the other. The class barrier between men and management, capital and labour, may become irrelevant. As robotics and other devices replace traditional labour everyone will become a technician or specialist, a much more closely knit working unit. This will call for the ultimate in communications. It will not be a case of the bosses making exorbitant profits but of whether they are making big enough profits to sustain our life style. The impetus for production will be information in both directions.

This will not happen overnight. It will come about through the development of internal public relations, by company communicators acting as the catalysts

245

in producing upward and downward communication until this becomes *mutual* communication. The frustrations and savagery of industrial relations are mostly the result of ignorance and a communication vacuum. The video-cassette, the electronic newspaper, the Viewdata system, and—on a larger scale—the satellite are providing the in-house PRO with the means to communicate instantaneously within one organisation locally, regionally, nationally or internationally.

It amounts to a freedom of information, much of which in the past has been locked up in boardrooms and shop stewards' meetings, or with people isolated and inarticulate. Management has scarcely known what it was managing, employees have not known how best they could contribute. True, there have been a few enlightened companies in which there has been participation through co-partnership schemes, works councils or worker-directors, but even these efforts have lacked the unity which constant communication can wield.

A start has been made. The International Association of Business Communicators has shown that a house journal editor should develop himself into a general communications manager. The British Association of Industrial Editors has realised that its membership should include internal PROs, not merely house journal editors. These organisations recognise that the printed word is only one form of communication and that electronic media have extended the ability of business communicators to communicate. One day, perhaps, all employees will receive their house journal in the form of a throw-away video-disc—not once a month but every working day—to play on the domestic television set.

We already have systems where employees can dial for internal information or watch video-cassette company magazines. In the Summer of 1980, the *Columbus Dispatch* (Columbus, Ohio, USA) became the first commercial newspaper to publish an electronic edition which subscribers could receive by telephone on their home computers. Similar services were soon introduced by newspapers in San Francisco, Washington, New York, Los Angeles, Chicago, Miami, Philadelphia and Detroit. The American Tivue system *reads* the Viewdata information as it is screened, an improvement on the British Prestel system.

But the first true electronic newspaper is published on Prestel in Britain. This is the Viewtel edition of the *Birmingham Post & Mail*, which provides national news. The viewer calls up numbered headlines on his Prestel television screen, and then selects the stories he wishes to receive. There is no page charge. Pages may also indicate advertisements, which can be received in the same way. There are also Viewdata trade journals such as *Construction News*, whose pages cost 15p each. Instant information is available about contracts for which tenders are invited. ICL have their electronic *ICL News*.

So, between computer terminal displays and television sets with decoders, there are already systems which the in-house communicator can adapt as a daily, maybe hourly, replacement for the laboriously produced printed house journal. He can become an editor/producer and, as with Prestel, there is no reason why there cannot be feedback and reverse communication. The means already exist technologically: all that is required is installation. All that is needed to bring down the prices of receivers, or to make them realistic rental propositions, is demand and volume production.

Educating People About Changing Life Styles

This is a universal application of PR. The Third World is being introduced to new concepts such as primary education, power farming, piped water supplies, air transport, census taking and democratic elections. Development is uneven between countries rich in resources such as Indonesia, Nigeria and Zimbabwe, and ones less well blessed such as Bangladesh, Jamaica and Tanzania.

In the industrial world—the 'West', although this includes the Far East, Australia, New Zealand and South Africa so far as development is concerned—we have new concepts such as space travel, the micro-chip, robotics, less industrial employment and greater leisure which require both an agonising and a beneficial reappraisal of everyday life. The necessity for commuter travel may cease, the petrol-driven car may vanish, the hypermarket and shopping by teletext methods may develop.

All over the world PR techniques will be necessary to familiarise people with revolutionary changes which, initially, will give rise to the classic negative reactions of hostility, prejudice, apathy and ignorance.

Corporate Responsibility

Big business is likely to incur public and political criticism because of its behaviour, effects on the environment, responsibility for employment changes, and involvement in changing life styles. Response to the demands of articulate activists, whether they be consumers, environmentalists or other pressure groups, will need to be equally articulate, intelligible and compelling. What is sometimes called 'public affairs' is likely to become an increasingly active area of PR, again dealing with the negative situations or attitudes mentioned above. Management will need to become more 'open', externally as well as internally, if its actions are to be understood and approved. This will also call for better and more communicative management, with PR built into management training and job specification. More than ever before, the chief executive will need to be an organisation's premier PRO.

Media Changes

Some of these have been indicated above. While circulations or printed publications will diminish, the historic Fleet Street system will disappear, and more economically produced computerised photo-typeset web-offset newspapers will supply the need for portable, more permanent and more in-depth media. But in an age of greater leisure people will be better able to watch screen media over a greater part of the day, and not necessarily in the home. Thus the PR practitioner may have to compose more for the computer terminal, feeding material directly into editorial offices or information banks. The style will be more terse than the present wordy news release!

Television itself will be subject to many influences and inputs that could make the existing television stations and *TV Times* redundant, perhaps like the modern cinema compared with the days when Odeons had audiences of 3000 cinemagoers. If they have to compete with screen material provided or selected by the viewer the present 15–20 million audiences for a single programme will no longer exist.

Coronation Street and *Parkinson* may well go on to video-cassette. Viewers will be able to show home movies on cassettes which they can wipe and use again. Video-discs will bring the latest full-length film or company house magazine. Satellites will invade with foreign programmes. And viewers will be able to plan holidays, do mail order shopping and get the sports results by Prestel. Ceefax and Oracle will be there, too, with minute-by-minute news. This could see the end of television commercials as produced and shown at present. They could be converted into the more informative teletext and Viewdata forms, or advertisers could sponsor inexpensive or free cassette programmes. Clearly, the viewer will become more selective and more capable of

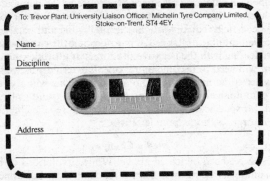

Fig. 12. An example of the use of a very well made audio-cassette tape to tell prospective graduate employees about the prospects with Michelin and about the company itself.

creating or choosing his own television entertainment or information. He will no longer be dependent on what the BBC and ITV decide to show him.

As an example of an aggressive move to take PR messages right into the home or school, the Royal Society for the Protection of Birds advertises RSPB films on VHS or Betamax video cassettes. Titles include *The Language of Birds, Round Robin, Osprey, Big Bill—The Story of a Heron, Speckle and Hide (Bird Camouflage)* at prices around £20–25. The ads carry the slogan: 'The wonder of nature—in classroom or home.' This is an excellent example of the documentary film finding a larger audience through the video-cassette and in direct competition with television contractors' standard programmes.

One may ask where do Third World countries fit into this scenario when they are trying to catch up with the West's 'old' industrial age? What will happen in, say, Nigeria when universal primary education will revolutionalise a country which used to be 80 per cent illiterate, and where dams, irrigation systems, power farming, a steel industry, a new power station, a rebuilt railway system and so on are modernising a country which has colour television and a growing press?

The answer may exist in a remarkable book published in France in 1980 which has been translated into 15 languages. *Le Defi Mondial (The World Challenge*, Collins, London, 1981), by Jean-Jacques Servan Schreiber, sees the solution to the world's problems in the microprocessor. He told a French radio audience: 'I am for the first time in my life resolutely optimistic. If we can manage our resources in the difficult years ahead a very exciting future will open to us—a job for everyone in the world.' He continued: 'The day of large cities is over. Within the space of a generation the backward populations of the Third World can make the change to a microprocessor society in which people can perform the relatively simple computer operations without leaving their villages.'

Education and Training

Three things are likely to occur to meet the changing situation:

1. The PR practitioner will need to be a technician capable of using the new technologies.

2. PR education will have to change from its present emphasis on training people *already in the profession* to preparing younger people for *entry into it*.

If the qualification is to gain the recognition of employers, if PR practitioners are to be regarded as properly qualified people, and if they are to have the breadth of training necessary for such a complex, demanding and responsible vocation, nothing less than a degree (whether university or CNAA) will be satisfactory. The CAM Diploma has been a disappointment, and because of its inadequate teaching time and lack of external examiners it is not recognised by many universities. The Open University, for instance, will not accept the CAM Diploma for credit exemption purposes. As a member of the Public Relations Committee of the Open University and holder of an OU honours degree, the author is aware of this paradoxical situation.

3. Such people will need to be qualified professionals like architects who combine vocational training with practical experience to gain admittance to the professional body.

This will call for an entirely different educational and professional system to the one currently operated by CAM and the IPR. It will put PR into its proper place in the curriculum of higher education, and it will enhance the status and role of the IPR.

Once again, this is not a 'pie in the sky' hope or a foolish prophecy for the groundwork has been done. It exists in the Hong Kong Document on Public Relations Education (*IPRA Newsletter*, October 1980) which resulted from the special meeting of public relations educators from 10 countries, including Britain, who conferred at the Chinese University of Hong Kong on September 4 and 5, 1980. Among them was the chairman of the education committee of the Institute of Public Relations, so Britain is already committed. Basically, the Document sets out curriculums at undergraduate and graduate levels. This is the most positive programme of public relations education ever conceived or published, and it is a foundation on which future education in public relations can be built. It is up to national public relations institutes to accept the challenge to establish the sort of education plus academic and professional qualifications which will enable future practitioners to function efficiently and to be respected as professionals. To be accepted as a member of a professional institute the candidate should have the appropriate degree and a determined period of practical experience. Ideally (like architects) this could consist of a first and a second degree, two years' experience and the passing of a professional examination such as the CAM Diploma.

Appendix 1

CAM EDUCATION FOUNDATION

CAM—The Communication Advertising and Marketing Education Foundation Limited—was formed in 1969 by combining the educational bodies of the Advertising Association, the Institute of Practitioners in Advertising and the Institute of Public Relations. Thus, the CAM Diploma embodies the vast experience and high standards of previous educational awards, the earliest dating from 1929.

CAM is now recognised and supported by a total of 27 organisations in the communication and education fields and the qualification Dip. CAM commands very high standing throughout UK industry and indeed the world.

More people than ever before recognise the need for proper training and sound qualifications, and the CAM Diploma is the nationally recognised qualification for anyone making a career in advertising, media, public relations, and related fields. The number of current students now far exceeds the total number of people who have qualified over the past 40 years.

The **CAM Certificate in Communication Studies** is awarded after the first part of the course (normally two years) on the basis of examinations designed to establish that candidates have a practical and basic knowledge of six Certificate subjects (see Fig. 13).

CAM Certificate in Communications Studies
Public Relations Syllabus

Aim. To provide students with an awareness of the many different publics with which an organisation is concerned, and a knowledge of the professional context in which people working full-time in public relations operate. Also, to provide an understanding of all means of communication by which those publics can be reached.

Note. There will be a compulsory question on the legal and voluntary controls which apply in this subject area.

Definitions of Publics (1)

Consideration of the various internal and external publics with which an organisation's public relations programme may be concerned:

Customers	Management
Distributors or agents	Media
Employees	Shareholders
Government: national or local	

PR as a Management Function (3)

The service nature of public relations	The PRO as a channel of two way information and communication

---

PR Practice in Organisational Frameworks (4)

Public Relations Departments within organisations	Local Government public relations
Consultancies	Counselling: Counselling services Services only
Central Government Press and Information Officers	Personal and product publicity

---

251

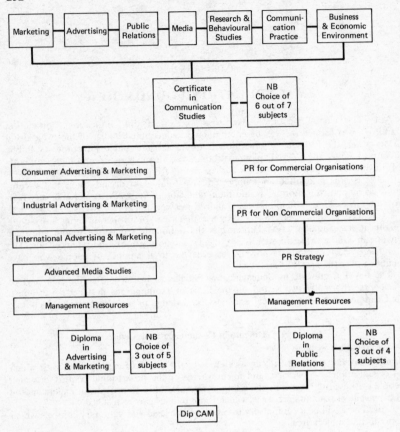

Fig. 13. The CAM Educational Scheme.

Operational PR (7)

Problem analysis

Programme Planning

Costing and Budgetary control

Case presentation to client or management

Programme execution

Assessment of results

Research and preparation of feature articles, radio/TV, video scripts and talks

Appraisal

Targets

Methods

Recommendations

Budget

Progress Report

Writing and Distribution of Press Releases

Lecture material

Types of Media (5)

Description, characteristics

Advantages/disadvantages

(a) Basic Media

Costs (capital and running)
Major 'public'/audiences

Person-to-person (public speaking, TV/Radio techniques)

Printed work (editorial, advertising, direct mail, print)

Annual reports, employee reports, house journals

Two-dimensional/graphics (photography, film slides, charts)

Film/audio/tape (tape recordings, discs CCTV, VTR)

Three-dimensional (models, displays, signs).

(b) Composite media

Press conferences
Formal meetings
Special events
Facility visits
Exhibitions
Export promotions
Conferences
Sales Presentations
Sponsorship of sport, art, books, films
Artistic or educational activities

Timing and Handling of Material (5)

News and features

Demands of all types of media

Public relations material—what is required, how it is used

Proof reading, sub-editing and preparing for press

Professional Attitudes (2)

Freedom of the press—including radio and TV

Society and the journalist—in all media

The journalist and public relations—in all media

Legal and Voluntary Controls (3)

The ethics of Public Relations

Codes of Professional Practice and the reasons behind each clause

Protection afforded to members

The Institute of Public Relations

The Public Relations Consultants Association

Laws affecting Public Relations practice

See also Business & Economic Environment and Advertising

Specimen Examination Paper

Communication Advertising and Marketing Education Foundation Limited

CERTIFICATE IN COMMUNICATION STUDIES

Examination in

PUBLIC RELATIONS

JUNE 1981

Time allowed: THREE HOURS

Candidates *must answer* QUESTION ONE and FOUR OTHER QUESTIONS.

Each question carries equal marks.

Marks will be deducted for bad presentation—including illegible handwriting.

Overseas students can base their answers on the situation and structure of their own localities.

Question Five carries equal marks for each digit.

Question One

Explain:

a) The laws of copyright as they affect the written word and photographs.

b) Give two examples of what may constitute a defence in a libel case.

Question Two

Several of the licences for operating commercial television companies were changed recently. Detail the main changes and comment on the published reasons on which the IBA made their decision.

Question Three

Discuss the Code of Practice of the Public Relation Consultants Association.

Question Four

Outline the decision making processes within the European Communities and show the opportunities for access available to public relations practitioners.

Question Five

Write a brief paragraph on the following:

a) ITCA
b) COI
c) Shirley Williams
d) Edmund Dell
e) Clive James
f) Ivy Ledbetter Lee
g) BECA
h) Sir Terence Beckett
i) Lord Thomson of Monifieth
j) David English

Question Six

How would you advise the management of a factory employing 500 people on its regular communications with the work force.

Question Seven

You are a staff public relations practitioner with a major international pharmaceutical house. The company manufactures and markets a drug which is prescribed as an appetite suppressant in obesity.

A daily newspaper reports that the drug is being abused by teenagers as a 'pep pill'. The article uses quotes from a headmaster and a psychiatrist.

Your Managing Director asks you for action proposals.

Write them.

Question Eight

You are a public relations consultant to a company manufacturing glass bottles for the brewing and soft drinks trade. During recent years the competition from can manufacturers for this market has increased.

Write an outline of your public relations programme to counter this competition and identify the key people to whom you feel this programme should be aimed.

Question Nine

Your Chairman has accepted an invitation to speak to a group of young businessmen on 'The Growth and Importance of Commercial Radio'.

He has asked you to provide him with 'background material'.

Give him the information he requires.

Question Ten

Discuss the public relations opportunities offered by the publication of a company's annual report and accounts.

Appendix 2

LONDON CHAMBER OF COMMERCE AND INDUSTRY

Higher Certificate in Public Relations Syllabus

Public Relations. Definition. How PR differs from advertising and propaganda. PR in relation to marketing. PR as a management function. PR for commercial and non-commercial organisations. Developing areas of public relations, especially internal communications, financial PR and public affairs (including e.g. corporate PR and relations with consumerist, environmental and other pressure groups).

Ethics of Public Relations. Code of Professional Conduct of the British Institute of Public Relations and versions adopted by Institutes in other countries. The Code of Athens (International Public Relations Association).

Publics of Public Relations. Basic publics—community, employees, suppliers, investors, distributors, consumers, users, opinion leaders. Special publics of different organisations.

Public Relations Departments. Role, responsibilities, staffing, place in total organisation.

Public Relations Consultants. Role, client-consultancy relations, services, methods of remuneration.

Budgeting. Costing PR programmes and individual activities. Value of budgeting in planning programmes and evaluation results.

Planning Public Relations Programmes. Problem analysis and preparation of proposals for PR schemes involving appreciation of the situation, definition of objectives, budgeting finance, labour and resources, selecting publics, choosing media and techniques. Feedback and assessing results.

Evaluating Results. In relation to planning by objectives and budgeting; feedback such as press cuttings and monitoring of broadcasts; use of research techniques such as opinion surveys.

Press Relations. Researching material for the media; writing and presenting news releases; negotiating publication, interviewing, and writing feature articles; organising press conferences, press receptions and facility visits. The establishment of good relations with the media. Adopting the criterion of supplying material of 'interest and value' to readers, viewers and listeners.

The News Media. Organisation of press, radio, TV, newsreels. National and international news agencies. Freelance writers, contributors, correspondents, stringers, etc.

Documentary or Industrial Films and other Audio and/or Visual aids. Making of films, PR purposes, distribution. Mobile film shows. Slides, including synchronised slide presentations. Multi-screen presentations. Video tape recordings.

House Journals. Internal and external, newspaper and magazine format, special PR uses, methods of distribution. Wall newspapers. Video cassette house journals and other new developments.

Exhibitions. PR support for consumer and trade exhibitions; private and touring exhibitions; exhibition press rooms.

Photography. Uses of photography in PR; briefing of photographers; captioning of photographs.

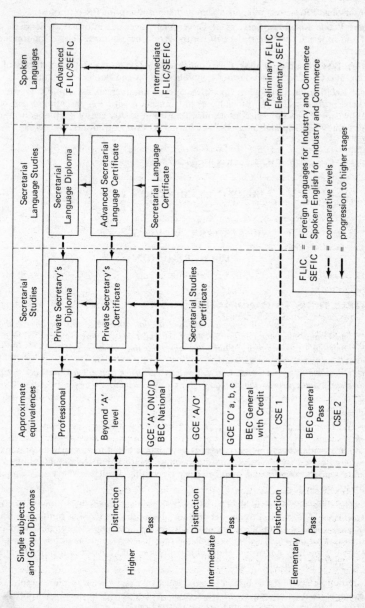

Fig. 14. London Chamber of Commerce Examinations. Distinction in a Higher Certificate in Advertising, Marketing and Public Relations qualifies for exemption in the same subjects in the CAM Certificate in Communication Studies examinations.

Printing Processes. Letterpress, lithography, photogravure, silk screen. Methods of typesetting.

Sponsorships. PR aspects of sponsorship and sponsorship for PR purposes.

Export Public Relations. Services of Government overseas information services, e.g. COI and External Services of the BBC or those of other countries. Use of international PR services.

Market Research. Use of desk, field, panel, discussion group and other forms of research; questionnaires; interviewing techniques; quota and random sampling.

Public Relations in Developing Countries. Special commercial uses of PR to educate markets. Special social and official uses in connection with e.g. parenthood and baby care, hygiene, farming, pest control, nutrition, road safety, census taking, educational programmes, tourism and internal and external government information services.

Specimen Examination Paper—Higher Stage

SPRING EXAMINATION 1981

WEDNESDAY 13 MAY—6 to 9 p.m.

PUBLIC RELATIONS

INSTRUCTIONS TO CANDIDATES

(*a*) **First,** *read through* **all** *the questions and do not attempt to answer any until you understand the scope and limitations of the questions you have selected.*

(*b*) *Question 1 is compulsory.* **Four** *other questions may be answered.*

(*c*) *All questions carry equal marks.*

(*d*) *Questions need not be answered in numerical order, but all five answers must be clearly and correctly numbered.*

---

1. COMPULSORY QUESTION

You are writing *both* a news release for newspapers and a feature article for a magazine. Choose your own subject, and demonstrate the different techniques required for opening a news release and a feature article by writing a suitable short opening paragraph for each.

2. The definition known as 'The Mexican Statement' reads as follows: 'PUBLIC RELATIONS PRACTICE is the art and social science of analysing trends, predicting their consequences, counselling organisation leaders, and implementing planned programmes of action which will serve both the organisation's and the public interest.'

What is especially important about this definition, and how does it differ from any other with which you are familiar?

3. Why is it necessary to brief a photographer on exactly what to photograph? Give an example, real or imaginary, of what could go wrong if you failed to work closely with the photographer, giving him precise instructions.

4. In spite of frequent editorial criticism of PR, why does the press in practice find PR sources of information genuinely useful?

5. Many employee newspapers are nowadays printed by offset litho—sometimes by web-offset-litho—instead of by letterpress. How do you account for this change, and what advantages does the offset-litho process offer to the editor and designer of an employee newspaper?

6. Public relations consultancy services may be provided by:

(*a*) an advertising agency with a PR department;
(*b*) a PR consultancy which is a subsidiary of an advertising agency;
(*c*) an independent PR consultancy.

What are the advantages and disadvantages of each to you as a client, assuming that you require only a PR service?

7. If you were responsible for PR for a voluntary organisation or charity with limited funds for your PR programme, how could you increase your PR activities through sponsorship by commercial companies or by joint PR schemes with other organisations of various kinds?

8. Throughout the world national PR institutes and associations have introduced codes of professional practice. Allowing for special national requirements, what principles are common to most codes of PR practice?

9. Describe some of the special communication problems which exist in developing countries, but which do not exist in Western countries.

10. How can the BBC External Services assist the PR practitioner, and how do they differ from the overseas radio services of the Central Office of Information?

11. Documentary films, various kinds of slide presentation, and video cassettes are visual aids which provide valuable PR media. Describe the special characteristics, advantages, disadvantages and PR uses of these three kinds of visual aid.

12. Give brief explanations of each of the following:

(*a*) Wire service	(*f*) OB
(*b*) Embargo	(*g*) IRN
(*c*) Special correspondent	(*h*) CERP
(*d*) Features Editor	(*i*) PA
(*e*) Lobby correspondent	(*j*) AP

13. If you were planning to take a party of journalists on a visit to a factory about 100 miles away from the starting point, what additional arrangements and expenses would be involved compared with those for holding a press reception at a hotel which was easily accessible to invited journalists?

14. What research techniques can be used to

(*a*) appreciate the situation before planning a PR programme and
(*b*) test the progress and results of a PR programme?

Appendix 3

ADDRESSES OF ORGANISATIONS AND SERVICES

BBC External Services, Export Liaison Unit, Bush House, London, WC2B 4PH (Tel. 01-240 3456)

British Association of Industrial Editors, 3 Locks Yard, High Street, Sevenoaks, Kent, TN13 1LT (Tel. 0732-59331)

British Overseas Trade Board, Publicity Unit, 1 Victoria Street, London, SW1H 0ET (Tel. 01-215 7877)

CAM Education Foundation, Abford House, 15 Wilton Road, London, SW1V 1NJ (Tel. 01-828 7506)

Central Office of Information, Hercules Road, London, SE1 7DU (Tel. 01-928 2345)

EIBIS International Ltd, 3 Johnson's Court, Fleet Street, London, EC4A 3EA (Tel. 01-353 5151)

EMA (Editorial Media Analysis), Bill Gibbs-PNA Group, 13/19 Curtain Road, London, EC2A 3LT (Tel. 01-377 2521)

Institute of Public Relations, 1 Great James Street, London WC1N 3DA (Tel. 01-405 5505)

International Public Relations Association, 40 Wellington Street, Covent Garden, London, WC2E 8BN (Tel. 01-836 4046)

London Chamber of Commerce and Industry, Commercial Education Scheme, Marlowe House, Station Road, Sidcup, Kent, DA15 7BJ

Media Information Group (PR-Planner, PR/Systems, Romeike & Curtis Ltd press cutting service), Hale House, 290–295 Green Lanes, London, N12 5TP

PIMS (Press Information & Mailing Services Ltd), 4 St John's Place, London, EC1B 1AB (Tel. 01-250 1779, 01-250 0870)

Public Relations Consultants Association, 37 Cadogan Street, Sloane Square, London, SW3 2PR (Tel. 01-581 3951)

Universal News Services, Communication House, Gough Square, London, EC4P 3DP (Tel. 01-353 5200)

Appendix 4

BIBLIOGRAPHY

Annual Publications

Advertiser's Annual, Kelly's Directories, East Grinstead, Sussex.
Asian Press & Media Directory, Syme Media Enterprises Ltd, Hong Kong.
Benn's Press Directory, Benn Publications Ltd, Tunbridge Wells, Kent.
Blue Book of British Broadcasting, Tellex Monitors Ltd, London.
Contact, IPC Business Press Information Services Ltd, East Grinstead, Sussex.
Hollis Press and Public Relations Annual, Hollis Directories, Sunbury-on-Thames, Middlesex.
PR-Planner, Media Information Ltd, London.
Television and Radio Annual, IBA, London.
Willings Press Guide, Thomas Skinner Directories, East Grinstead, Sussex.
Writers' and Artists' Year Book, A. & C. Black Ltd, London.

Periodicals

Advance (alternate months), Themetree Ltd, Windsor, Berkshire.
Campaign (weekly), Haymarket Press Ltd, London.
Conferences and Exhibitions (monthly), International Trade Publications Ltd, London.
Exhibition Bulletin (monthly), London Bureau, London.
IPRA Review (quarterly), International Public Relations Association, London.
Media Reporter, The, Financial Times Business Publishing, London.
PR Bulletin (monthly), Woodpecker Press, London.
Public Relations Year Book, Financial Times Business Publishing, London.
UK Press Gazette (weekly), Bouverie Publishing Co. Ltd, London.

Books

Advertising Law, R. G. Lawson, Macdonald & Evans, Plymouth, 1978.
Careers in Marketing, Advertising and Public Relations, Norman Hart and Gilbert Lamb (Eds), Heinemann, London. 1981.
Corporate Personality, Wally Olins, Design Council, London, 1978.
Dictionary of Marketing and Communication, Frank Jefkins, Intertext, Glasgow, paperback edition, 1981.
Effective Communication Made Simple, E. C. Eyre, Made Simple Books, Heinemann, London, 1979.
Effective Press Relations and House Journal Editing, Frank Jefkins, Frank Jefkins School of Public Relations, Croydon, 1980.
Effective PR Planning, Frank Jefkins, Frank Jefkins School of Public Relations, Croydon, 1980.
Effective Publicity Writing, Frank Jefkins, Frank Jefkins School of Public Relations, Croydon, 1981
Introduction to Marketing, Advertising and Public Relations, Frank Jefkins, Macmillan, London, 1982.
Marketing and PR Media Planning, Frank Jefkins, Pergamon Press, Oxford, 1974.
Media and Mass Communication in Nigeria, Dayo Duyile, Gong-Duyison Publishers, Ibadan, Nigeria, 1979.
Planned Press and Public Relations, Frank Jefkins, Intertext, Glasgow, 1977.
Practical Public Relations, Sam Black, Pitmans, London, Fourth Edition, 1976.

Practice of Public Relations, The, W. P. Howard (Ed.), Heinemann, London, 1981.

Printing Reproduction Pocket Pal, Advertising Agency Production Association, London, Fourth Edition, 1979.

Public Relations, Frank Jefkins, Macdonald & Evans, Plymouth, 1980

Public Relations For Marketing Management, Frank Jefkins, Macmillan, London, 1978.

Public Relations For Top Management, Reginald Watts, Croner Publications, London, 1977.

Public Relations In India, J. M. Kaul, Naya Prokash, Calcutta, 1976.

Setting Up a European Public Relations Operation, Philip Currah, Business Books, London, 1975.

Synonym Finder, The, J. Rodale, Rodale Press, Aylesbury, 1979.

Index